Nothing Broken Nothing Missing

VERONICA OBY WADDELL

Table of Contents

Dedication

I dedicate this book to Evangelist Sena Price, Patricia Evans, Minister Beverly Brown, Shirley Herron, Eloise Murphy, Gayle Waters, Prophetess Cassandra Bradshaw, Elder Capatoria Wilson, Janice Reid, Janice Mason and Margaret Brown

I want to give a special tribute to my Eloise Murphy for being such a great friend and sister to me. Thanks for the support you have given me when others put me down. Thanks for the wisdom that you have shared with me in my walk with God, and a special thanks for the Salmon Croquettes no one cooks them like you. I want to say thank you and I love you big sister.

Special thanks to Mother J. Carrether thanks for your listening ear. We argue constantly, and she never takes it personal. Special thanks to Pastor Lida Ratcliff; you have truly been an inspiration to me. Your words of wisdom were much needed and I love you. Special thanks to Evangelist Claudia Terrell; you have walked with me for the many years I was hurting. You heard my cries. When no one understood me, you did. Thank you for holding my hand. Thank you Prophetess Cassandra Bradshaw for being the angel in my life. You are truly a blessing.

No matter what you are going through, all is not lost. God wants you to know that He is with you in everything that you are going through. He knew what you would go through before it was ever presented to you. Everything you have been through is a part of God's plan for you. Keep moving forward and persevering. The blessing is about to manifest before your eyes! If I made it, so can you! God Bless You!

Introduction

We are born when the seed of life is planted into our mother's womb. Although we are predestined, no man knows his destination or what lies ahead of him. We are nurtured, taken care of up to a certain age at which time it is expected for us leave, and become the man or woman God has predestined us to be. Each individual's life is a mystery, waiting to be unraveled by the person chosen to travel its road. Only God knows what we will experience and do during this journey.

Many of us go through life getting hit by all types of balls; curve balls, sinkers, fast balls, or foul balls. Some of us may find ourselves feeling like we've struck out or that there is no one around to make a fair call. Some of us are hurt by others for many different reasons or at times, no reason at all. Many of us travel through life appearing happy, smiling as though nothing is wrong, with hurt and pain building its empire inside of us. In the end, we all continue through life, carrying the scars of life's battles.

This empire of hurt and pain within us tears at our hearts and destroys our brains. It is important that we continue life's journey, free of worry regarding the opinions of others. Others are unaware of our past battles and our search for peace within. They are unaware of the shellshock we may be experiencing and our preparation for future battles. While our outer core may be hard as steel, our inner cores remain soft as cotton.

Satan has thrown everything but the kitchen sink at me, so I decided to throw the kitchen sink along with God's word back at him. He has done everything he could do to stop me from writing this book, but I wrote until I finished. Satan remains powerless when my Father has all of the power, even the keys to Satan's house. God Bless!

In life, there are two types of people. There are those who allow the balls they've been hit with determine how they will live their lives. They use life's pitfalls as an excuse to explain why they life the way they do. They spend much of their journey angry at themselves and the world. These people have either turned away from God or were never introduced to Him. Some have no interest in knowing God or returning to Him. This is a result of feeling that God has betrayed them by allowing unfortunate events to happen to them.

Many have been hurt in different ways and for different reasons. Some have been hurt by their spouse, children, other family members, friends, and even the church. After being hurt, many don't know how to get up from this fall or become comfortable in this new miserable position. Unfortunately, many Christians make the mistake of feeling that because they are believers that negative things shouldn't happen to them. These people have conformed to the negative aspects of life's journey instead of following God's word. In Romans 12:2 Paul says, "Don't copy the behavior and customs of this world, but let God transform you into a new person by changing the way you think." Then you will learn to know God's will for you, which is "good and pleasing and perfect." It is at these times that the wounded should seek the help of a caring Christian who can assist them in coming out of these desolate places by relying on the love of Jesus. It is the responsibility of Christians to reach out and assist those who are having a hard time getting up. Those that refuse help and ignore God's word do so because they know by accepting Jesus as their personal savior a change in their lifestyle must follow.

Then there is the second type of person: Those who bounce back and continue life's journey no matter the type of ball they're hit with. These people don't allow their downfalls to dictate how they will live their lives; they will triumph over any situation they encounter during their journey and continue to work towards their goals. Many of these people have been hit with just as many, if not more, sinker balls than the next person. However, they are able to turn their sinker balls into home runs and straighten out their curve balls. They always return to home plate after a foul ball with a huge amount of confidence, ready to take another swing. These people take their downfalls, pitfalls, trials, and tribulations and turn them into something positive. They know that in every bad situation, there is good that can be taken from it. They understand that there is always a lesson to learn from each fall, even if it means starting over. Their faith teaches them that they can conquer anything. They know the voice of their shepherd as stated in John 10:27, "My sheep hear my voice, and I know them, and they follow me."

I must admit, I have been both of these types of people. I was once the one that knew Christ and turned away from him. I am now the person who's focused on my goals and determined to achieve them. At the age of fourteen, I began to write poetry to express my feelings about the things I found myself going through. I found myself writing like I'd never written before; as God spoke to me I would write, similar to how this book was written. I'm writing this book because I was instructed by God to do so. He told me this book would be therapeutic for myself and others. My intentions are not to bring hurt or shame to anyone. My only goal was to tell my life's story. To those involved, I pray you understand that I'm following the orders giving to me by the Lord.

I refused to strike out during my journey. If I hit a foul ball, I continued to return to home plate until I score. If I found myself hit by a ball, I keep going despite the injury. If I struck out, I simply waited for the chance to return to home plate. Once I hit a homerun I found myself able to move closer to my dreams. If I were lucky enough to hit a grand slam, I'd bring others with me but ultimately I refused to fail! F=Focus.

We were created in God's image, yet He is the only perfect one. We are not perfect; therefore we should be allowed to make mistakes without being beaten down. We should be allowed to have differences without fearing being labeled. We should be free to be ourselves without others attempting to change us into an image that fits their ideal. We are all the same imperfect creatures; therefore God created 7 billion imperfect human beings. God utilizes imperfect people for perfect purposes. He may also use imperfect people to strengthen us, everything is not of Satan. Sometimes God will put things before you for the purpose of building strength before moving you to your next assignment. This is stated in Isaiah 45:7 and Ephesians 6:10-20 shows us that we are protected with God's armor.

I love each and every person I've crossed paths with throughout my life's journey. I thank each of you for assisting in making me the person I am today, without you all it couldn't have been done. Each of you have served as a brick in the building of me and without each brick, my building wouldn't have been completed. Our meeting was predestined by God and because of this we couldn't miss meeting each other. I will take you on a journey to experience many of my personal battles and victories. I will expose my deepest secrets that I've held close to my heart. I will expose mountains that I've encountered and moved through my faith in God. I will also show how God delivered and protected me from many things while on my journey.

God had given me the order to write this book seven years ago. Instead, I went on to release my first CD in 2005 entitled "How Well Are You Playing Your Part". It was a poetry CD from God which allowed me to pour my inner soul into words. While the CD was comforting for me and others, I found myself unable to rest because there was a burning sensation within me that needed to be released. However, with little free time, I found myself unable to write and satisfy this sensation. In June of 2009, God granted me the time needed. After being laid off from my job, I retreated to the country and began writing this book.

There have been people that I've encountered, some were good, and others were bad. Nevertheless, they've all served a purpose in my life as I served in theirs. I thank God for them all. I pray that this book will be a blessing to all. We must realize that our experiences can assist others out of their desolated place. Please note that this book was not written in chronological order, it was written by God's order.

CHAPTER 1

Genesis

I called my friend Pauline Bass, whom I have known for over twenty years. (We were once coworkers, which is how we met.) I told her that I was headed to Mississippi. July 10, 2009 would be the day. I was on the Amtrak headed to Kosciusko, Mississippi, the hometown of Oprah Winfrey. Kosciusko is where the train would arrive. My final destination, which is where Pauline resided was a town named McAdams, Mississippi, located just outside of Kosciusko. The population is about 150. Yes, I was headed to the country to relax and hear from God. I arrived on July 11th and began writing my book on July 13th. I completed the book on July 30th.

I was so upset that I didn't have access to a computer to type the book. Instead, I began to write the book in a notebook. Although, I preferred the luxury of typing on a computer, I actually enjoyed writing in the notebook. I would wake up about 7 a.m. to start my day. I drank water throughout the day. I wouldn't eat until about 4 o'clock in the late afternoon. (As it turns out, I was fasting. I didn't realize that I was fasting until after I had completed the book.) I would sit on an enclosed back porch, with a cold glass of water. The temperature was every bit of 100 degrees. God began to speak to me like never before. I could hear His voice so clear. Sometimes, I would get up throughout the night and write pieces to the book. It didn't take me long to realize that I was on a true mission from God. I left Mississippi on August 9th, almost 15 pounds lighter. I listened to the different animals every morning. One animal that caught my attention was the Mockingbird. I loved the sound of the Mockingbird. I enjoyed God's creation while writing my book.

My visit was an experience that I would never forget. I really enjoyed myself. The things that I encountered were just what God wanted me to see. It was totally different from being in the city. My friend Pauline has more than enough love to give. She also has a lot of responsibilities. She has two daughters, Anastasia and Alyssa. Anastasia was 11 years old and Alyssa was 8 years old. They are very intelligent girls, who are both in gifted classes. Then, there are her parents, Daddy Peteet and Mama Peteet. She moved to Mississippi to assist in the care of her parents. Pauline has three dogs that barked at everything moving, from cars to people. The last time I visited her, she had approximately five cats or more. I told Pauline she was running a breeding farm and it also reminded me of animal farm. When I arrived, I was prepared to hear the dogs bark. However, I didn't hear a sound. The dogs were silent.

After I was there for eight days, Pauline's dog by the name of Chucky decided that he was going to attack me. He was trying to bite my legs. I used profanity to express how I felt about this. His actions attracted two more dogs. They too tried to attack me. Chucky's behavior was abnormal, but he had just met his match. He started to run, ready to attack me. However, I surprised him when I dropped my purse and told him, "Come on so I can pull all your teeth out. I dare you come on!" I was so angry, he was in big trouble. Chucky stopped in his tracks, looked at me, and took off running. He never barked at me again. The other two dogs ran away as well. When I was preparing to leave, Chucky tried to attack again. He didn't scare me this time. I felt that he didn't want to see me leave. I was totally unaware that during the incident of Chucky attacking me that Mama Peteet overheard me using profanity, cursing and screaming. She said in her calm voice," Now Veronica oh my God! Don't cuss like that. My God you sound terrible that's not godly." I felt so ashamed and I apologized. I told her I wasn't myself I was acting like a crazy woman because I was in a panic.

I found those dogs to really be strange, I watched them as I wrote. They would eat and go off into the woods. Once, just before dawn, the dog named Queenie came back from the woods, and I heard strange sounds. I asked Alyssa about the sound. As I stood up to get a closer look from the porch, I noticed that the dog had a kitten in his mouth. Alyssa jumped up, grabbed a baseball bat and ran towards the woods, after Queenie. I was screaming for her to come back, she kept running and screaming to the dog, "Drop it or I'll kill you." I screamed for Pauline. I told her that Alyssa had run into the woods and she better go get her. I wasn't going. It was just getting dark at this time. Alyssa came back with the kitten in her hands. The kitten had been injured from the dog shaking it like a toy. It could have been no more than two weeks old. It was a tiny little thing. I cried out, "Oh Lord I didn't come down here for this. I came to write a book!" Alyssa tried to nurse it with a pet's bottle that they already had in the house.

I watched her care for the kitten as if it was her child. She wrapped the kitten in a blanket and kept it in her room. She named the kitten "Blessed Kimberly". I had told her the kitten was blessed, because a little later after she had rescued the kitten, the dogs made three more trips. Each time they returned they had another kitten that they had killed. They seemed to be eating the kittens and I couldn't believe it. I had never seen anything like this. These dogs were fed more than enough every day and they still went out to hunt as if they were starving. These were not large dogs. They were small dogs, about the size of a Poodle. One of the dogs had puppies and they were all given away except one, because it would hide in a hole under the house and no one could get to her.

I watched how determined Alyssa was to bring the kitten back to health. She was so smart she had even made a call to the veterinarian. She talked the doctor into giving the kitten a free appointment. Wow! What an amazing little girl! But there was one problem: she was trying to get me to assist with caring for the kitten. I was not interested at all. Every time the kitten would cry, she would bring it to me. I thought, "What is going on?" I had been around dogs all my life, never cats. I wasn't afraid of them, but I didn't know anything about them. I asked God to please help me with this because I had to help her. She didn't have anyone to help her. Although I don't like cats, I agreed to help her. Alyssa assigned me to feed the kitten from the bottle. Alyssa was like a mother with a baby, she never got any sleep. She was up throughout the night and every morning her eyes were red from the lack of sleep. Once, I went in the dining area after hearing the kitten cry. Alyssa was sleep with the kitten on her stomach, she never woke up. I cried out to the Lord again, "I didn't come to nurse a kitten, nor did I come to chase a puppy". I complained, but I assisted Alyssa. Pauline and Anastasia laughed at me because I was fussing every step of the way. The best investment you can make is investing in a child. The payoff is priceless.

One night, I went to a revival with Pauline and her daughters. When we arrived home, I went straight into my room. When I heard Alyssa scream, I knew the kitten had died. She said the kitten moaned "meow" and closed her eyes. It was as if the kitten was waiting for her to come home to say goodbye. I knew the kitten wouldn't make it. That morning, she looked so weak, and I had a strange feeling. It took two days for Alyssa to grieve. The reason that I'm talking about Alyssa and the kitten is because of the love that she had shown this kitten. She demonstrated more love than many mothers show their own children. It was amazing to see an 8 year old with so much love in her heart for animals.

Now the puppy that made her home under the porch was past the weaning stage. The mother would take food to her puppy to eat. The mother continued to look after the puppy. I thought, "Wow God is showing me that his love still rules".

Anastasia decided she was going to write a book. Week one was good, but by the second week of her book writing adventure, she put the book down. I know in my heart she will eventually write a book, I'm just waiting. It's not going to be a surprise to me. God had planted the seed, as she watched me write. She, like all of the other children in our lives, is watching. You have to be careful what your actions say to children. They are watching everything that is done around them, and to them. Are your actions those that you want a child to imitate? The children see a lot and imitate what they see. What are they seeing when they watch you? I pray that they see the good and discard the bad.

Seeing Pauline's day-to-day ordeals, it doesn't take a rocket scientist to know that God has blessed her with amazing strength. God gives her much patience because she allows me to be in her life! I watched her run errands from 6 a.m. to 9 p.m., doing for her parents and others. What she does is not easy and many people would not be able to handle it. Nevertheless, I know God is pleased with her. The bible says that we should honor our parents so that our days will be lengthened and that it shall go well with us. Are you honoring your parents? As I look at the professionals in this type of career, everyone is not cut out for that type of work. You must be dedicated and hopefully have God in your heart. It may look easy from the outside, but there is nothing easy about it at all. For instance, I took care of my 94-year-old grandfather. No, it wasn't easy, even though we lived in the same house. Pauline had to leave her house and run across the road to take care of the needs of her parents, which makes it difficult. My hat goes off to Pauline, and all of those who assist those that are in need. Many are not fortunate to have a person with a heart like Pauline's in their family. You may have to place your loved one in a nursing home because you are not equipped to handle their needs properly. We must pray to God to place our loved ones in the hands of those who love them. You will be in a position to visit the nursing homes and will be in a better position to appreciate the work that they do. We must keep them lifted up in our prayers.

Pauline loves to cook and she is a very good cook. People would stop by her house to eat, and I would get angry. I asked one guy, "Why you don't ever bring a bag with you?" I also asked him, "Why don't you bring something in with you sometimes?" I guess I was running all of Pauline's friends away, but I saw them taking advantage of her. Pauline would continue to feed them and I just wanted to knock her head off (smile). I knew she was being used. Yet, God knows. He made her in His image, not in my image, and God is love. Pauline would tell me I was too mean, and I would tell her she was too nice.

Her mother is a very nice, soft-spoken lady, and I had a good time laughing with her. She is a very strong woman to put up with her lovely husband and have so much patience. She would fuss with him and her tone of voice never changed, it was always calm. He would be in a rage and her voice never changed. This is true love and patience at its best.

Now her father was a different person. He was always kind to me, but he had pit bulls guarding his heart. He did this because he knew his heart was like a marshmallow and I told him that. He looked at me with a frown on his face, and began to laugh. He had a part of him that he would let people know, but he wouldn't let everyone in. He was no punk! I loved him so much. Every time he said my name he would pronounce it incorrectly. He called me Baronica, instead of Veronica. This didn't bother me one bit.

One morning, I heard a shot. I looked from the porch and saw Daddy Peteet loading his rifle and shotgun. I hollered, "Daddy where are you going?" He told me that he was going to shoot this white man, if he doesn't have his money. I then said, "Daddy put that gun down or you are going to jail". I got on the phone and called Pauline and told her to hurry up home. The man was supposed to be repairing Daddy Peteet's lawn mower. He was angry because he paid the man three months prior and he kept delaying by giving him excuses. He told me, "I'm tired and he's not going to take my money". His nephew, brother-in-law and Pauline had to go and talk to the man. The man didn't know how much danger was ignited by his unreliable ways.

I loved Daddy Peteet and all of his ways. One of the funniest things that he said to me was, "Woman what's wrong with your hair? Do you ever comb it?" I laughed because my hair was done in a certain style. The style is called "spiked". He thought it was just sitting on top of my head. Daddy Peteet had taken ill, and needed to go to the hospital. As he was being taken to the hospital, he wouldn't leave until I prayed for him. As God would have it, I stopped and prayed for him. As it turned out, I missed my flight back to Chicago. When I finally did arrive in Chicago my phone rang. It was Pauline saying that her father went into a deep sleep and they couldn't wake him. I felt in my spirit he would be fine, that was the reason he wanted prayer. He woke up the next day. Pauline's father and mother made my stay so beautiful.

While writing this book, Daddy Peteet went home to be with the Lord. He will truly be missed, and visiting Mississippi will never be the same. "I will miss your beautiful smile, I will miss you fussing, and I'll even miss praying for you. I know the angels are rejoicing in heaven, Daddy Peteet!"

I completed this book in 2009, and begin to type it up February 2010. I accidentally pushed a button on the computer, erasing all 79 pages. I recall being in Mississippi, how I was angry because I didn't have a computer. God knew what was best for me. After it was erased, I still had a copy of my book on hand. This is why God wanted me to write the book on paper. Praise the Lord! Now let us travel into the journey of the unknown.

When God has something for you. No devil on earth, or in hell can stop you from receiving it. Only **you** can stop it!

God decided to create a beautiful child. He began his fearful and wonderful creation and nine months later Veronica Waddell was born to Tyrone Loyal Oby and Barbara Jean Waddell. I'm the eldest of my siblings, my father had two boys and two girls, and my mother had three girls. My father was killed when I was 9 years old. He died of gunshot wounds. My father was shot 22 times by the police. I can still hear my grandmother saying, "How are we going to tell Ronnie?"

(Ronnie is one of my many nicknames). I got up that morning, as I did every morning. Part of my daily routine was beating my grandmother to getting the newspaper. I loved to read the paper before I went to school. I got the paper before my grandmother could stop me. I looked at the front page and there was my father lying on the ground, dead. There was a jacket covering the upper portion of his body and head. I couldn't see his face, but I knew it was my father. At about 2:00 o'clock a.m. that morning "something" woke me up. I felt someone sat on the side of my bed. I turned around and there was no one there. Before I woke up, I had a dream that I was talking to my father. He told me, "Everything is going to be alright 'Slim', (this is a nickname that he gave me). I am gone, but you will be o.k. and I want you to know that I love you." I gathered up and thought about everything that happened that day. I knew without a shadow of doubt that it was my father.

Although, my father and mother never married or lived together, I was very close to my father. I felt as if my life was crushed. I felt empty inside, as if I had lost one of my vital organs. My entire body was numb, I couldn't explain to anyone how lost I felt. My father was killed in January 1969, and by July, I was baptized at the "31st Street Beach", in Chicago. I had also begun to practice hiding my feelings. I was ashamed to cry because of the way my father died. I wanted to appear strong, so whenever my younger sister or cousins teased me, I could defend myself. I can still hear them saying, "That's why the police killed your father", whenever they became angry with me.

My mother worked, bought us clothes, and kept our hair styled nice. She took us places and gave us money. However, she was a party animal. She enjoyed herself and to me, that's what was important. So the home of my mother's mother is where my younger sister and three of my first cousins stayed. This is where the "nurturing" took place.

My grandmother Maxine (we called her mama) had five of her six grandchildren living with her. She took good care of us. My middle sister and my younger sister had the same father. My middle sister was raised by her father's mother. I thank God for mama. She had rules in her house and we had to go to church every Sunday. We attended Quinn Chapel Methodist church for Sunday school, and attended a Baptist church for morning service. If we didn't go to church, we were not allowed to go outside and play all week. Although we really didn't want to go, we attended church. When I went to visit my father's mother, I attended Catholic Church. When I visited my stepfather's mother, I attended the Church of God In Christ. I was knowledgeable of the bible and got to know Jesus at a very young age. It was never a surprise to me that my grandmother would make us go to church. My grandmother's father was a pastor, her brother is a pastor, her nephew was a pastor, and her stepmother was the principal of a school. My grandmother had two years of college, which was something outstanding in her day. She attended Lane College in Jackson, Tennessee. Her mother died when she was 5 years old. My father's mother was a beautician, and her father was also a pastor.

I was very bright as a young child. I guess this is why no one thought I needed counseling after my father passed. At the age of 8 I could go downtown on public transportation, and would take my friends almost anywhere in the city. No one thought I needed any type of help, but I was hurting on the inside. No one thought about me because I was very good at hiding my hurt and pain. This caused me desperately to try to fill the void in my life. I was truly missing my father. He would pick me up in the long black Cadillac on Sundays. I would ride in the front seat and we would head to the old Maxwell Street area. He would order two Polish sausage sandwiches, two orange pops for himself, and he would order two hot dogs and an orange pop for me. We would sit and eat having our man and woman conversation. That one-on-one time made me feel so special.

The other hot dog stand we would visit was located on the corner of 79th and Morgan, just down the street from my grandmother's beauty shop. I would stand outside the shop and wait on him to come down the street. At that time, the street would be so crowded that I could never see his face, because I was so little. I would watch the legs of the people and I could pick his legs out of the crowd. I knew his walk. I would run down the street and jump right into his arms and we would go to the hotdog stand and eat. After my father died, I prayed throughout my life that no one would hurt like I did. I didn't want anyone to experience the pain I was having.

As I mentioned, I was a very intelligent child. I did exceedingly well in school. I was an excellent speaker, reader, and was outstanding in vocabulary. I took my 6th grade test, to pass to the next grade, and I did very well. I did very well on everything, except math. I hated math with a passion. My mother and grandmother couldn't understand how I could score 8.8 in reading, 9.0 in vocabulary, 9.0 in spelling and a 4.9 in math, while in the sixth grade. I knew why, because I hated math and loved to read. Anything I didn't like, or held no interest in, I would not put any effort into it. I was no dummy by a long shot.

Mama would trust me to take care of her business. I was sent to the Social Security Office when I was 9 years old, to get my sisters' and cousins' Social Security Cards. Although I lived with mama in the Harold L. Ickes projects, I had very prominent people in my family. I also had very influential people in my life. Let me introduce you to my family members. My maternal grandfather Robert Waddell was born in Grand Junction, Tennessee, a town right outside of Memphis. He worked in Chicago at Humboldt Bottling Company for over 35 yrs. My maternal grandmother Maxine Reed Waddell was born in Brownsville, Tennessee. Her father was Rev. Robert Reed; he served as the Pastor of Woodlawn Baptist Church in Brownsville, Tennessee (her mother died when she was 5 yrs. old and she was raised by her aunt, Willie Ann Barber). We called her Aunt Will and she was something else. My paternal grandfather was Claude T. Oby and he worked for International Harvester for 30 yrs. My paternal grandmother Bessie Oby owned a beauty shop, named "Le Femme" and her father was Rev. Scott.

My father was a very intelligent man who worked for International Harvester until he was murdered. The story given was never proven. But when God has a plan for your life nothing can alter it, except you. My father was affiliated with the Black Panthers; he took me to many of the meetings. My father was one of the few Black men to assist in designing the Dan Ryan Expressway. My father was an excellent artist, he designed his motorcycle and had it built.

My mother Barbara Jean Ford worked for Internal Revenue, she then transferred to Social Security Administration where she worked 30 years. (this where she retired from). My step-father, Charles Ford, worked for Hertz and later went to work for Chicago Housing Authority. My step-grandmother, Mary Matthews, worked for a local furrier and she made fur coats for them. She was also a gospel singer. There are many Pastors, Ministers and Evangelists in my family. There are so many that I can't name them all. So now that you have met the influential people in my life and let us move on.

CHAPTER 2

Deuteronomy

I was now about to learn the laws of life. When I was 5 years old, my mother married Charles Ford. He was the father of my sisters, Raya and Renita. Charles was very nice to me. He never treated me any different than he treated my sisters. I truly loved him. But he had a terrible temper and it reared its ugly head when he got angry, even with my mother. Once when I was 5 years old, I heard my mother screaming. I walked down the hall and he had the barrel of the shotgun in my mother's mouth. I pleaded with him, "Please don't shoot my mother"! He put the gun down and told me how sorry he was. I made him promise he wouldn't hit her again. It was at that moment I made up my mind that no man will ever put his hands on me, and live. I went into a protective mode. I prayed every night that he wouldn't hurt my mother. However, it happened again. When I was 8 years old, I saw him beating my mother again. I walked up on him and told him, "you broke your promise and you will not get away with it this time".

Later, I was sitting and talking with my Uncle James, who was actually my cousin. We believe he was a hit man. He seemed so cold and heartless. Many people in the family were afraid of him, but I was too young to know that. (I would find out later about James from my grandfather.) I went to many Black Stone Ranger meetings with James. He took me everywhere. He called me "Noinky" and I enjoyed being with him. I told him what had happened with Charles beating my mother. James and Charles were very close. But yes, I was trying to hire a hit man at 8 years old, to take care of my stepfather. As a child, I couldn't conceive of the enormity of what the results could really be. If I had known, I don't think I would have kept it a secret. I was just that angry and hurt. James went to talk to T.T, and she pleaded with him not to kill Charles. T.T was very angry with me for telling her business. I was just as angry with her and at that time I asked to go back to mama's house. I didn't want to be there to see it happen again. Then later, she eventually left him and moved with mama for a while.

Now came the time for me to enter high school. I attended Wendell Phillips High School, where I was on the honor roll in my first year. I was the principal's pet. I worked in the office on my free time. The principal took an interest in me because he said I was a very bright young lady. Favor was upon me. Once, my world geography teacher and I got into a confrontation. He was giving a test and the lead on my pencil broke. I asked him if I could go to the locker to get another pencil. He told me "no", that I would have to fail the test. I was not about to let this happen. I went to the locker anyway. I didn't understand his attitude because I never gave him any problem. When I returned, he told me he would pull all the "nappy Nigger hair out of my head". He pushed me, and I defended myself. This was a grown man who had pushed me. It wasn't a little push. I picked up a chair and hit him with it. I was about to hit him with the desk until a student grabbed it. I was then sent to the principal's office. Mr. Estelle kept me there the rest of the year. My class assignments was sent to the office for me to complete

Mr. Estelle was an inspiration to me, He would take time to talk to me and he would actually listen to what I had to say. I remember him telling me that I would go far in life. He believed in me and said he saw a great future in me. But the enemy of our souls had another plan for me. I was confused and evil seemed to be around me a lot. I was so tired of fighting and tired of the boys bothering me. I fought on the way to school, in the school, on the way home, and after I got home. I didn't care whether it was a boy or girl. I even fought the teachers, if they did something to me. Life without beautiful people around is like a room without light. Beautiful people lighten up your life. The beauty that I am talking about comes from God and shines through His people. It seemed that I didn't have any of that.

I found it strange many of the boys I knew called me Smiley. I didn't feel it because I fought so much. I became fed up with fighting. I asked T.T if I could I attend an all-girls high school and she agreed. I transferred to Visitation High School for my second year. T.T had bought a house in the 7500 block of South Winchester Street in city of Chicago. My Aunt Yvonne Palm bought a house right next door. I was happy because now my cousins (Capatoria and Norman) were right next door. I grew up with these two cousins at mama's house. My sister Nita and I now had company. I felt that we were back to being a family. My cousins Norman and Steven (Jody) decided they wanted to stay in the Projects with mama.

My sister Raya stayed with her father's mother (Mary Matthew), she had been with her since she was 2 months. (Raya is the middle child) I couldn't understand how my mother could give her away and have another child 11 months later. I asked so many questions about this that I stayed in trouble. I was told she cried too much and she couldn't get any sleep. I asked T.T, "Didn't my little sister cry also, so why did you give the other child away?" I would then get "cursed out". I just felt for whatever reason she was given away that the purpose was defeated, by having another child.

I was now in my second year of high school at an all-girls Catholic high school. It was so different for me, but I loved it. I had one problem: the religion classes that I were mandated to take. I asked too many questions. As a child, I had all of these pastors, ministers, and evangelists in my family. I attended Church of God in Christ, Methodist, Catholic and Baptist churches. I was in Catholic High School now. I was always put out of the class because of the questions I asked. The teachers felt like I was putting them on the spot, but I truly wanted to know why we weren't praying to Jesus. I really didn't understand why we were praying to His mother. After all, He is the Savior. I also couldn't understand this place they called Purgatory. I couldn't find it in my bible and that was a problem for me. I tried over and over to find it in my bible and I couldn't find it.

One day I took my bible to class with me and raised my hand. I asked the teacher if she could find Purgatory in my bible. Once again...out of the class I went! The teacher was right behind me saying that I was trying to be the class clown. There was another time that I raised my hand and I asked the teacher why was she always throwing me out the class? I didn't wait on an answer, I answered it for her. I told her, "I know why you are always throwing me out. It is because you are teaching us a lie. You can't find it in my bible because it doesn't exist. You are lying to us. Why would you lie?" I was out of the class again, but fortunately it was near the end of the school year. I was so afraid to look at my grades. I knew I had failed the religion class for sure. God saw different. I received an "A" and a letter from my religion teacher saying, "Keep up the fight you will do well in life."

Oh Jesus what a sweet name! Oh Jesus what a powerful name! I dare not fail to call your name! Demons tremble at the name of Jesus! Things begin to move at the call of your name! When the waves are raging and the tides are high, I can call on him and he never gets tired, or tells me to stop calling him. I thank God for Jesus!

While I was in school, I organized the "Say No to Drugs" program. It was later used in all of the high schools. I also began to write and perform a one person play. The play allowed me to place 3rd in the 1975 Miss Elk of Illinois pageant, 2nd in the 1976 Miss Elk pageant, and 10th in the 1976 Miss Black Teenage Illinois pageant. There were close to 500 contestants. This made me so proud to be in the 10th place.

In my first year of high school, I found that I had a gift. I found it out after I injured my back in gym and was out of school for two weeks. I became very bored and began to write poetry. I wrote close to 100 poems in two weeks. I enjoyed writing because it brought me peace. I was able to express how I felt and not get in trouble. I went on at the age of 16 years old to write a 300 page book entitled, "Have Anyone Seen Ivory Brown?" I never did anything with the book. My sister really enjoyed reading the book; she still talks about it today. I continued my journey in high school and I was a straight A student even after I completed my math. I solved the "math problem" by going to summer school every summer to take two classes.

I loved going to school. I needed 16 credits to graduate. However, I had 19 credits in my junior year. The Catholic high school would not allow me to graduate early. If I had stayed in the public school, I would have graduated at sixteen years old. When I finished my senior year, I had 4 A's, and was waiting for my Spanish teacher to give me my grade. There was competition between myself, and a Hispanic girl to become Salutatorian of the class. My Spanish teacher gave me a B plus and the Spanish girl an A- so that she would graduate in the "number two" spot. I felt I was cheated again. The Spanish teacher told me, "We look out for our own sweetie". If only she could read what was going through my mind, I don't think I would have been "sweetie" then.

I decided I would go away to college, since I had been accepted at many of the best in the United States such as Harvard, Yale, Princeton, and Mississippi Valley State. I was applying just to see if I could get accepted. T.T looked at the tuition to Harvard and said, "The cost of their tuition is more than I make." I decided to go to Mississippi Valley since it was a black university. Mama's nephew and his wife had ties to the school. When I arrived there, I noticed that the dormitories were extremely hot. I immediately called mama and told her I wanted to come home.

Once I was in my room. The monitor came into the room and told me to pack up I was moving. I asked her, "Where am I going?" She never answered me, she just walked off. I thought maybe my grandmother had made a call and I was being moved to the sophomore dorms, since they had the air. I packed up, went outside, and there was a car waiting for me. I got in the car, and the man drove off, passing the sophomore dorms. My thoughts were maybe he's taking me to the bus station so that I could go home.

We pulled up in front of a mini mansion and a lady was standing in the doorway. I got out of the car and the lady called me by my name. She introduced herself to me as Ms. White, the wife of the founder of the college. I was told that I would be staying with her duration my college stay. I was given a four-year scholarship. I hated everything about the college. It was just too hot for me. Not to mention, there were frogs everywhere. I was so afraid of the frogs that a 5 year old to hold my hand once. That was the last straw for me! The people did everything they could to satisfy me. However, I was never going to be satisfied. The truth is that I had left the man that I loved behind. Mr. Jay was that man. No matter what they did I wasn't going to stay. If I had only known what was ahead. Here are some words of wisdom: Don't turn down sure opportunities for possibilities of "IF he loves you, he will wait". I met Mr. Jay in my second year of high school and I was madly in love with him. I returned back to Chicago, and a year later we were married. (Well, it was actually three years later. We told people we were married when we weren't.) That was another mistake on my behalf. My thoughts were "If I gave up college for him, he should have given up something for me."

Rebuke the devil at the door because once he gets in he will spread out, and will become too large to exit out the same door. He will rearrange your life and your house until you force him out. It's easier for him to come in, than it is for him to leave. Don't allow him an opportunity to enter.

There are twists and turns, hills and mountains, pitfalls and darkness, hail and storms, temptation and frustration on the path of every good man's journey. We have already overcome all these things with faith and endurance. These things may slow us down but they won't stop us. It's not about who will be first, it's about going forward and not giving up. These things are designed to give us strength.

Revelation: Hurt and pain as a child, if not addressed, will grow into other problems. The problems will follow you throughout life, until you allow God to step in and guide you. God will allow us to go through things to teach us, and to strengthen us for what's to come. Yes, I made many other mistakes, but God was right by my side giving me instructions. It was up to me to follow His instructions, and when I didn't follow, I paid dearly for being disobedient. Being intelligent does not mean that I would not make mistakes in my life. We must allow ourselves room for mistakes. If I had listened to the advice of my elders, I would have stayed away at college and many things I went through would have never happened. I guess God said, "You will get tired of being beat down before I get tired of forgiving you".

I have not always been dealt the best hand in life, but with the presence of God I've played with such great wisdom. Although I was not always a winner, by the time the next hand was dealt, everyone knew not to underestimate how I played my hand. My presence was known, even when I was not aware of what I was doing. God will allow people to know who you are before you recognize who you are. God has truly blessed me and I learned to recognize a blessing when I see it. Your blessings can lead you to greater things when you appreciate them. The elders giving advice was no more than a blessing. Stay behind your blessings, it's your guide to greater things. Don't get ahead of your blessings or you will lose direction. God is in the blessing business at all times, we must learn to recognize them.

CHAPTER 3

The Joseph Experience

I was about to enter a hole. I was asking for help, yet nobody extended a helping hand. I was stuck until God had revealed to me my strength to pull myself out of the hole. I was being sold for less than a coat only because I loved and he didn't love. Maybe I should say that he loved the only way he knew how to love. He cared nothing about me, only himself. T.T and my aunts were too busy partying to give me advice. It was not until I got older that we would sit down and have a talk. They were not in the best relationships themselves. For them to give me an ounce of advice would be pointless. After all, what did they know about relationships and problem solving? My grandmothers believed that once you are married, you should remain in the marriage until death. T.T would talk to me about my husband. She would also discuss with him, many things that she and I discussed. I was a blind fool. You are powerless when you don't realize how much power you have.

The day we got married, my husband and I were on the bus. He got up before our stop. I asked him, "Where are you going?" He replied, "My woman is waiting for me at the motel." I didn't believe him then, but later found out that he was telling the truth. I stayed with him because I had married him. In all actuality, I was searching for love in the wrong places. It was more of lust than it was love.

I realize that Emmanuel (God with us) was in my life from the beginning to the end. For example, God allowed me to have many good jobs in my early years. By the time I made 19 years old, I had worked three good paying jobs. At the age of 17, I obtained a job with Chicago Transit Authority during the summer. I went to work for Social Security Administration at the age of 18. I transferred to the Post Office at the age of nineteen. Many of my co-workers were unaware that they could transfer from the Social Security Administration to the Post Office until I did it. Many of them followed me. I was always good about gathering information and about exploring new things to learn. While working at the Post Office, God blessed me with two beautiful daughters, Tyra and Taineeka. Many of my family and friends had children. They were waiting on me have a child. I was age 24 when my first was born, and 26 years old when the second child arrived. I wanted boys, but God wanted otherwise. I thank God for my girls.

Bearing children didn't change Mr. Jay. He actually left me in the maternity ward while I was in labor. His reason was that I wouldn't stop crying. He even told me that if I had any more children that he would leave me. That was something I would never forget. He was controlling, yet he was out of control. I did everything to satisfy my husband, it was never enough. He was never physically abusive. Nevertheless, he was emotionally, mentally, and verbally abusive. He couldn't manage to stay out the bed with other women. As a matter of fact, he was with another woman every chance he got. Many would question my reason for staying with him. I stayed with him for the reason that many women give for remaining toxic relationships: I was hoping that he'd change. I was caught in a web of finding love because I didn't love myself. I was hurting.

Mr. Jay was taught that his children would always be his children, but his wife would not always be his wife. He had no values for marriage. He was never at home and he lied to me on a constant basis concerning his whereabouts. I was basically serving as mom and dad to our children. He felt that paying the rent was his only obligation. He was very self-centered. I can remember a time when our children needed shoes because their shoes were worn down. Mr. Jay walked in the house smiling; he had purchased a brand new pair of expensive, designer shoes for himself. I fussed so much, the children and I ended up with new shoes.

I wanted to go to school for nursing. Mr. Jay had told me that if I quit my job that he would stand behind me 100%. It wasn't until after I left the Post Office that I would learn otherwise. He was setting me up for failure. What he didn't understand was that God was allowing him to set me up for the comeback. God had a ram in the bush and I didn't know it.

Mr. Jay would have affairs with people of whom I knew. He did not discriminate. He had affairs with family members, so-called friends, associates, and strangers. After we separated, three of my associates called me on three separate occasions, to let me know the reason that they had stop coming around. They had stopped because he was "hitting" on them. "Hitting" used in this context, is a street term for flirting. Mr. Jay also had an affair with a woman for 25 years. After our divorce was final, he married her. She waited 25 years for Mr. J and I to divorce. Now, she finally has what she always wanted… a husband. To God Be the Glory! When they got married it was a secret. His children weren't invited to the wedding. I was astounded; I thought he was only concealing it from me.

I had to move on. After all, I was the one who had filed for the divorce. I was very optimistic about continuing my journey. There was one problem: my divorce papers were returned me. I failed to put my signature on them. The next day after, a letter came in the mail. The letter was from my husband's lawyer stating that he was filing for a divorce! This was awesome, now I didn't have to file. I began to thank the Lord. I knew he was by my side.

The day I went to court for the divorce, I made sure I was dressed in my best. I was in such a joyful mood. I felt I was going to my freedom party; I was being set free from the plantation. When I got off the elevator at the Daley Center, the first person I noticed was Mr. Jay. I walked over to him and asked, "Why aren't you dressed up for this special occasion?" He looked at me and began to cry. We went into the courtroom;

my attorney was running late. Mr. Jay's attorney turned around and said to me," Why don't we just go before the judge? You both agree to the divorce. Why don't you sign the papers so that we can leave?" I told his attorney, "Why don't you leave the papers here and let my attorney handle it?" He replied, "I can't do that." I told him, "Then turn around and be quiet. You and I have nothing to talk about." I couldn't believe that he would think I was that stupid. I didn't come this far to allow my final decision regarding my marriage to be a foolish one. I had made too many mistakes in my life. This would NOT be one of them.

My attorney walked in with two other attorneys behind her. Mr. Jay's attorney looked very uneasy; both of them were in shock. I laughed as I thought to myself, "Look at God! He didn't just send me one attorney! He sent me three! The Trinity" has just walked in the courtroom!" I knew God was about to favor me. Mr. Jay's attorney went before the judge. He pretended as if he forgot to bring the most important form for the divorce. This form was needed in order for me to be paid. The judge told him to get on the bus, go to the library, and get the form. My attorney told me if I had went in front of the judge, before she arrived and the paper wasn't signed I would not have received any money. I would have forfeited everything. My attorney informed me that I didn't have to wait. I could go home. God was still walking with me.

The company that you keep is delegates that you have chosen to represent you. You may not think they can change you, but they can surely change how people view you. Little by little, they are chipping away at pieces of you, good or bad. The next time you choose delegates, make sure what they are chipping away, they can replace it with something greater than what you have already obtained.

Now I want to back up for a moment. I must tell what led to the divorce. I found out that Mr. Jay had a baby with a woman that I knew. I was told that the baby was his mother's foster child. Due to the fact that his mother had custody of the child, I was allowed to babysit on several occasions. I received an anonymous tip that my mother in law's foster child was my husband's child. I asked him if the child was his. He denied it. What led me to believe him were these words that came out of his mouth. He put his hand up and said, "That child is not mine! If I'm lying, God could take the breath out of my mother." Never did I think that he would ask God to kill his mother unless, he was telling the truth. I knew I would never say anything like that about my mother. The next day, I called his cousin's house looking for him because he didn't come home. A child answered the phone, and told me that he went to the hospital. I didn't think anything of it. The Holy Spirit spoke to me, telling me to call back and find out if he went to the hospital, or did he go with someone. I did just that. The child told me that the ambulance took him to the hospital because he couldn't breathe. I went to the hospital and he was on a ventilator. The doctor said that his heart had stopped three times on the way to the hospital. I stood over him not knowing whether he could hear me or not. I told him, "You are not going to die until you tell me whether that child is your son." I didn't expect him to respond. After all, I was making a declaration. The hospital kept him for further observation. The next day, I was riding around in my car. My thoughts were racing. The Holy Spirit had instructed me to go by the hospital. When I arrived, they were taking him off the ventilator. I asked him once more, "Is that baby your child?" Once again, he denied that the child was his.

Two days later, he was discharged from the hospital. He came home and confirmed what I already knew: he was the father of the child. I had put up with so much during our marriage, but this was a hard pill to swallow. Words could not express the feeling of devastation that had come over me. I was torn beyond words. I had no family to turn to. My mother had passed away on May 27, 1999 (this was November of 2000). Once I found out that he fathered the baby, his family had become very angry with me. (Now there were a few of his family members that were not angry with me. They actually were a blessing to me and I thank God for them.) This left me baffled. After all, I was the one who was betrayed. I didn't understand how they could hate me for no reason. I had been around this family since I was 15 years old. I considered them as being my family. I would not be the only one affected by this situation. Our children were too affected. No one cared about the emotional disturbance, or the hurt that the situation caused my children. During this time, there was so much confusion being kept up, our children were no longer able to visit their grandmother.

If you allow the devil to hold your hand, he will eventually become your dancing partner. He will step on your feet, spin you and let you go, trip you up, and when you think he will catch you he'll let you fall. Instead of helping you up he will dance on top of you. Know who's holding your hand.

It was right around the time of our anniversary. I decided that I would go out and eat on my anniversary. He had told me he wanted to take me out. Instead, he took his woman out. So I went out alone. While I was out, I couldn't stop thinking about what was going on. I knew that this would be the last anniversary that I would spend with him. I looked in the booth next to me and there set a man who I recognized. I couldn't think of his name right away, but it finally came to me who he was. He was out to dinner with his wife. As they were preparing to leave I asked him, "Are you Congressman Bobby Rush?" He told me yes. I knew that he was not only a congressman; he was also a Pastor. I asked him could he pray for me and I began to cry. I explained to him what I was going through. He and his wife prayed for me. That was so nice of them. He did get me to smile. He looked over at my plate and told me that I better eat my food because it looked like it has gotten cold.

I went to a friend's house and talked to her for a long time. She told me, "Girl God has you". When I got home it was 1 a.m. My husband was in the bed sleep as if he had done nothing. I looked on the floor next to his coat and there was a piece of paper. I picked it up and saw where he had bought two steaks, one for him and one for his girlfriend. I woke him up and told him, "Pack your stuff. It's time to go and make sure you take everything because I don't want you to come back here. You told me if I had another child that you would leave me. You had the child and now things are being reversed; you are leaving." I was struggling to be strong for our girls and hurting at the same time. The more I was hurting, the more his family dug more to hurt me.

The woman that he was having the affair with was calling my house. She had no respect for me as his wife. I guess she didn't feel she needed to respect me because he didn't. She was calling my house as if I was supposed to be afraid of her. I was never afraid. I actually felt sorry for her. I knew that it was going to come back on her and everyone that was involved in their unholy alliance. All I had to do is sit back and watch. I know that this is how the devil worked. He will let you feel like you're on top when actually you are on the bottom. I knew that when groups come against you, Satan will have them fighting amongst each other in the end. This is how Satan worked. The same thing that makes you laugh will eventually make you cry. No one can fight like God. When God fights for you no one can help your enemy.

I wasn't thinking straight and I knew that trouble was coming. I knew someone was going to get hurt. I decided to move away from Chicago. I had a friend who lived in Nashville, Tennessee. I decided that I would visit, and not to let him know that I was coming. I left and went to Tennessee on January 23, 2001. I would go there to find me a place to live. I didn't care where I lived, I just wanted out of Chicago. I went to the Tennessee Housing Authority while I was there. I found out that Section 8 applications were being given out. I went there and completed an application for Section 8, thinking it wouldn't hurt to be on the waiting list.

I then returned to Chicago. I received a call in about a week, Housing wanted me to come down and look at a place. I thanked God for the quick response, not knowing God had other plans for me. I left Chicago, going back to Tennessee on February 5, 2001. I was given a list of places. I didn't like the places because they were not safe for my daughters. They were now ages 16 and 14. The 16 year old was now pregnant. Yes, she was pregnant. I found out one month after I found out about Mr. Jay's child! Yes, that was another blow and I was just a walking shell, not knowing where to turn. I had looked at the last apartment on the list and I stood in that yard with tears rolling down my face. I cried out to God, "Lord I need you! I can't live here, Lord please what am to I do now? Lord you told me you would never leave me and you would be with me from the beginning to the end. Lord, please help me! I need you, I'm hurting. Lord, you are all I have I need you right now!" Then something strange happened, it was something that I can't explain. I do know it was God. There were six men in front of the liquor store across the street from where I was standing. I was crying out and I didn't care who were watching. Peace came upon me and I began to wipe my eyes. I looked across the street and the six men were staring at me, not saying a word. They appeared to be looking at me, but they were looking pass me. I looked behind me there was no one there. As I was turning around, my cell phone rang. It was my youngest daughter calling from Chicago. I answered and she said, "Mama you have a letter from Section 8." I figured they were letting me know they had put me on the waiting list, since it had only been about three weeks since I filled out the application. I told her to open it. She did. She told me that they had reached my name on the list and they wanted me to come down in a week. I fell to my knees. I couldn't believe it. I prepared to go back to Chicago so that I could come back to Tennessee next week.

When I returned to Chicago, I noticed that I was in pain, physically. My stomach and thighs were hurting. They had been hurting for a while, but I tried to ignore it. I decided to go to the doctor. I was diagnosed with gonorrhea. I was informed that I had been infected for a while. I called my husband to ask him about it. He told me that he had already been treated. I asked him, why he didn't tell me. He told me that it wasn't up to him to tell me anything; he was going to let my doctor tell me. Here I was, the mother of his two daughters and this is what he thought of me? I was dealing with a modern day Pharaoh. Yes, he had a hardened heart. This was no surprise to me because I couldn't count the numerous other times that I went to the hospital for infections. My chart was so long that I was ashamed to go to the doctor. I remember once, a Nurse Practitioner asked me, "How long are you going to allow your husband to abuse you." I had never looked at it as abuse, until she asked the question. She shook her head and said, "You will be dead and he will still be alive. If he gave you something and you didn't know it, he would never tell you. You are dealing with a monster. He's the devil. You better get out while you can."

T.T and mama never told me that I was being abused. They told me that this is something you go through with men. I thought about my father's mother, Grandma Oby. Whenever I told her how my husband was treating me. She would become very quiet but one day she spoke up. She told me, "I will never tell you to leave him. The day you get tired, you won't come to get advice. You will be coming to tell me that you have left. No one will know you have left until you have done it sweetheart. You just follow God and your heart, you won't go wrong." I said to myself, "what a women of wisdom, she is awesome". I thought about what my husband would tell me. I would ask him why he was so cold and he would say, "I'm the devils right hand man." I can remember when his son was 6 or 7 months old, every time I looked at the baby, he would turn his head, as if he didn't want me to see his face. Mr. Jay and his family would laugh.

I went to Tennessee and I received my moving papers. I found me a beautiful place. I received a three-bedroom apartment with two bathrooms, and a swimming pool, located in a beautiful apartment complex. I was scheduled to move in on June 14, 2001, but I had to put the "move in" date on hold. I had to have surgery. There was damaged tissue from the STD I had gotten from my husband. I put the date off until July 23rd, after the surgery. I asked God to give me peace, and I thought I was going for peace. The divorce judge had given me temporary maintenance, to give us time to think about what we were going to do. The divorce did not go through until I returned to Chicago to live, which was two years later. That was fine with me, as long as I was allowed to leave and go and find peace, so I thought. I moved to Tennessee praying to have peace restored in my life once again.

Revelation: "Therefore what God has joined together let man not separate", Mark 10:9. God never put my husband and I together. We put ourselves together. If God had put us together it would have never began with him getting off the bus, to be with his lover. When we do things out of the order of God, things continue out of order. We also lived a lie, yet God knew the truth. We lived together telling people we were married, when we weren't married (Deception). This is not how God operate. He doesn't bless lies. I was operating under the rules of Satan and I was getting what he had to offer. Satan doesn't give blessings, he give lessons. Once you have received your lesson, you can be blessed by learning from it. Yes, God will turn a lesson into a blessing. I thank God for his grace.

I was hurting and there was no medication that could stop the pain. The only medication that could give me relief was Jesus. I knew that God had a plan for my life, because he would continue to bless me when I didn't deserve to be blessed.

I learned that love has to be shown. Therefore, a person should not just tell you that they love you; they should demonstrate their love through actions. God is love. God is perfect love. I have learned that people will turn on you at the drop of a hat. The average person operates out of surface love and that is not in the heart. I learned that the scripture about God that says, "I will never leave you nor forsake you" and He will not. God's word is the only one that never changes. Although there were many that were wrong in this situation, I decided to let God handle the situation. I knew that I wasn't fighting the people; I would have been fighting Satan. They may not have realized they were being used by Satan to try and destroy me, but they were. I was in a spiritual fight for my life. Satan was trying to kill me and he had lost the battle. I don't have any animosity against anyone. I was made by God to pray for them even when I was hurting. I am mandated by God to continue to love to those that hurt me and have caused me pain. I knew that vengeance was the Lord's and I had to move on with my life. God moved me away to reach me. I had been running for a long time. I was reaching out to a man to fill the void of losing the only man in my life. I just wanted the pain of losing my father to go away.

I learned that God was all the love that I needed in my life. Not to say that I didn't make more mistakes afterwards, yes I made more and I paid for them. My definition of marriage was developed. God begin to speak to me about marriage. These are some of the words that helped me move on, and he spoke to me after I moved away. I couldn't hold anything against those that spoke to me such as: my mother and grandmothers. This is what they were taught. I learned that people reacted according to what they were taught.

In order for Satan to do his work, he must have a vessel. He must have an entrance into your life, whether it is drugs, alcohol, sex, or money. Once he gains entrance, he then blinds you, gives you a deaf ear, and ties you up, to steal your joy. "No man can enter into a strong man's house, and spoil his goods, except he will first bind the strong man; and then he will spoil his house." Mark 3:27 NIV

Lord, thank you for being my life jacket when I was sinking, my parachute when I was falling, my light in the time of darkness, my peace in chaos, my healer in sickness, my crutch when I couldn't stand, my shoulder to lean on, for loving me in my sin, wiping away my tears, making a way out of no way, and being a Comforter when I needed it. Lord I thank you for all the attributes that make you God. No one can do all these things but you.

I don't agree with women having affairs with married men or vice versa. It's wrong regardless of what the excuse may be. I know there are many that wouldn't agree with me, but this is my own personal opinion. He will give you the lie that you are his helping him through a bad marriage. He will tell you that the marriage is in shambles and they are going to leave their significant other as soon as the children are older, as soon as they find a decent woman, or as soon as she signs the divorce papers.

They will tell you their mate does not satisfy them, they are there for children and they don't love their wife. They will talk about their wife like she is the worst thing that ever happened to them. But you will be talked about next. You are being used because men don't think that you are important. Don't be a fool and fall into the serial infidelity trap. Many feel great by their actions. They are no more than person with low self-esteem, for someone to latch on to.

Many need someone to share their misery with and you are the perfect victim. If they are not happy with their mate, there's nothing in this world that will make them stay. There are outside lovers that would prefer to stay hid from the mate, and family members. They don't want anyone to know who they are. Those are the individuals who are convicted by their actions and some consider themselves respecting the mate. If you are not comfortable with your actions, why do you stay in the mess?

Then there are those who want to be known as the lover. They smile and glow when they are around the married person. They feel like they are important in their presence. They are in need for love and use the person they're with to complete their desire to be seen. They are filling a void in their own life and actually both are using each other. I call these people brazen and very dangerous. They use every excuse of why they do the things they do. They have no respect for themselves or for the mate. These people have it in their mind that their lover belongs to them and they will go to any length to keep them. These are the people that are more than likely to let the mate know, if their lover tried to break the relationship off. It's not about love; it's about what they can get out of the person. They only care about material things.

I wouldn't lie to you and say I've never dealt with a married man. I did it unknowingly. The guy told me that he was divorced. When I found out two years later, I had a chance to get out. I paid dearly for it. I thank God for the wake up early in my life. I thought this is not right, and wouldn't want anyone to do this to me. I don't want to cause another woman pain of no sort. A mistress is a secret woman, and I'm too great of a woman to be someone's secret. What man is so great that he can have me and another woman? On every throne there are two seats: one for the King and one for the Queen. The seats for the prince and the princess seats should be for the children if there are any. PLEASEEEEEE! There's God, my husband, and then there's me. Our children are looking to us for guidance, and to be an example to them. If I can't walk next to my husband, who will catch him and who will catch me if one of us falls? These are my own personal views.

Marriage is a divine institution designed to form a permanent union between man and woman, that they might be helpful to one another. True love is possible through people that have a relationship submitted to God. God grieves with those that have lost loved ones. God is the only one that can replace the void in the heart of those who lose someone they love. Reach out to God when you are feeling alone. He will be whatever you need in your life. Love is God's highest commandment. Without the love of God, it's useless to try to love.

The word of the Lord came to my spirit saying, "I created you and you are beautiful inside out, because you were created in my image. You are a priceless gem that I designed you to be. I created you not to be flawless, but to follow me. I will erase your flaws as you travel your journey. You will go through the fire, you will be put under pressure, but you must realize you are being molded for my kingdom. The carats in a diamond are determined by the fire and pressure that they go through. You are going to go through more fire and pressure. When I'm complete, you will be priceless. No jewelry case can hold you neither will you ever be found in a store on display. You are not for sale. You belong to me and you are one of a kind.

You are my diamond that I created just for me. You have been running and you are not going anywhere, until you hearken unto my voice. I will lift you up when you are down. I will be the shoulder for you to cry on. I will be your support when you are weak. I will lead you through the wilderness. I made you of many carats so that you may shine in the dark places you are about to go. Remember, I will be with you always". He spoke to me so loud and clear, and I wrote every word as he was speaking to me. I cried as the words were being spoken to me because I knew it was God that was speaking to me. The voice was so peaceful and calm, just what I needed at the time. I thought of what had I done to deserve this type of treatment.

I often wondered did these people ever think at one time that what they were doing would come back on them. Did they even care? I wonder did they ever sit down and think about how heartless they were. The fact that Mr. J's woman was going around speaking in the church really embarrassed me. As a matter of fact, I was afraid for her. I knew God would not allow her to play with him long before he turned things around.

The voice of God was bringing peace into my life. I could feel my spirit calming down. I knew I was going to be just fine. After He spoke to me, I felt stronger. I began to pray and read my bible more than ever. This situation bought me closer to God. Many times we think things are really hurting us and actually we are being help. God is molding you to be what He predestined you to be. Sometimes, you have to go through to get there. I loved the verse in Psalms 105:15 "Touch not mine anointed, and do my prophets no harm." I knew this verse was not only for me not to be touched, but I couldn't touch anyone.

I knew that my tears would not be in vain. For every tear that came down my face, my "offenders" would shed more than I did. I knew that things looked good for now, but things were going to change. I often wondered where the words of God in them were. They read the bible, went to church, and they didn't have any parts of God in them. What was the purpose of going to church and reading the bible if you are not going to apply it to your life? I know I'm far from being perfect, but I never enjoyed watching others hurt. I was always afraid of things turning around on me and my family. The scripture in Genesis 12:3 stayed in my thoughts, "I will bless those who bless you, and whoever curses you I will curse; and all peoples on earth will be blessed through you."

The words of God were enough to keep me in line. His words contained many blessings and many curses. I knew He had me and that He would see me through. I knew that He died on the cross for everything that I was going through. If He could bring me to it, He could take me through it. I learned that you can't trust everyone's word, you can only depend the word of God. Everyone that says, "I've got your back" doesn't have your back. Some are trying to get in front. I knew I had nothing to worry about because people would have to deal with God. "Therefore what God has joined together, let man not separate." Mark 10:9. God does give a word that someone should obey. There are consequences for those who know His word and don't obey His word.

It was a learning experience for me and I'm quite sure it was for my offenders as well. One lesson that I learned is to not get caught up in the tornado moment. This is when you are caught up in a whirlwind of chaos; you are so caught up you don't realize you're caught up. Satan has put blinders on you, where you don't realize what you are doing. You become so busy for him that, you are doing things you won't normally do. After the tornado releases you, that is when you realize what you have done and begin to have regrets. There are many that have been hurt in your tornado moment. This is why we must ask ourselves, "Would I want someone to do me this way?" We must not allow Satan to blind us; we must stay focused because it's easy to get caught up.

CHAPTER 4

My Abraham Experience

God said leave and I went under his orders, not knowing what I would be facing once I got to Tennessee. He made it possible for me to find housing and all I wanted was peace. I knew it was God because when I went to the Section 8 office, I was talking to others that had appointments. Many said that they had been waiting seven to eight years to be called. They couldn't believe that I received mine in a couple of weeks.

My granddaughter, Latavia was born August 11, 2001 and it was a joy to have a new arrival in the family. Lose one and gain another, that's how God work. When I arrived in Tennessee, I slept for one whole month before I had realized how long I had been there. It was just what I had asked for... peace. I could hear the birds, grasshoppers and all of the animals. I moved about five miles outside of Nashville, Tennessee, in a town called Smyrna, Tennessee, right off Interstate 24 South. It was a nice peaceful town, part city and part country. When I realized how long I had been there, I jumped out of bed one day. My thoughts were, "I must get up and find me a job. I've been here for over a month." I was sleeping and enjoying it, I knew I needed the rest. I looked in the paper and saw that a company was hiring. I went to a company and filled out an application. The company called me two days later, stating that I had the job. I started working and preparing everyone for school. I worked 16 hours on Saturdays, 16 hours on Sundays, 4 hours on Mondays, and

4 hours on Tuesday. I would take on this schedule so that I could babysit Latavia while my Tyra went to school. I would always have a headache on Mondays. The reason being that I wasn't getting enough sleep; the baby wouldn't stop crying. There had to be a solution to this problem, and there was. I found out that there was a high school that would allow my daughter to bring her child. I transferred both of my daughters and this would allow my youngest daughter to assist my other daughter with my granddaughter. Taineeka was angry, but I was teaching her we must help one another, because we were all we had.

There was no bus to take them to the school, but I was willing to drive them there. In doing this, I could get rest while they were in school. Everything was working well. I was enjoying my new location. I was adjusting to a new way of living. There were no relatives there, although I had a couple friends there. I had one friend that planned on following me and she beat me there by a month. I had another friend that had moved there from Chicago years before I had come. He was an old boyfriend. I had never told him that I was coming.

Tyra was soon graduating from high school. Both daughters had planned on going back to Chicago for the summer. They left for Chicago in May of 2002. I found me a part-time job around the corner from my house. I was working both jobs now and I was able to set my own schedule on the part-time job. Everything was going well until Taineeka called me from Chicago and told me she was sick. It was July 1, 2002 when I told her to come home. She came home on the bus. She was having headaches and she couldn't hold anything on her stomach. I waited until after the fourth of the month and took her to the hospital. The doctor ran the tests and gave us an appointment to come back. I took her home, praying that things would change. While we waited, things got worse. Her tongue had swelled up, her hair began to fall out, and she was losing weight very fast. I took her back to the doctor. The doctors prescribed her some medication for her stomach.

Now we were well into August. The doctor had not

diagnosed Taineeka's problem and she was continuing to lose weight. The doctor sent her to see a psychiatrist. He felt that she was suffering from depression since she missed her father. I took her to see the psychiatrist. I explained to the psychiatrist that she refuses to eat her favorite foods. She responded, "She is depressed, she is imagining her sickness (Psychosomatic)." I jumped up from my seat and told her, "I'm her mother and I know something is wrong. You are the one who need to see a psychiatrist not her". I left the psychiatrist and took Taineeka to another hospital. I was told they could not see her unless I got a referral from her doctor. The doctor wouldn't give her a referral until her test results came back. Meanwhile, her symptoms were getting worse. Her urine turned the color of tea and she was experiencing difficulty urinating. I was really getting worried because she had stop eating; to eat was causing her stomach to hurt. I decided to take her to the hospital where the doctor worked since the clinic was closed.

When I arrived, I was told they couldn't see her. Reason being that she was too young. She was sixteen and children were not admitted into that hospital. This baffled me. How could this be, when the doctor who was seeing her is a doctor at this hospital? I began to pray and ask God for guidance. It wouldn't be until the next morning that I would call the clinic. I was told the doctor was not there. I then asked them for a referral. I was told the only way I could get a referral would be from the doctor, and he wasn't there. I found out that there was a doctor present, in the place of Taineeka's physician doctor. I demanded that I see her. After arguing with the people behind the desk, I was allowed to see her.

Thank God it was a female. I felt she would be more compassionate with me. I realized the original doctor knew he couldn't do anything for her but he kept us coming for the money. I couldn't believe he would let my daughter die on the account of his greed. The female doctor gave me a referral. With that referral, I was able to take my daughter to the hospital. When I did, they ran tests, and sent her home.

The next day, I called the clinic, asking for another referral to a different hospital. I told them that Taineeka was two shades darker, and she still wasn't eating anything. The workers were very rude towards me. They told me there was no doctor available, and hung up the phone on me. Immediately, I called back. I began to get prepared to go to the clinic, which was about three minutes away. As I was getting dressed, I said to the women on the phone, "I am on my way there and when I arrive, I expect a referral from you please in the name of Jesus don't be empty handed." My thoughts were I was not going to allow my daughter to die without a fight. I had "lost it" and I didn't care what happened at this point. My plans were to jump through the opening in the window and clean house! I was a mother in a panic to save my daughter's life and these were an office full of young white girls playing with a crazed, Black woman from Chicago!

Tennessee was not ready for what was coming their way. I looked in the room at Taineeka; she had gotten darker. I told her that I'd be right back. She was too weak to respond, she just looked at me. I made it to the clinic in thirty seconds. I pulled up to the door; I never parked the car. When I opened the door to the doctor's office, there was only one woman behind the desk. The other six had disappeared. I walked up to the window and asked to see the doctor. She looked at me with a frown on her face and said, "I told you on the phone he was not here, now what else do you want because I don't have time for you".

I noticed she had the window closed, and all the doors were locked. I went back to the window where she was sitting, and told her, "I will be here when you all go to lunch and when you all go home." While I was talking, the door behind me opened. When I turned around, I noticed it was the police. It was a Hispanic, and a white officer both men. They came and told me that they would have to arrest me for threatening the workers. I looked at both of them and told them, "If you take me to jail my daughter will die, so therefore you didn't bring enough people with you to arrest me. I have a dying daughter at home and all I want is help". My thoughts now were to grab the gun to shoot both police officers, shoot the locks off the door and shoot everyone in the clinic. I didn't care what happened. I felt that if I shot up the clinic that my daughter would get the help she needed. I was ready for anything. One officer took his baton out, the other grabbed his handcuffs. I just stood there, ready to tear them to pieces. I had my keys in my hand. I was going to blind the officer with the keys and cut his throat. He was about to lose his sight and his life. Then the Hispanic officer looked at me and asked are you ok. I told him no and when I looked behind me, the six women were standing back laughing. I told them, "Open the door! I want to make your smiles prettier! These two men can't stop me. They have not realized yet that they will need help with me." The white officer he was ready, so he thought. I was ready too. The Hispanic officer held the other officer back and said let me talk to her. He asked," Where is your daughter?" I began to cry telling him, "She is at home dying." I told him why I was at the clinic and how the women were treating me. The door to the doctor's office opened and Lord behold, it was the doctor. The doctors asked the officers what was going on, and who called them. The officers proceeded to tell the doctor what was going on. The doctor told the officers they were no longer needed, and they could leave he would handle it from here on. He took me to the back in his office and I told him what had happened when I called. He called the office manager in and asked her who called the police, and who answered the phone. She gave him their names. He called the whole staff in the office, and these were his words. "No one calls the police on my patients, and no one refuses anyone services without contacting me. Who do you all think you are? I'm the man that owns this office not you. Now don't you get it confused do you all understand me? You don't run this office I do." He told the office manager and two of the medical assistants to get their coats, go home and wait on a call from him. Ms. Smiles forgot their smiles. One of them asked him, "Are we fired?" He told them to get their coats and get out of his face. Now it was me that was looking at the staff with a big smile on my face. God took care of this problem, I didn't have to fight, and I guess God said, "Let me step in and save this fool". I never realized how I was looking, I had my shirt fastened wrong, my hair was sticking up on my head and I had on mismatched shoes. I looked as if I was ready to be admitted.

The doctor gave me a referral. I had never experienced a healthcare system like this. This was not like the healthcare system in Chicago. You couldn't see another doctor, not even in the emergency room without a referral unless it was what they called "an emergency". I took Taineeka to the best hospital in Tennessee and waiting while they ran another test. I sat and watched doctor after doctor run in and out of her room, I was praying throughout the entire process. Two hours later the doctor called my name. I didn't like the look on his face. I felt a cold breeze come over me as he told me, "Your daughter has no function in either kidney. They are gone completely out. We are going to have to admit her. She is not doing well at all, and she will be placed in the intensive care unit." I fell to the floor and begin to talk to God out loud as everyone watched. "Lord what is going on! I asked you for peace and you only gave it to me for one year! My child is just 16 years old please, Lord heal my daughter! I can't take anymore! Lord, you are going to have to take full control of this situation! I don't have the strength to go any further! I need you to please step in Lord and help my child! Lord, why would you make it possible for me to come here, only to allow me to hurt more?"

I left Chicago hurting and now it's worse for me here. I have no one here to help me. I said, "Lord if my daughter dies let me go with her! I don't want to live! I'm tired of hurting!" The nurses picked me up off the floor, helping me to my feet. The doctors informed me that they wanted to give me a sedative. I refused the medication. I wanted to be in my right mind, and my daughter needed me to pray. I thought to myself, "My daughter's urine turned dark in July. This is September 29th, one day away from October. What was that original doctor thinking? Was it that important that my "brother" make some money? Was it that bad that you don't even value a life?" I felt as though he allowed her kidneys to go out so that he could make the money treating her. If he didn't know what to do, why didn't he send her to another doctor?

The next morning a very large bouquet of flowers was delivered to Taineeka. I read the card, they were sent by the doctor. I really went through while she was in the hospital. She was in and out of the hospital for four months. I never knew that this was the beginning of some more of my troubles. To be honest, I never thought it could get any worse. There was a test on Taineeka to see why her kidneys went out because her kidneys were in perfect shape. There were no scars on them at all. The doctors found out that she had "Systemic Lupus", a disease where the white blood cells become confused and begin to attack the vital organs, shutting them done one by one. I was told there was no cure for the disease. She was assigned to the head doctor of Nephrology (kidney doctor). The doctor was confused, she couldn't understand how perfect her kidneys looked and they had just stopped functioning. The doctor told me she would put her on dialysis and see if they will kick in. She said once the kidneys go out they usually won't function anymore. I looked at the doctor and told her, "My daughters kidneys will function again. They are only 16 years old and they have a lot of work to do." She looked at me and replied, "I don't know please don't get your hopes up". I told her, "My God said we will have life and life more abundantly and they will function again". There was another doctor standing by. He told me, "If her kidneys begin to function again, I'll serve your God." I looked at him and told him, "Be careful what you say. You will serve him because her kidneys are going to function again. Now what you do is go and find you a church." He gave me his card and said to me, "Call me when they start functioning".

I knew then that God was getting ready to show up and show out! I knew that God was going to perform a miracle and it wouldn't be long. They begin to give Taineeka dialysis. They gave it to her every other day. One Sunday morning, I was trying to decide if I should go to the hospital or, go on to church first. The Holy Spirit told me to go to church and pray, and I did just that. I wanted to also inform my pastor and his wife about Taineeka's condition. Pastor Ronnie Simms and his wife Pastor Terrie Simms were a great help to me. They were there with me from the beginning to the end. They even came to be with me at the doctor's office. When Pastor Terrie saw the color of my daughter's urine, tears came down her face. She looked at me and said, "I have a child and I don't know if I could be as strong as you are." I didn't see what people were talking about; I didn't see the strength they saw. There were members at the church that helped me with my daughter, while she was in the hospital and after she got home. They went and sat with her, washed her hair, and prayed for her. I had to work and they made sure she wasn't alone. They were truly a blessing and I knew God had my child and me. He sent people to help me through my hurting and pain.

I went to church at 8 a.m. that morning and prayed. Afterwards, I continued on to the hospital. When I arrived at the hospital, my daughter wasn't in her bed. I went to the nurse station and ask the nurse, "Where is my daughter?" The nurse replied, "She was in her room." The nurse came into the room with me. Taineeka spoke from the bathroom. "Mama I'm using the bathroom again!" I begin to thank God and cry. God sent me to the church to pray because he had taken care of the problem!

I once again felt the presence of God. I knew he was there all the time but I wanted to feel him near. Although, God had shown up and showed out... let me call the doctor. I called him and asked him would he come to Taineeka. He walked in the room and I asked him, "Did you find you a church? Her kidneys are working again! Are you ready to serve the God that I serve?" He was really confused; I could see it in his face. I know he couldn't believe it because my daughter only had two dialysis treatments; it had only been three days. He said I will find me a church this Sunday. Wow! God used Taineeka and I to bring another soul into his kingdom! This was evangelism at its best. It couldn't get any better than this. I knew then that God was going to use my daughter and also myself to display his power. I knew I had to be ready for what was to come. The attacks will come and I begin to prepare for them. I begin to pray and read my word more.

Many fail the test that God places before them because they don't study for the test. God gives everyone an answer sheet to study (the bible). Some never bother to glance at it. The bible contains every answer to life. Faith is the beginning of knowing God. If you have faith in Him, He will not let you down. I don't care what the situation maybe, put it in God's hand. Believe it is already done in Jesus' name.

Revelation: There were times that I felt as though God was not there with me. When I was alone, he showed up to let me know he was there. We never know how God will use us to draw others in. This is an indication to us that our trials and tribulations can be a blessing to someone other than us. God wouldn't allow me to get into trouble, He told us in his word that vengeance is his. He said, "I will never leave you nor forsake you." If we keep the faith, God will not let us down. God sent people my way to assist and comfort me in my times of hurt. He sent people to pray for us, they were our extended family members. God shows us that nothing is too hard for him, what's impossible to many is made possible through Him. God had opened the door for me to move to Tennessee and was not going to allow doors to close on me.

When the Holy Spirit told me to go to the church and pray, I was obedient. Because of my obedience, my daughter's kidneys began to function. I knew in order for my daughter to make it through her ordeal, I didn't have time to be angry at the doctor or his staff. I had to forgive them and move on. I had to continue to listen to the words of God. I was being strengthened and taught to hear his voice. I talked to the doctor about the origin of the disease. The doctor told me that depression could have sent the disease my daughter's way. He told me sometimes we have things in our body and all it needs is something to trigger it.

The fact that I moved Taineeka away and my husband and I had separated could have brought it on. Although, they had hurt me, I prayed that they never would go through what I went through. I knew it could be my child today and could be their child tomorrow. I doubt if anyone had ever thought of that. I knew they would not be able to handle it like I did. It would be a harvest from the seed that they had sown into my life. The harvest is always greater than the seed that is sown. You can sow one seed and receive a bushel in return.

I knew it was my place to pray and ask God to forgive them for the hardship they had caused me. I knew this was also a lesson for me. God was trying to get my attention. Yes, God will use whoever and whatever he wants to get your attention. In this case, he was using my daughter. He had my undivided attention because I needed him most. I prayed to God if he healed my daughter, I would serve him the rest of my life.

God allowed me to continue working and I was given instructions not to take off. I did that and he made it possible for me to spend time with my daughter. I knew in my heart God was not finished showing his power. He was going to use me in ways that I had never been used and I was being prepared for it. I knew that I had to be prepared for the next level of imps that Satan was going to send my way. I knew I had been elevated to another spiritual level. The anointing of God was upon me and I had power like never before.

If you give up the fight, you are a loser. Why even get started? If you lose the fight without giving up, you are a winner; you fought to the end. If you fight with Jesus on your side, you will always be a winner. He will give you direction and fight your battles. Get out the way and let Jesus do the work.

CHAPTER 5

The Miracles of Jesus

Taineeka was still in the hospital. It was working for me because I had to work. When they decided to release her, it was the first week of December 2002. She came home and Tyra would watch her while I worked. Tyra was 18 years old at the time. I had quit one job in September and began another job in October. The hours were better and the company was closer to my house. I was now working 6 p.m. to 2 a.m. I had been working at this company and had only missed three days. They only allowed you to miss four days.

One day while I was working, my supervisor called me into the office. When I arrived, the police were standing in the office. They told me that my daughter had been rushed to a hospital in Nashville and I was being arrested for neglect. I asked them, "How is that? When did I neglect her?" They told me, "You left her at home with a minor." I replied to them, "My daughter was an 18 year old adult." They then said, "Well you need to get to the hospital." When I arrived at the hospital, the doctors told me that my daughter had developed a blood clot on one lung, and the other had collapsed. The right side of her brain was swollen and her pancreas was inflamed, making it impossible for her to eat. She was having seizures, and her tongue had swollen making it almost impossible for her to breathe. Her hair was falling out due to the chemotherapy treatment that she was receiving. The doctor continued saying that her heart was beating too fast, her blood pressure was very high, and she would have to once again be placed intensive care. I knew she would pull through. God had prepared me for such a time as this. I begin to pray to God. I was letting him know that I was putting the situation in his hands.

God told me, "There are seven things that are named and you will begin to pray for her. Follow my instructions. You will pray for one organ a day and it will have to line up according to your prayer". He told me to get the blessed oil and begin with the brain. I got the oil and prayed that the swelling of her brain would go down.

The next day, I went to the hospital. The nurse followed me into my daughter's room. She said to me, "We got the swelling out of the brain." I begin to cry uncontrollably, thanking God. I told the nurse, "God got the swelling out of my daughter's brain and tomorrow the swelling in the tongue will leave. That's what I'm about to pray for." She looked at me and she began to speak in the heavenly language of tongues. I was shocked that God sent a Christian nurse to take care of my baby. She asked, "Can I stand in agreement with you?" I agreed, and begin to pray. She asked, if it's ok if she called me and I told her she could call me anytime. The next day I was getting prepared to go to the hospital, when the phone rang. It was the nurse, speaking in the heavenly language. She said, "The tongue has gone down. What time are you getting here?" I told her in the next hour. She said, "I want to be there when you pray." When I arrived, she was standing down the hall. When she saw me coming, she ran to the room. I began to pray for the pancreas. The next day the pancreas had gone down. The following day, I prayed for the blood pressure. Sure enough, the blood pressure went down the following day. I put oil on her head and prayed that her hair would grow back more beautiful, than it was before. I came the next day and prayed against the blood clots and they disappeared. It was the seventh day. That was the experience of a lifetime. I was prepared to pray for the heart to slow down. The nurse came into the room with me. She told me that God wanted her to be present. I put the oil in my hand and placed it on her chest.

The power of God was strong; it felt like a bolt of lightning went through my arm. The impact was so strong; it knocked me away from her. I rebuked Satan and went back to my daughter to try it again. I put my hands on her chest and I fell to the floor. I laid on the floor, as I began to pray, God said, "Get up! It is already done in my name!" I said, "Lord I never got a chance to pray." He said, "You believed in me, you trusted my word, your faith in me sufficient enough." The nurse looked at me while helping me up from the floor. She then began to hug me and said, "It is already done."

I begin to remember when Taineeka was 3 years old. She was diagnosed with lead poisoning. Her lead level was the highest reported in the state of Illinois and she had no brain damage. There were doctors coming in from other hospitals to see my daughter. She had to receive a shot in her thigh every day for one week. The needle was longer than my fingers because the needle had to touch the bone. She went through this pain for two months. They started the procedure as an outpatient procedure. Her lead level was abnormally high; hence, she was hospitalized for further treatment. There was a little boy who she shared the room with her while in the hospital. His lead level was half that of my daughter and he was a vegetable. This experience caused my daughter to develop a phobia of needles. This phobia stalked her throughout her life, even in adulthood. Many didn't understand it, but I did. I would cry along with Taineeka when the shots were being administered.

I can recall when I would take her to the Board of Health for treatment; she would began to cry when the nurse pulled the needle out. She would push the nurse's hands away from her. The nurse hit Taineeka on the thigh that she had gotten the shot in the day before. It was not just a tap; she hit her hard. I immediately slapped the nurse in the face just as hard as she hit my daughter. She dropped the needle and ran to get her supervisor and security. I told her supervisor what had happened. She looked at the nurse and told her, "We have been through this before. Go to my office." The security officer told me, "It is against the law to hit an employee." I told him, "There are no laws when it comes to me or my child being abused. If you hit my child I will hit you too... now what?" I couldn't believe that this woman would work in pediatrics and be so mean and heartless. There are some very mean people that are angry for other reasons and take it out on the people. A pediatric nurse should have compassion for children and most do. However, that nurse didn't. Did this woman think that I would allow her to hit my daughter? I never took her back to that clinic. After this incident, I asked the doctor to place her in the hospital for her treatments.

Now that Taineeka was back in intensive care, I knew things were about to change for me once again. I had no doubt that she would pull through. My faith and trust in God was overwhelming. Every day something would go wrong. I would stand by; watching how the devil was trying to shake my faith. Yet, I stood strong. God had molded me to withstand the fiery darts of the devil. He was in trouble now. I begin to pray like never before. Everything that I prayed for began to manifest.

The doctors told me that she would be in the hospital for at least a month. I told them that she would be home within a week. Taineeka was released from the hospital in a week. I was told that I would have to bring her back to the hospital next week; they wanted to perform a procedure on her to reduce her heart rate. I told them, "Sure I would, but God is going to handle that also."

Mr. Jay took a leave of absence from his job, to come from Chicago and be with our daughter. I allowed him to stay at my house. His women had no compassion for our situation. You would think that they would at least have respect for me because my child was sick. God spoke to me and said, "How can they have respect for you and they don't have respect for themselves." They were calling, using profanity to express their anger at him for leaving Chicago. It was sad. They didn't understand that getting back with him was the last thing on my mind. I was making it possible for him to be with his child and that was it! If only they knew how stupid they looked and how many other women were calling him. I was so happy to be out of that mess. I was free and planned on keeping it that way. I didn't hear anything they were saying because I had to keep my mind on God. My focus was for my child. God even had me to pray for them. Mr. Jay would go to the hospital and sit with our daughter while I was working. It sure took a lot of pressure off of me. I felt good to know that there was someone with her while I worked.

When Taineeka was first admitted into the hospital, I would come to the hospital to visit her after I got off work, which was at 2 a.m. I would stay with her until 12 o'clock noon. I would then could go home and prepare to be at work at 4 p.m. I received a call one day to come to the hospital. They wanted to know what time was good for me. They wouldn't tell me what they wanted; they just told me it was to sign some papers. I chose my off day and went to the hospital, not know what was waiting for me.

The Holy Spirit had already warned me that there was trouble awaiting me. I began to pray before I went. I was directed to go to the doctors meeting room. When I opened the door, there were three white women, two security officers and two police officers. I knew then that the devil was up to his old tricks again. They began to introduce themselves as the Social Worker, the Nurse Administrator, and Children and Family Services. They asked me to take a seat and I refused telling them, "I don't plan on being here long, so I might as well stand". The nurse administrator started off by saying, "My nurses have been treating your daughter for three months and they have not seen you but once or twice. The social worker began to speak, "In the state of Tennessee, this is called child neglect and that's what you are being charged with." The last woman who was from the Children and Family Services begin to speak, (it was if I was watching a play and everyone had their parts rehearsed) "I want you to sign these papers. You are turning your child over to the state of Tennessee, and you will have to go to court to get regain custody". I got quiet and

I looked around the room. I saw the seven people as a sign of completion. I thought to myself, "They don't know who they are messing with." I begin to think about the number seven. It took God seven days to create the world and it was complete, Joshua and his troops marched around the wall of Jericho seven times and the wall came tumbling down. The seven-fold blessing of Abraham consisted of seven parts, therefore; the number seven was significant in the bible. It meant completion and perfect. I thought in this situation I was complete, and they were the perfect group to display the power of God to.

I felt the sense of power coming over me as I did when Taineeka was hooked up to the machines. I wasn't feeling myself. I wanted to get angry, but God wouldn't allow me. He wanted me to be used in a different way this day, and it was a way that they would never forget. When I snapped out of my trance, I heard the nurse calling my name. I looked at her, "I told her I want to ask you a question. If my daughter was to be released from the hospital and I had no home for her to return to, would you take her away from me?" She nodded her head and said, "Unfortunately yes". I then asked, "If she is in the hospital, aren't you responsible for her?" She nodded her head and replied, "Yes". I asked, "So I am being punished for working, or is it my race that allows you to attack me?" They got quiet and each of them was waiting on the other to answer the question. I looked at the Administrator and asked her, "Have you done your research"? She asked, "Research on what"? I replied to her "Research on Veronica. Furthermore, you must have evidence of child neglect. You can't tell me what the second shift says. What about first and third shift?" She responded, "All I need is one nurse to tell me about you" I responded, "When you are prejudice, it wouldn't matter if they gave you a report or not. God gave me a message to give to all of you." I began to recite verses from the bible: "No weapon formed against me shall prosper." "I can do all things through Christ Jesus who strengthens me." I then told them, "I am blessed going in and blessed going out. Now I am about to leave this place and I am not signing any papers. I am not giving you my child. Do you understand me? If you touch my child, this hospital will belong to me and new workers will replace each one of you. I have been through enough with you people and I'm tired of you all. It's by the grace of God that I can hear his voice. If you only knew what I am going through you wouldn't have dared to asked me to come in this office, to listen to your ridiculous accusations. I pray that none of you ever have to experience what I'm going through. You wouldn't make it! You don't have God in your lives and that's who you would need." I looked at them and said, "Satan I rebuke you and plead the blood of Jesus on you. I rebuke each one of you in the name of Jesus. Stop allowing Satan to use you and try God. Goodbye and have a nice day. Remember, it would be safe for you all to leave me alone."

When I walked out of the room, I looked back through the glass. They were all standing there, looking as if they were in shock. I went to my daughter's room to show them that I was not running and I meant business. I was not playing with them. I was now there on second shift, dealing with the nurses that had reported me. One of the nurses walked in the room. When she seen me, she turned around and went to the nurse's station. I heard her tell the other nurses, "She's in the room. Can you believe that they didn't do anything to her." God whispered to me, "My child hold on. There is more coming your way, but I have your back. You have nothing to worry about. Just keep me before you and keep the faith." I never questioned God about what was next. However, I knew I had to be prepared for it. Two days later, I was called to the hospital. They wanted me to sign papers to do surgery. I was told that Taineeka's reproductive organs had fallen out. I asked, "How did that happened?" They told me this is something that happens a lot when people are very sick. I sat and talked to Taineeka. I asked her did she remember what happened. She told me, "Yes, the nurse came to take the catheter out. I told her it was hurting, and she just snatched it out". She continued to tell me that when she began to bleed, they told her it was her menstrual cycle.

I told Taineeka I would be right back. I went looking for the Chapel. I needed to pray immediately.

I went to the Chapel and prayed, asking God for direction. I told him that I was about to become a murderer and I needed His help. They intentionally did this to get back at me. He whispered, "You go back upstairs and sign the papers. I will handle everything else". I went upstairs and asked for the Administrator. She took about two hours to come. I told them, "I would not sign any papers until she arrived. I needed to talk to her first." When she finally arrived, I told her, "This was done intentionally. The nurses knew that in order to properly remove a catheter, they would need to remove 10cc of water first. If the water is not removed, it will cause problems for the patient. The nurses knew this also. This was far from a mistake. Now I'm talking to you for the last time as a human being. I don't know what type of animal I will turn into the next time. I want a sitter in my daughter's room at all times at the expense of the hospital." She agreed to put the sitter in the room with my daughter, until she was discharged. They had to sew my daughter's reproductive organs back in place.

The hospital released her to me the next day. Wow, that was quick! I was told to bring her back for the procedure to slow down her heart. I asked, "Why wasn't the procedure done already? As long as she has been in the hospital, it should have been done." They were so busy worrying about how to destroy me, they forgot about their own duties. When Taineeka was sent home, I had to give her 38 pills a day and 16 shots a week. I also fed her through the nose.

Taineeka's heartbeat had not slowed down. It was time to take her to the doctor's office, so that they could perform the procedure. They were going to put her to sleep and run a needle to her heart, putting medicine inside of it to slow it down. It was boggling why I was able to lay hands on every part of her body, but God wouldn't allow me to touch her heart. We went to the hospital and they placed Taineeka in a room. They hooked the heart monitor up to her. I was in the waiting area.

The doctor came out of her room and came over to me. The doctor said, "We are not going to do the procedure. When we hooked her up to the monitor, her heart began to beat at a normal rate. I have never seen anything like this." it was nobody but God! He had his own time and place to show his miracles. He wanted others to see his work. I told the doctor that God told me he would take care of Taineeka's heart, and he did. I thought that when he told me to go and pray for my daughter, the heart would get healed along with the other problems. God wanted me to wait for His time everything is not done in our time. We must be obedient and wait on the Lord. Taineeka was doing well. Her hair was growing back, she was gaining weight, and she would go to the hospital once a week for chemotherapy treatments.

Taineeka's medicine was very expensive. The doctors prescribed two blood thinners for her because her blood was very thick, and they were trying to avoid more blood clots. One was to be administered in the form of a pill; the other one was to be given by a shot. She ran low on both medications. I went to the pharmacy to get a refill, and they told me they were not authorized to give a refill. They said they would have to put in a request for the insurance to pay for it and it would take seven to ten business days. I told the pharmacist that my daughter couldn't wait that long. I was afraid there would be more blood clots. I had three hundred dollars in my pocket and I told the pharmacist I would pay for it. He smiled at me and told me, "Let me ring it up." He came to the counter and told me $1,543. I said, "What?" He told me the pills were $243.00 and the medicine for the shot was $1,200. I looked at him and asked him, "What I am supposed to do?" He told me that he would put me in for an emergency supply for two weeks. I couldn't believe that medicine cost so much.

Revelation: Although it seemed like I was never going to get out of the turbulent waves, God was holding me up and doing construction on me at the same time. I was learning how to depend on Him. I had read about the many trials and tribulations of others in the bible over and over. However, to experience it myself was more strenuous. The reading helps you remember the things that you are to do, it is no more than a road map. It gives you directions to follow when you are in the wilderness. I never thought my daughter being sick would teach me so much. I learned that people that you would think were compassionate, because of the work they did, could be the cruelest people that I had ever encountered. They took on their careers to help others, yet more were hurt than helped. Oh, but God had the ram in the bush for me. I will never forget the nurse, the prayer warrior who spoke in tongues.

My journey was not easy up to this point, but my job was to stay on board regardless of what was thrown at me. I was not worried about them taking my child. I knew if they had grounds to take her from me, they wouldn't have needed my signature. Also I would not have to appear in court for them to do it. This was a sneak tactic from Satan trying to get me to sign my rights over to him. If I didn't have God on my side, I would have signed the papers, making my problems much worse. If my husband was in the room with Taineeka every night how could I neglect my child? God demonstrated to me that no matter what a situation looked like do not faint. I was being put through a test that I couldn't pass without forgiving those who hurt me. To hold anger would imprison me inside of a box created by no one other than myself. I got the chance to experience one of my favorite scriptures in the bible. "I will answer them before they even call to me. While they are still talking about their needs, I will go ahead and answer their prayers!" NLV Isaiah 65:24. I was too far into the fight and it was too late to turn around. I had to remember that it was not easy for Jesus. I could hear a voice saying to me, "Don't throw in the towel before the battle begins. The battle is where you pick up your rewards." Each time Jesus went to bless or heal, he had an encounter with controversy. He overcame it and you can too. I had made a promise to God that I would serve him the rest of my life, if he healed my daughter. I believed that my daughter would be healed, so I couldn't give up. I knew you could never get rewarded at the beginning of the battle. It's at the end of the battle that you receive your reward

Faith= trials and tribulations. Matthew 6:31-34(NIV), "So don't worry, saying, what shall we eat? Or what shall we drink? Or what shall we wear? For the Pagans run after all these things, and your heavenly father knows that you need them. But seek first his kingdom and his righteousness, and all these things will be given to you as well. Therefore, Do not worry about tomorrow, for tomorrow will worry about itself. Each day has enough trouble of its own." Many people will not pass the test because they will fall apart on the journey.

When the devil comes to attack, remember this: In the book of Job, God sent His angels to come in for the good report and Satan showed up. God asked him what had he been doing. He told God he was walking to and fro the earth, looking for someone to devour. He has heard your good report, and his job is to ruin you. Rebuke him and get your blessing.

Chapter 6

My Esther Experience

W hile living in Tennessee, I had a male friend. He didn't live with me but he came to visit me every day. He was very nice to me. However, my biggest problem with him was that he was very jealous and controlling. He never wanted to go anywhere, just sat around the house. He didn't want me to speak to my male neighbors. When it would get cold outside, he would drive my car because he owned a motorcycle. One day I needed a tire for my car. He had $2,000 in his pocket and refused to buy me a tire. I couldn't believe this man! I went to get a Payday Loan Store to take out a loan. I had no choice. In doing this, I was able to buy me a used tire. He had the nerve to call me two days later, asking me to come to his house after work. I told him that my wheels would never park in front of his house ever again. After leaving my husband of 25 years, I was not about to be abused in any shape or form by another man.

The following week, we would meet at a restaurant. He told me that we could no longer see each other. These were his exact words: "You are too damn strong for me. I've never seen a woman that was as strong as you are and I can't handle it. Baby I love you and will always love you, but I can't handle it. I don't understand why haven't you broke down, I have never seen you cry. You act as if nothing is happening and your daughter is near death." I looked at him and said, "It's not me I have nothing to do with who I am, or how I react to things. It's

God. I'm just a vessel being used by him." He gave me a hug and walked away. I stood looking at him thinking he's walking away from me when I need him the most. I smiled and waved at him, I knew that this was a part of God's plan, not mine. I had known this man for twenty years and we had been through a lot together. When he was at his worse, I was there for him. He walked away and so did I. I never looked back. Yes, I was hurt but I couldn't stop persevering. I was on a mission for God and nothing could stop me. I thought maybe I'm one not meant for relationships. I had been with my husband for 25 years. No I had not stopped having relationships, until one day I learned my lesson. It wasn't going to work for me to live out of the will of God. I couldn't say the flesh had been subdued because I was constantly fighting the flesh. I still battle with the flesh today. I had to learn it was a day by day process.

Lord I'm holding on to your "unchanging hand". Throughout the pain, sickness, personal attacks, loneliness and the desolate places that I sometimes go. Knowing that I have You, I really don't need anybody else. I know you will bring me closer to be in your likeness. I know the healing of my heart and body is already present. I found peace in Psalms 37 and 73.

I'm persevering, pressing, and praying Lord Keep lifting me up and giving me the strength to continue this journey. Many go through life searching for help they really don't need. When God has something for you to do, He will send you help. If help is not sent your way remember for every assignment He has given you, God has equipped you with everything you need to complete the task. Pull it out and begin to work.

Well it was January 2003, and my probation on my job was over. I was told that I didn't reach my production numbers and they couldn't keep me. I laughed and began to thank the Lord for the time I had on the job. I then applied for my unemployment benefits, the company denied me. I had to attend a hearing to get my benefits and I won it on a technicality.

I found another job two months later, working with mentally and physically handicapped adults. I loved this type of work.

This is the work that I did when I first came to Tennessee. The only difference was this work was with children. Tyra couldn't take watching her sister suffer and she decided she was going back to Chicago to live. I asked her why she didn't stay and register for college. She could help me with her sister, and I could help her with my granddaughter. She refused and became very angry with me, because she didn't want to follow orders. She was now 19 years old and didn't want to listen to me, because she was now grown.

She wanted me to keep her child until she got on her feet. I told her, "I must worry about my own child and you worry about yours. I will not allow you to put more pressure on me while I make things comfortable for you. Also you will not leave here and bring another child back. The best way for you is to get on your feet is with your child on your hip". Latavia was 17 months old and I loved her but I had my own problems. I took her to the bus station. Taineeka wanted to go along with her, so I allowed her to go, since she was feeling better. Family members were very angry with me. They were telling me you need to have the baby there with you. I told them she's walking out on me and mine, I need the help she doesn't need help. I'm dealing with a situation that can't be helped. Her situation is her decision, not mine. This will be the best birthday present and learning experience she will ever receive. She got on the bus two days after her nineteenth birthday. All I could say is Lord be with her and happy birthday. Tyra told me, "You would never see your grandchild again." I replied, "Watch what you say, you may not see her." I never felt bad about it, because I had to keep moving. I couldn't fight her fight, I had my on fight and the best way for her to learn to fight was to make mistakes and correct them. When it was time for Taineeka to come home, she called and told me she couldn't find her sister. Everyone she told us she would be staying with had not seen her. I told Taineeka to come home don't worry about it.

I was working on my new job for about a month, and I received a call from my husband telling me that a former supervisor's daughter had died from Lupus. She told him to tell me that there was a hospital in Chicago with a treatment for the disease. I called the hospital and they told me that I must send her records to the hospital so they could find out whether she was a qualified candidate. I sent the records and received a call, saying that she was a candidate. I begin to prepare to move again. I didn't want to move back to Chicago, so I found a house in Indianapolis, Indiana. I thought three hours wouldn't be far, since she was only going to receive treatments for three months.

Since I was working a weekend shift, which consisted of eight hours on Friday, sixteen hours on Saturday, and sixteen hours on Sunday, it allowed me to spend time at home with Taineeka. I had to take time off of work. I went to work Friday and the lady I was relieving asked me could I work the entire week for her. She had to go in the hospital for throat cancer. I told her I would be happy to do that because I needed her to work in my place. She would work for me on my weekend and that gave me a week off to go to Indianapolis and Chicago. Taineeka and I left on a Saturday. We had planned to leave that Friday and I waited. I wanted to wait until Monday, but God said go today and we left.

This was May of 2003 and I was in Chicago. Taineeka received a phone call saying that Tyra was in trouble. She had lost custody of my granddaughter to the state of Michigan. Never at one time did I regret my decision. I called my daughter to inquire about the situation. She told me, "Yes she is gone, and I guess you are happy now". I told her, "You know you are crazy as hell. Now it's time for you to woman up. I didn't have a child, you did. I have my baby with me and you told me I'd never see her again, now what's happening with you. I told you to watch what you say, didn't I? I gave you alternatives and this is what you chose sweetheart. Now what are you plans? She became very quiet. I told her I can assist you. When is the court day? She told me it was in July. I told her that's good I have two months. I should be moved by then.

While I was in Chicago, I was getting calls from my employer and the lady I worked for. I returned the call to the lady and she told me that I was under investigation for hitting the client at the house. I was out done I couldn't believe this! I would never hit a client. I wanted to know where they got this from. I called the employer and they told me I had to meet with the investigators. When I returned, I was to give them a call. I was told that the client told them I hit her. I knew this was a lie because these were the only words she spoke and everyone, even the manager knew that. I later found out that the lady I filled in for is the one that set me up. Her friend wanted my position, so she lied on me to get me fired.

I later saw the lady that set me up. I walked up to her in Wal-Mart and spoke to her. I asked her about her throat. She was surprised to see me, and she began to shake. She told me she had to have another surgery. She then said, "I'm sorry you are not there to work in my place." I looked at her and told her, "You are a lying demon, you are the reason I'm without a job. I thought I was helping you and you took it upon yourself to lie on me! You mean to tell me, that you have cancer and you are lying on people. If cancer doesn't stop you from lying what does it takes? Death is knocking on your door and you need to repent for your wrong doing. Now you have a blessed day and I want you to know that you didn't hurt me. You actually blessed me. Let me say this now that I never told them that your husband was there with you every day; neither did I tell that you were cooking your family dinner at the house. I never told them that you were washing your family clothes at the house and was taking food out the house to feed your family. There was a lot that I could have told, but I know God will teach you better than I ever could teach you." I walked away and she was standing in shock, she had turned pale in the face.

If I never had a gift that was so helpful to me, it was the gift of discernment. The gift of discernment never lied. I always knew when something was wrong. I went to Northwestern Hospital to talk to them about Taineeka's treatment. I was told that the treatment alone would cost $100,000 and that did not include the stay in the hospital. I was told that Public Aid would pay for it, but I must live in Chicago. I thought then why do I have to move? Why can't the state of Tennessee pay for it? I went back to Tennessee and file a request for them to pay, they denied it. I put in for a hearing before a judge. I was told to bring an attorney with me. I wasn't taking an attorney when I could do it myself. I had two weeks to prepare for the court date. I went to the medical library and did my research on the laws of Tennessee insurance. I also researched how many people that Tennessee had paid for to have procedures that were similar to my daughters.

I then called my employer and was told to come in the next day. I went to meet the investigator and was told that the lady I had worked for, who had cancer had called them. She told them the client had told her I hit her. I told the investigator have you all checked the books? She says this every day and everyone knows this, it's notated in the books. There is not a day that this client does not say someone hit her. She said I am aware of that. I asked her, why am I really here? I have more important things to do than this. She told me the charges were unfounded but I could not return to the house. I must report to my supervisor for further instructions. My supervisor called me the next day and asked me if I would I take a 3pm -11pm, Monday through Friday. I told her, "No. When I was hired I explained to you I couldn't work all week because I had a sick daughter at home." I went to the unemployment office once again. They denied my unemployment. Therefore I had to go to a hearing. The hearing was over the phone and the supervisor fought against me receiving my benefits. OH BUT GOD! The arbitrator told her that when I was hired, there was an agreement to which days I could work. He said, "It's not that she does not want to work, you can't accommodate her. Therefore I rule in her favor".

The court date for my daughter had arrived. I went before the judge and represented Taineeka and myself. I was fighting the attorneys from the state of Tennessee's insurance and there was a doctor that was also there with the insurance (Public Aid). I had a chance to question them and it was great. The whole courtroom begins to laugh because they were speechless. They were lost for words; they were not expecting me to be so sharp. The judge was a black female. She asked me to come to her chambers for a moment. I went to her chambers and she told me, "You are doing a great job. Have you ever considered going to school to practice law"? I told her that I wanted to be a lawyer when I was younger but that dream left. She told me, "I suggest you reconsider. You are a natural at this. You will not win this case, only because the laws that are set in place will not allow you to. If there were no laws, you would have won the case. Nevertheless, don't let this discourage you. Think about what I told you and if you need a reference for law school, look me up. I will give you one". We went back into the courtroom. The Judge announced that the state of Tennessee had won the case. The attorney and the doctor begin to smile. There was a white man that hollered from the audience, "I don't know what you all are smiling at she lost to the state, not you!" He was then asked to leave the courtroom. I left feeling like a winner. I had done all I could do, but I must keep moving to the next thing on the agenda.

I received a letter stating that I had to come into the unemployment office to speak to an adjudicator. I walked in and I was sent to the manager's office. He told me that I had been approved to receive six checks and he needed my signature. He also told me to go and speak to the adjudicator. (Taineeka was with me.) At this point I was so tired of fighting and just wanted peace and to move. When entered the office, there was a white woman sitting at her desk, looking at a computer. She never turned around to see who had come into the office. This woman talked to me with her back turned. She asked me questions. As I would answer, she typed them into the computer. I really felt strange because this lady never took a look at me. It was if she was making her decisions on my race because that's the first page she clicked on when I entered the office. After she would finish typing, she would ask another question. Not once did she look at my daughter or me.

By this point, I was boiling angry. She said, "I'm sorry, you don't qualify for any benefits. You have a nice day." Her supervisor had already told me what I was going to receive. I was furious with this lady. I jumped out of my chair and grabbed her swivel chair, giving it a big push. The chair turned at least three times before it came to a stop. I had both hands on the arm rest. I looked her right in her eyes and asked her, "Don't you want to know what I look like Miss? Don't you want to even see my face? Don't you want to know who snapped your neck? Today I'm not in my right mind. I've left home and don't know how to get back." The lady jumped up, her glasses fell to the floor, and she took off running down the hall. I was right behind her. My daughter was behind me screaming, "Mama please stop you are going to go to jail, they are going to call the police on you." I screamed to my daughter, "She needs some help now, Lord knows she needs help. Let them call the police to help this heifer because I feel sorry for her myself". The lady ran right into her manager's office screaming. I explained how she treated me and told him that she had taken my benefits that he said I had. He looked at her and asked her, "Why did you take the benefits that I had given her?" She couldn't answer him, she was shaking looking like she was about to have a nervous breakdown. The manager told me he would take care of it and I could go home. He told me I would receive my checks in about three days.

I went home thinking I could get ready to leave. Everything was set in place. Then Taineeka had an appointment to receive her chemotherapy treatment. We went to the hospital and the doctor asked me if I was planning on leaving. I told her I had not set a date as of yet. She asked me if Taineeka would be there the following week to get her treatment. I told her yes, she then said the hospital in Chicago can't do any more than I am doing now. I told her my daughter can't continue to receive chemo all her life. I want her to become medication free. The next week I had packed and was ready to go. All I needed was to get Taineeka to the hospital for her treatment. I went to the hospital and the doctor told me that she had gotten papers from the hospital in Chicago. She was not going to release Taineeka from her care. The doctor said she was too weak to take the trip. I knew this was all about money. Every time Taineeka would make a doctor visit, the doctor was making $3,000. Taineeka was originally going to the doctor twice a week. The doctor then broke it down to once a week. She had informed me that since Taineeka was doing so well that she would make it once a month. Now for some reason she was changing the time again. The doctor informed me that I would be getting a court order in the next 24 hours. I told her, "That's fine." I knew as soon as we left the office we would be on the road within an hour.

We left the office and headed to Indianapolis, Indiana. I had rented a house there. When we arrived to Indianapolis, we unloaded the truck and left for Chicago. I figured that Taineeka's treatment wouldn't take that long and we could come home right afterwards. I was wrong. After the treatments, Taineeka was not permitted to travel. Therefore, I spent the majority of my time in Chicago. I had to now transfer my section 8 from Indianapolis to Chicago. I had waited for Section 8 for three months, so that I could find me a place to live in Chicago. I never got the chance only to enjoy my house Indianapolis. I had stayed there for a short period of time. I moved in July of 2003 and moved out Dec of 2003.

Two days later, the doctor from Tennessee called. She wanted to know why I didn't answer the door for the police when they came to serve me the papers. She then told me, "I will take over her treatment with or without your consent by Monday morning." (It was on a Friday that she had called.) I told her, "It does not matter what you do. Taineeka had already been admitted into the hospital. God Bless You and thanks for saving my daughter's life."

Taineeka was in the hospital to receive a Blood Stem Transplant. There was only one hospital in the United States that did the procedure and it happened to be in my hometown, Chicago. Lupus is when the white blood cells becoming confused, and start attacking the vital organs. The procedure would involve removing all the white blood cells out of the body, freezing and treating them and finally placing back into the body. There was going to be a tube placed in her neck to draw the white blood cells out. Once this procedure was done, she would not have an immune system. Therefore she couldn't be around children, plants, animals, sick people or carpet. This was very dangerous because if she caught any germ with no immune system to fight it off, she could die. There was a 22 years old young lady sent into the room to comfort Taineeka, letting her know that there wasn't anything for her to worry about. She told Taineeka that she had a Blood Stem Transplant seven months ago and there was nothing to it. After Taineeka had her transplant, she inquired about the young. She wanted to thank her. She was told that the young lady had died. She went home to Florida and got sick. She couldn't fight off whatever virus she had picked up. This is a very dangerous procedure but we were ready, especially after we found out there were people that had the procedure done and were Lupus free for fifteen years. I felt we had no other choice unless she wanted to continue the chemo treatment the rest of her life. The chemo treatment made her very sick. I explained to the social worker that we didn't have a place to live. The hospital was trying to place us in a hotel for five days near the hospital. They thought that it would be safer for her to be in a hotel. It also made it much easier for them to monitor her for that week.

Revelation: It appeared to me that I was really having a hard time getting out of Tennessee. It seemed that everything that could come my way came. I knew that I had to keep going I was leaning on the promises that God had given me. I knew that God was removing all of the people that he didn't want around me. He knew that they would be a hindrance to the journey he had me on. I was taught during this experience, that there was nothing I couldn't do with God on my side. "I can do everything through him who gives me strength." Philippians 4:13. I guess many would ask why I described everyone by race. It is not because I am prejudice in any way. I want people to see that it was not only other races, that mistreated me, but my very own. There were many white that were very nice to me. Actually they outnumbered my own race. I never mentioned the white woman who helped me by putting $1,000 credit on my utilities. Neither did I mention the white woman that had come by with Thanksgiving with dinner that she had ordered. When I lived in Tennessee, there was a white woman who lived in my complex. She would always come by to see how Taineeka was doing. She then said, "Everyone is always concerned about your daughter. We really want to know how you are doing." She had to hold me up because no one had ever asked me that question. She held me in her arms and cried with me and said, "My child, you are taking a beating that many of us wouldn't be able to stand. You have shown me strength like never before, I will always remember you. Don't worry about the weight loss, just keep following the Lord he will never let you down. If anyone asks who my hero is, I will tell them her name is Veronica." By this time, I was on the floor. I was praying and crying out, "Lord Help me give me strength, hold me up Lord." She then lifted me up off the floor and told me, "I want to pay your rent next month." There was calmness in this woman's voice that I can't begin to explain. There were also others of my race that helped me. They brought fruit baskets, balloons, and food to my house. Many prayed with me for Taineeka and myself. I thank God for them. I realize that even the nurses learned something from me because of my boldness to speak the truth. I was on an evangelistic crusade and I never knew it. I was being shown my gift for healing and the gift of a prayer warrior. I was taught to listen to the voice of God and yes, I could hear him so clear. When I was lied on I really couldn't get angry. If there is something God wants you to have, no man could keep you from having it.

People were being used by Satan to build God's Kingdom and to strengthen me. When people think they are hurting you, they are actually blessing you. I always went to the story of St. Stephen when the crowds begin to beat and stone him for proclaiming the word of Jesus. He looked to the heavens. Jesus was no longer sitting at the right side of his father. Jesus had stood up and was watching what they were doing to him. This is how Jesus does when his children are being talked about or mistreated. He stands up to see what's going on with his children. He is now standing up and looking down at my situation.

People don't realize that they have caused so many to be blessed, and Jesus will even make them out to be a blessing. I may have lost in the courtroom, but in the end I'm a winner with Jesus. Everything I went through I was supposed to go through, for my faith to be tested and I passed. I learned of the many gifts I had, and if I hadn't went through I would never had known I had the gifts. God allowed me to teach many from my trials and tribulations. I always said how can a man teach unless he is taught? You can't teach if you have nothing to teach. We must learn to pay attention to the instructions of God and not to worry how looks like. I was a pupil in the Lord's classroom, and I was indeed learning.

The picture can't be painted for you. If it is painted for you then you won't need faith. You can't see Faith; you must believe it is done even when you can't see it. If you can see it, then it is not faith. I was going through, but God was blessing me. Just remember to ride the wave and don't allow the wave to ride you. When people learn who they are and whose they are, there will be less confusion in the world. I am not angry with anyone that was used as an obstacle in my life. I thank God for you and pray you get to know Him. We must learn to become a blessing to others that are less fortunate. Do not put your foot on their throats. There are people that may need a hug, a smile, or just for you to say I love you. Love goes a long way. Your dark places are not created to keep you down. It is created to activate the Kingdom of God in you, to strengthen you, and make you appreciate the light. It is created to prepare you for the upcoming blessings. If you never went into a dark place, how would you recognize the Light?

Life without God is like a rowboat without oars, a sailboat without sails, or a motorboat without a motor. You are tossed by the waves without direction. When God is in your life you can anchor in him and peace will be still.

CHAPTER 7

My Mother Teresa Experience

I was now in Chicago and Taineeka was about to go through her transplant. The hospital placed us in a hotel. The room had three beds in it, one in the bedroom and two in the living room. It had a kitchen and bathroom. I invited her dad to stay there with us so that he could be of assistance. I took Taineeka to the hospital. Afterwards, I went to the Section 8 office. I gave her dad the keys to the room so that he could get Taineeka back to the room once the procedure was over. When I arrived to the room, his girlfriend opened the door. I was blown away when he arrived asking, "What do you all want to eat?" The thought that went through my mind was, "Did he actually think that him and his woman were going to stay with my daughter and me?" They ate, laid in the bed next to my daughter, and went to sleep. I couldn't believe it! This is when I realized that God had been working on me. I didn't care about them being together. But I did care about them being so disrespectful. If this had happened when I was younger, they wouldn't have wakened up. He even had the nerve to later ask me if they could spend the night. My answer was hell no! My daughter had just had every white blood cell taken out of her body and this was very serious. This was no time to be playing games with her life. I knew that God had done a remarkable job with me. I was so close to peace I could smell it.

Taineeka and I were basically from house to house. I was doing my best not to be a burden on anyone. I knew it was very hard for people to deal with a sick child. I was still waiting on Section 8 to find my papers, they claimed they had lost. I was in for a surprise of my lifetime. I found out that when you had no place to go, people were at their best behavior... NOT! They were as mean as a snake. No one that Taineeka or I stayed with was exactly nice. It was as if they knew I had nowhere to go and they were taking advantage of it. If we did something personal to them before we moved, they were coming back for the kill. I could deal with the attack on me, but I couldn't deal with the attack on my child. I had been through a rip tide and I made it. But when you are mean to a child who is sick, it really shows you the kind of heart that these individuals possess. They were so conformed to being evil that they thought they were doing the right thing. Taineeka was put out of relatives houses for very petty reasons and I was attacked for almost no reason. We would leave one house going to another, and we were treated just as bad or worse than before. This was done by people that I thought would understand, or people I had assisted in one way or another. Each person claimed to read the bible, or attended church. The biggest problem that they had was the fact that Taineeka couldn't help them clean. They knew that she was not to be around dust or chemicals but they didn't care. They didn't care that the dust would kill her if she caught an infection. They didn't care that she was this sick. It was as if this was their perfect opportunity to attack. These people either didn't realize how sick Taineeka was, or they really didn't care. I prayed for them because I knew they were going to go through. I knew that you reap what you sow. I felt a lot better being attacked in Tennessee by strangers, than to come to Chicago and be attacked by family and friends. These people didn't know they were being used as a vessel by Satan and they didn't seem to mind being used. They always had advice for others, and myself yet they couldn't see their way to being nice enough to have compassion for someone sick.

I then realized the reason I had such a hard time in Tennessee with strangers. God was preparing me for the people that I knew. He wanted me to be strong. He knew my hurt was not over. In fact, he knew it was just beginning. I cried many nights. I couldn't let them see me cry. They may have killed me then. My tears may have been used as fuel for the fire. They were so heartless, yet so righteous. Remember they read their bibles and some even went to church. I begin to pray to God and he has shown me the people that I had reached out to.

There was one time when my cousin called me, telling me about a member of her church that was in need of a place to live. She asked me if could she send her to Tennessee so that I may assist her. I agreed to help. She came down with her three sons. Her sons were ages 7, 9, and 11. I failed to mention that the mother was blind. She received Section 8 in Tennessee and she also had gotten it in Chicago. She decided to go back to Chicago and live. They were an experience to me. Her boys were rough but they were very nice to her. They were very protective of their mother and they would fight. I think the school system and my apartment complex were very happy to see them leave. I loved the way they treated their mother. When they went places, they were her eyes. I recall coming home once, only to see the mother and her three boys outside. There was a crowd. As I walked up, I heard the mother telling this lady, "Come on! I will give you the whipping of a life time." Her boys were in position behind the woman, as if they were going to push the woman into the hands of their mother. Now this was a blind woman ready to fight for her children. This shows me the love of a mother does not have eyes. They left and I begin to miss them. There were plenty of days that I thought about them, and it brought a smile to my face.

I had been seeing this unfamiliar number on my phone. July 4, 2002, I happened to be at home to answer the phone. It was my brother in law from Minnesota. He was in Tennessee in a shelter. My sister got tired of her husband and sent him to Tennessee, where I was. Why would she send her husband where I was? I had my own problems. He was her responsibility. I couldn't turn my back on him because he was mentally challenged. I went to the shelter and picked him up. He stayed with me three months until I found him an apartment. I ran errands for him and took care of Taineeka. I didn't have time to complain. He wasn't easy to get along with, but he would eat you out of a house and home. I had only seen one man that could eat as much as he did and he didn't live with me. A pound of butter, a loaf of bread, and a pound of bacon only last two days. A pack of hot dogs lasted one day. The seasoning and garlic didn't last a week. My sister should have factored all of this into the equation before she married him. After all, it was for better or worse. When I decided that I was going back to Chicago, she decided she that wanted to take him back. I told her, "If you don't want him, don't have him to come back to you." I was afraid he would lose his apartment. He moved back to Minnesota with her in October, and was homeless in December.

My cousin called me again about assisting another friend. She told me that her friend would help me with Taineeka. I took her in and we really had a good time. She was a lot of help with Taineeka. The only problem was she didn't stay long. She came to Tennessee and found her job right away. I hated when she decided to move.

The reason that I mentioned these people is because when I was being mistreated, God had shown them to me. He told me, "Don't worry, you have helped many and I have not forgotten." I never thought that I would become homeless after helping these people. I was never mean to these people and they were not sick. I treated them with love even when they made me angry. I didn't believe in allowing people to come into my house then mistreat them. I don't allow others to mistreat me in my home and neither do I allow others to mistreat my guest in my home. I sat back one day and counted the people I have allowed to stay in my home. I counted 22 people in a lifetime. I am so happy God created me with a heart. I realized that God was watching everything.

This is what people must remember. You may think no one is watching, but God is omnipresent; he is everywhere and he sees everything. You can't hide from God; even your heart can be hidden from him. I believe those that were mean to me were being taught because they have changed the attitudes; they seem to have changed hearts. They have become very kind people and they are helpful. I thank God for change.

Revelation: When people are selfish and mean, begin to pray for them. Many will not be able to withstand what is coming their way. There is no getting around it. The word says it will come back one way or another. Many expect their payback to come in the form of which they gave it. They don't know that punishment has no form and it does not read how you have done things. Punishment is orchestrated so that you may learn from it. It may come back the way you put it out it can also come back on you through your loved ones. It can come back in sickness and even in hardships. What people must recognize is the reason for karma. They must know why and who they mistreated and usually God will allow them to see that person. There are many things that we go through for learning, and strength. We as individuals know why we go through. We don't want to recognize it, but God puts it on our hearts. We realize that there isn't anything wrong with apologizing to the person that you have caused to hurt.

Many will try to show they are sorry in many different ways, by doing things for people or just being nice. There's nothing wrong with that. However, you must know that in order for you to ask God for forgiveness, you must apology to the party that you have offended. Many will say, "God knows my heart." Yes, he sure does. He also knows the heart of the person you have hurt. He knew their broken hearts and the pain you caused in their hearts. Now what makes your heart so special that He has to know yours and He didn't feel any pain for the other person's heart? God love each of us and He doesn't love you any more than he loves the person you hurt. They are just as special to Him as you are. You can't have eyes when you are doing the hurting, and become blind when it's time to apologize to a person you have hurt. If you do that, God will become blind to your request. Many have not been blessed because they are carrying the heart of Pharaoh. They possess a heart of stone. These are the same people that want others to be kind to them. The way they treat people, they will not allow people to treat them that way. If people will show more love, they will realize they are spreading one of the most important elements that was ever created besides man. Love spreads faster than cancer, love can even heal cancer.

CHAPTER 8

My Jonah Experience

I finally made it out of Tennessee and was headed to Indianapolis, Indiana where I had found a four bedroom house. I didn't want to go to Chicago, because I was still trying to have the peace that I had asked God for. The wait for her treatments, the appointments, and traveling back and forth made me realize that I had to move back to Chicago. I had never unpacked the truck when I moved from Tennessee to Indianapolis. It was November of 2003. I had gone to Tennessee to visit some friends and take care of some business. I drove from Tennessee to Chicago, to pick up a rented truck and my "help". I then drove back to Indiana to load the truck, and then back to Chicago to put my furniture in storage. When I totaled the distance I had driven over 1,000 miles that day.

I had to have another surgery. The scarred tissue that I had developed from STD that Mr. Jay had given me had to be removed. I was having problems from it two years later. I asked him if he could he pick me up from the hospital. I didn't have anyone else to do it. This was the worst thing that I could have done. He came to pick me up and he had his son with him. His son was about 3 years old at the time. He drove over bumps in the streets and I asked him could he try to avoid them because I had stitches. He then began to drive as if he were looking for the holes in the streets. He hit every pothole he could. It seemed as if he was even creating potholes to hit. I was in so much pain. He would even make sharp turns trying to hurt me. His son was being thrown all over the truck, I told him to put him in a seat belt and he refused. I put the baby in a seat belt so that he wouldn't get hurt. I thought as we were riding, his son and I were the most hated people in his life. He was angry at me about receiving his money. He was angry with his son because he felt as if he was responsible for everything. He never acknowledged that he was the one that messed up. It was neither the son nor my fault. He refused to take responsibility for his doing wrong. I felt so sorry for the little boy because he was so mean to him.

It was time for me to find a place to live. I had to wait for my Section 8 papers to be sent from Indiana to Chicago. I waited for five months for the papers. Indiana told me that they had sent them to Chicago. Chicago was telling me that had not received them. I was in between houses living with people that didn't really want me there. I had been doing this since July, after I had moved from Tennessee. I had nowhere to go and these people knew that. I was thankful they allowed my daughter and me to stay there. There were times when I slept in my car and I knew it was dangerous. I was willing to take a chance just to have a peace of mind. I cried out to God, "How could this happen to me as many people as I have helped, and many of the same people that were mistreating me I had helped?" People told us we were welcome but didn't make us feel welcomed. I think they were telling me this to be able to say they helped in one-way or another. These were my friends and relatives who knew how sick my daughter was. I had been through so much before I arrived in Chicago, and the devil was really using people to attack Taineeka and me. They didn't realize they were being used by Satan, but I knew what was happening.

It seemed like years of waiting on the papers and finally they came. I had to go to a congressman crying for help. I explained my situation to him. He made a call and mysteriously my papers appeared. While I was in the Section 8 office, the worker told me about a house that was just put on the market. The house had not been shown to anyone. She gave me the owner's name and number, and told me to call her. I called when I got home and was allowed to look at the house the next day. I loved the house it was a four bedroom house just what I needed. The owner said that I could have it once I gave her a $1,500 deposit. She asked when I could bring her the money. I told her I would have it Monday, and this was on a Tuesday. I had no idea what made me say Monday. I had said it without thinking. I walked away asking myself, "Now where am I going to get this money from?" I had no idea where it was coming from. I didn't mean to tell that lady Monday. What was I thinking? I began to pray asking God to assist me with getting the money. There was a peace upon me. Although I had nowhere to live, I felt a breakthrough coming; I knew God was about to bless me. I remembered his word "Now faith is the substance of things hoped for, the evidence of things not seen."(Hebrew 11:1) I had faith that I would get the money. "Delight thyself also in the LORD; and he shall give thee the desires of thine heart." (Psalms 37:4) I had done everything I could to delight the Lord. I had passed the test and was being moved to the next level. I could feel it.

It was on a Friday when Taineeka and I were out eating, and my phone rang. I answered it to hear my Aunt say, "You have mail at my house, and Taineeka has what looks like a check." We went to her house and got the mail, Taineeka opened her mail and it was a check for $5,000. We both begin to praise God. We deposited the check into the bank and wrote a check to the owner of the house for $1,500. Look at God! No it wasn't me giving the lady a date, it was God speaking through me. He had heard my prayers and seen every tear I had shed. He had a plan all the time for me and Taineeka. He knew we had suffered enough and He was doing just what his word said that He would do. The lady gave us the keys when we gave her the check. Taineeka and I didn't care that I didn't have the money to get our things out of storage. We decided that we would sleep on the floor in the house until the check cleared. We did it with comfort. We finally got a chance to move in. Don't allow opposition to move you out of position.

Yesterday is in your heart; tomorrow is in your hand. Don't let the future become your past. Reach out and grab the blessings that are coming your way. They're in your reach. Bondage is created for you to be set free. If you are never allowed to experience bondage, you will never know how to break free. You will never know how it feels to be free.

It was now time for Taineeka's four month checkup after her blood stem transplant. We went to the hospital and the doctors took blood from Taineeka. They came back into the room confused as ever. I asked them what was wrong. They told me, "We must draw more blood from her." I knew what was happening, I was just waiting on them to tell me. I could feel the Holy Spirit in the room with me and His presence was heavy upon me. I wanted to begin shouting and praising the Lord before the doctors came back.

They entered the room and they asked Taineeka what medicine was she on. Taineeka looked at them and told them, "God told me to stop taking the medicine in January." This was now May and she had not taken any medicine. I was praying to God about removing her off the medicine and she had removed herself while I was praying. It was already done and I didn't know it. The doctors then ask for more blood, when they returned they looked confused. They looked at me and said, "We don't see a trace of the disease, and usually if a person stops taking the medicine, the disease would be present. It would be going wild by now." I begin to praise and thank the Lord for healing my daughter. This was a very beautiful day for me. This was a day I will never forget. Now it was time to go and fight for my granddaughter and I was ready. I couldn't wait to get started. I knew it was already won. I just had to go through the fire and be tested to see if I had faith that I would be victorious.

Revelation: Although, I felt as if people were mistreating me, God was there all the time. He knew just how much I could take. If I had not went through the fire I couldn't come out a priceless diamond. I realize that those people were being used by Satan, and God was allowing it to happen to bring me to where he wanted me to be. Satan had blinders on those people. He didn't want them to know they were being used by him. I asked for peace and God was teaching me how to have peace in my life, in the midst of a storm. I sat one day and God had shown me, the same ones I shared my mother's insurance money with, are the ones that turned on me in my time of need. WOW! How soon people forget!

Sometimes, the things we ask for we have to be taught how to obtain them. We usually are the one that blocks what we are asking God to do for us. This is because we are in the way. We must learn to step aside and allow God to do the work Him to do. I had faith that my daughter would be healed and God healed her. I was speaking her healing and many other circumstances into existence. God was allowing them to manifest right before my eyes. You can look at it this way I was in school and Jesus was my instructor.

There were different problems to be solved and there was a certain formula that had to be used. I had to follow the steps to follow the formula. Many of the steps were not easy to follow. Nevertheless, I had to trust in God and stay on the course. Revenge is for God to handle, not me. When God fights your battle there is nothing the offender can do to stop it. Many came to me later for help and I never turned them down. I never brought up to them how they treated me. If I had done that it means I'm still bitter towards them.

I knew I was on a mission. The mission was possible if I stayed on the course. I knew in order for my child to be healed and for me to be blessed, I had to be obedient to God's word. I knew that Job had suffered and he continued to be obedient to God's word. People turned against him during his suffering and he never gave up on the word of God. In the end he received more than he had before he suffered. I knew that if God was faithful to Job he wouldn't treat me any different. I had to continue to focus on God and keep moving. I knew that God had a plan for my life. I just I knew it was in his timing and not mine. I had to be patient and wait on him.

Lord, I thank you for giving me all of my life. I thank you for lifting me up and for not allowing me to fall. I thank you for bringing so many beautiful people into my life. Lord, I ask that you touch any person that has nothing to eat during this holiday season. Remove any demonic thoughts and add joy into their lives. Let them know that you are a way maker and it's not over. I realize it's not about me. Lord, I thank you for being who you are, the Alpha and the Omega, the Comforter, the Wonderful One, the Almighty One. Everyone, enjoy your holiday and be blessed.

CHAPTER 9

My Prophetess Deborah Experience

I t was time for me to go and battle with the state of Michigan for my grandchild. I asked Mr. Jay to go along with me and he left me to battle on my own. There was no one there except Taineeka, myself and God. Yes I was about to hurt again. Nevertheless, I was prepared for what was to come. I went to court on the day that was set. When I walked in, I was not allowed to talk. The people in the court treated me as if I was nobody. I asked the social worker, "Why wasn't my grandchild placed in my custody?" She looked at me and said, "You need to ask your daughter why and ask her to tell you what she told us." I asked my daughter and she told me that she had to tell a lie to get into the battered women's shelter. She told the people I abused her as a child and I was on drugs. I could have fainted when I heard this. The main reason she couldn't call me was because she had blocked me out, by saying I was the abuser. I was flabbergasted. I was the only one who had tried to help her. Her father never came to court on behalf of his daughter and grandchild. The judge at one time asked about Tyra about her father. She wanted to know why he wasn't coming to court to show support. She was speechless. What a lesson she was about to learn from this. I was so hurt I couldn't cry. I had been drug free for 7 years and I had never abused her. I didn't argue with her at all. I figured she was getting the beaten of a lifetime, not to have her child. I realize this was something she would learn from.

This was better than any lesson than I could teach her. The entire courtroom was against me but I had to gird up and get ready for battle. What was done was already done and there was nothing I could do about it except pray.

The social worker was very rude. They told Tyra that if she gets a job and an apartment they would award her custody of her child. She got a job as a CNA and got an apartment. She was doing everything they asked of her. The director of Nursing and the social worker were very good friends. The social worker called the nursing home and had her friend to fire my daughter, so that she wouldn't have a job. The Director of Nursing was telling my daughter what a beautiful job she was doing, until the social worker found out where she worked. She admitted that the Director was a very good friend of hers. When the next court date came, I went into the courtroom and sat behind the social worker. I asked her why did she call and have my daughter fired. She looked at me in shock, as if "she was thinking, "How did she know what I did?" She denied it, I told her she was lying and that God was going to deal with her. I told her, "You are being very mean because you couldn't control my daughter." This social worker later admitted that she had never been around blacks, and the town she was raised up in had blacks. She even admitted that there were no blacks at the high school she attended. This young lady had no children, and so she had no knowledge of how it hurts a woman to be separated from her child. The social worker and Tyra were just 3 years apart in age. She wanted to talk very nasty to Tyra and she was not going to allow her to talk to her any type of way. The court still would not allow me to say anything in the courtroom. I went home and prayed to God for a change on the next court date.

The court date was approaching. I asked Mr. Jay could I use his truck to go to court. He told me yes. The day before the court date, he wouldn't answer his phone. When I finally talked to him, I asked him, "Why didn't you answer your phone? You know I had to be to court." He asked me, "Why you don't let the State have her? It's not your child."

I asked him, "Why didn't you allow the State to keep your son." He didn't let me use his truck for court. However, God made a way for me to get there. Upon my arrival, I learned that everyone was recommending that my grandchild be given to me. I was given the privilege to sit on the stand and tell my side of the story. I let them know that my daughter left because she couldn't stand to watch her sister suffer, dwindling down to 90lbs. She felt like her sister was going to die and she was afraid. Latavia had been removed from my daughter's care since February 11th 2003. The reason she was removed from my daughter's care is because the workers in shelter decided to call the agency on my daughter. The agency took the shelter's word, stating that the workers in the shelter are always accurate when reporting on someone. My grandchild was returned on November 2, 2004. Around that time, my 93-year-old grandfather was also sent to stay with me. Now I had to take care of my daughter, grandchild, and my grandfather. In the midst of all this I decided to go and find me a part-time job and I decided to go back to school. April 21, 2005, Tyra regained full custody of Latavia. I looked around at how God worked things out in my life. I had to fight, shed tears and pray to get everything in place. I took care of everyone in the house that God had provided for me, while I worked and attended school. It was not easy but I did it, in spite of the trials and tribulations. You have so much power, that the people who set themselves against you in a war will lose before you arrive on the scene. NOW THAT'S GOD GIVEN POWER!

I expanded the prison ministry that God had given me. When I first moved into the house, I was unemployed. I asked God what was it He wanted me to do. He gave me instructions to start a pen-pal prison ministry. I started the ministry by writing one inmate that I knew. The ministry then expanded to over 500 men. I wrote all 500 men without any help, I wrote men in each Illinois facility. I even wrote men as far as Kentucky. Writing the men was a learning experience for me. We had a bible study by mail and many of the men taught me the bible. They had a lot of knowledge and were eager to share it with me. I felt like they were a part of my family. I cried many nights for the men. They were asking for help, yet I was not able to provide them with any.

I would like to take a little time to share a few of my experiences with the inmates that were a part of the pen-pal ministry. I went on the Internet and God had chosen whom he wanted me to make contact with. I sent out twenty letters and I had five men to respond to my letters. There were twenty letters sent to the women inmates and I only had one response. I found the men to be very lonely; many of them had no one to write them in the last twenty years. There were some that had not gotten a visitor in twenty years. I was the only one that they would hear from on the outside, so I was their only connection. I really felt the heart of many of these men. I realized that many of them were either innocent, or had gotten too much time for the crime. I got a chance to see how the Justice system really offered no justice to minorities. Many of the men could not afford a lawyer and were railroaded by the penal system. Some of the men sent me their records to look at. I'm not a lawyer but I knew that many of the cases would have been beat if they had good legal representation. For example, one man was charged with murder. His records stated that they were looking for a white man six feet tall with a blond ponytail. The man charged was a Black male, 5 feet, 6 inches tall with black hair. The witness claimed she saw him through a fence at approximately 9 p.m. Now this was a fence made of wood with three cracks in it. She claimed she was 20 feet away. I know I couldn't identify anyone standing 20 feet away, especially at 9p.m. Reading through the paperwork, I noticed that she changed her story at least three times, giving a description of the assailant. She even said she was high at the time of the incident. The man didn't have a clean record, but I thought you had to be guilty beyond a shadow of a doubt. His record didn't have a murder on it. Even if his record contained a murder charge, does that mean that he is guilty of another murder without the evidence to prove he's guilty? There was one man that had owned his own construction company and he actually built the prison he was in. I had one pen pal who was a C-number. (This means he has been in prison before 1978.) These men and women were given open end sentences, to ensure they would never get out. The person that has done the same exact crime after 1978 were given 20-30 years, less time than the C-number inmate. The C-number inmate must appear before the board to ask for parole and they are denied time after time. Many of these men are in their 50's and 60's. They went to jail as teenagers. If many of the C-number inmates were sentenced under the new law they would be out by now. Many of them are the trustees in the penitentiary, many of them have degrees. There is approximately 200 C-numbers in the penal system.

I had a C-number as a pen pal. He was a very compassionate man. He was also remorseful for the crime he had done in his twenties. This man was one of the oldest C- number inmates in the penal system. He had been locked up for about 50 years. His wife visited him every week for the last 50 years. She had never remarried. When I talked to her, she told me there was never another man in her bed since her husband was arrested. She said that she only intended to marry one man, and it will be to death. She told me she will wait and pray for her husband until, either he dies, or she dies whichever comes first. My heart went out to the couple. They were still in love with one another. The man said that it was a usual thing to go before the parole board to be denied. It was a waste of time. He said every time he went before them, he already knew the answer; they would hardly look at him. He felt they were there just to say that they had done their job because it was so predictable. He stated that they could have done the paper work blind folded. I made one mistake when writing him. I sent all the men a picture of me at Christmas. There was nothing exotic about the picture I was wearing a red sweater and a big smile on my face. I received a letter from the man asking me not to write him anymore. He said that he couldn't stand looking at another woman besides his wife, and the picture bothered him. He told me that he had not really seen another woman in fifty years and the only woman he wanted to see was his wife. I apologized to him, but he insisted that I follow his orders. I did just that.

My heart goes out to him and others that are facing the same circumstances. I was really hurt that he wouldn't allow me to write him anymore. I learned not to take everything for granted and to be careful how I dealt with the inmates. You just don't know where they feel in their hearts and minds. I also learned that there was a thing such as true love. How many women would wait that long for their husband?

There was another inmate that really touched my heart. He wrote me a letter and asked me to take care of his mother. He wanted me to stay in contact with her. He explained that he was a loner growing up. He had been burnt in the face and people teased him. As a result of that, he didn't like being around people. When we begin to talk, he had about a year and a half more to serve of his five-year sentence. He sent me his mother's phone number. His mother and I would talk quite often. His mother began to share her story with me, telling me about her children that had died. This woman was a very strong woman; she had suffered two heart attacks and a stroke. She told me one of her sons had been killed in front of her house, one of her daughters was found dead on her back porch, and another daughter was found in a dumpster. She had one son that had just gotten out of prison and one in prison. One daughter died on her birthday, another one died on Valentine's Day, and her son died on Mother's Day. She asked me "How you would like to remember those days when you have lost your love ones on those days?" I couldn't respond to the question at all. She explained that she loved each one of her children but the one that was in prison was the child she held closet to her heart. He was the child that never had friends, and he was afraid to go outside, out of fear of being teased. I kept my promise to my pen-pal, and kept up with his mother. She told me once, that she had no food or heat. I got in touch with a ministry in her area and they went to her house, taking her food, and assisted her in getting her heat turned on.

Her son, my pen pal had sent me a letter, asking me what was that in my hand. I didn't understand what he was speaking of. That was until he sent me another letter stating, that there was healing in my hands. I then searched my bible for the quote of what is that in your hand. I found out that was question asked of Moses. I sent a reply letter back to him and never got a response. (This was in July.) In September, I decided to call his mother. She told me that he had died of a massive stroke in July. This happened right after he had sent me the letter, asking what was in my hand. I was blown to pieces. I cried. It felt as if I had lost a family member. The mother had forgotten to call me and let me know he had passed away. I often wondered why did he tell me that there was healing in my hands. I have a file cabinet with each letter the inmates had written to me. I kept them as a record, hoping that someday I would be able to help them. I was one day looking at their folders, and I asked the Lord when He will send help for the men. He replied saying, that "I've already sent help." I was confused until he spoke again, saying, "You are going to help them. You will go to law school and help the men that should be out". I said, "What Lord? My brain can't take all that, my plans were to go and get my Doctorates degree in Ministry. Well I am praying to God which way I should go. I will know whether it will be law school, or ministry after God answers my prayer. Due to the fact that my ministry had gotten too large, and I didn't have help, I had to put it on hold. I began this ministry in November of 2003. My time was limited because God told me to begin working on my CD. Once I completed that, I went back to school. I eventually graduated from school, receiving my Bachelors in Christian Ministry. Shortly after graduating, I obtained employment at a mental health center. I eventually left the job, and I was told I couldn't get unemployment. God moved once again through His favor in my life and I received the unemployment benefits.

Revelation: I couldn't hold anything against my daughter, although I was hurt from her actions. But this is a lesson for her to learn also. My daughter was 19 years old at the time. Many young people make very immature decisions at that age. This is the way they learn how to live. I figured that she hurt herself more than she hurt me. I knew that his would help her in life up the road and she would become a better person. I thought it could be worse where it could have caused her to sit in prison the rest of her life. This is something that can allow us to move on with our lives and try to practice to better people. My daughter is now in her senior year of college. She's majoring in Elementary Education. She has a job and her own apartment She is taking very good care of her daughter and has turned out to be a wonderful mother. If I had not allowed her to go through her trials, she may not have become the person she is today. The situation has made her a better person and a stronger person. God always has His plan when we think we have a plan. I learned that all bad things are not bad when God is behind you. He will allow these things to come into your life for a reason. I realize that God created chaos and if He created it, He had a solution to bring peace.

Chaos was created to allow solutions to be created. There is peace in the midst of chaos, and chaos is how we learn to solve problem. Without chaos, we wouldn't be able to solve problems. Therefore, chaos is should be used as tool to allow Jesus to come in and show His power. We tend to get upset when things are chaotic, when we should understand that Jesus is watching how we will handle the chaotic situations. This is where our faith is tested and we are strengthened for the next task that's coming our way. Every time Jesus went to bless or, he was confronted with chaos. He overcame it each time. Jesus was being an example to us and showing us that chaos is nothing new.

We must learn that everything that we encounter in our lives, whether it is good or bad, is a learning experience for us. We can learn from all things that we encounter. Writing the in-mates had shown me how we all take freedom for granted. Anyone of us could end up in jail just being at the wrong place at the wrong time, just like many of them were. I thought about how many of them are forgotten by their family members. I was also shown that the penal system is more concern about money, than they are rehabilitation. There is no rehabilitation in the penal system. Each man is a commodity. The inmates are looked at as money, and there is money made off the inmates. They are "set up" when they are sent to prison. When they are released from prison, there are no jobs available to them. They now have a record and no one will hire them with a record. This gives them no option but to return back to the lifestyle they once had. The penal system knows they are coming back because many of them lack the knowledge to open their own businesses. Each way they turn, the doors are closed in their faces. This is no more than being in prison again, but only it's worse. They are prisoners without a cage, and they will return to make money for the prisons. The prisons make money off the family by allowing the inmate to use the phone, and the bill will be charged to the love one. The hotels are making money because many of the love ones will stay over. The average prison is three to five hours away from Chicago. There are restaurants that have been placed around the institution to make money off the families. The phone companies have gotten in on the money making deals.

The prison industry has become a business. They are no longer interested in rehabilitation the inmates. They are set up in the courtroom because many of the judges have stock in the penal system. This alone lets us know that many will be guilty, if they don't have representation. Many of the men can't afford legal representation. Therefore, they are given time to keep the stocks up. I went to court for a friend, it was after Memorial Day holiday. The Public Defender walked in and you could smell the alcohol from the front of the courtroom. When he tried to sit down, he missed the seat. I thought Well, he allowed this man to represent my friend. I called his supervisor and put in a complaint against the Public Defender. She told me it was right after the holiday and that he may have had too much to drink. We don't know; it could be that he just had the smell of liquor from the holiday on him. She did everything in her power to defend him of being drunk and representing men whose life depended on him. I couldn't believe what I was hearing and seeing. This is when I realized that the men and women are in trouble if they don't have any legal representation.

The law is against them before going into the courtroom. I have seen the judges ask the attorneys about golfing, which lets you know they golf together. It is very sad to see our men and women being railroaded into a dog pen and you can't help them. They will not listen to what you have to say, when you try to tell them what is going on. Satan has blinders over their eyes and they don't want to hear anything you have to say. Even when you tell them the State makes up to $56,000 per inmate that is incarcerated. The State makes more off the youth, when they are incarcerated. We must pray for our people.

We must love one another; although there are some that we feel don't deserve love. God mandates us to love one another regardless. We are supposed to visit the prisoners, the sick, and take care of the widows. We must not forget those that are not as privileged as we are. We all make mistakes throughout our lives; hence we don't know who will have to visit us. No one is perfect. Many make mistakes and get caught. Meanwhile, there are some that make mistakes and they don't get caught. The realization is we all make mistakes. Let not the desire to love your brothers and sisters candle is passed on to others it then becomes a fire which can't be blown out.

Chapter 10

People who made me who I am

As I mentioned earlier, my grandmother whom raised my sister, my cousins, and me was named Maxine Reed Waddell. My grandmother was mama to us. We would call her mama. She made us go to church and taught us the values of life. If we didn't go to church, we were not allowed to go outside for the entire week. She would drink on the weekends, but we still had to go to church on Sundays. We were happy to see her drink. This meant more time outside and we would have McDonald hamburgers. We thought we were in heaven to get McDonald's and were angels if we got White Castle burgers. I was an adult when I realized we were poor. I never thought we were poor because we never missed a meal. It was the fact that we were rich in spirit that kept us from being poor in the mind. We were so happy that we didn't realize we were without. It was the love we had for one another that kept us so happy and at peace.

Mama was about 5'1 light skinned with long wavy hair and was the sweetest person you ever wanted to meet when she was sober. When she had a drink, she was nothing to play with. As a matter of fact, she was dangerous. You may have got shot or stabbed. Whenever she pulled her weapon out, it was time to go. Everyone that knew her would get out of the way. When she would be returning home from her card games, you could look out the window and see her walking down the street with her gun in her hand. Everyone outside would step to the side, getting out of her way. When she knocked on the door and we didn't answer, she would shoot in the house to wake us up.

I remember waking up and letting her know I was on my way to the door so that I wouldn't get shot. I remember the card games that she would host. They would last the entire weekend. The police would raid the parties and all the card players would jump in the bed with us, playing sleep. I can't count the times I looked out the window and saw the police putting my grandmother and her friends in the paddy wagon. Once, early in the morning before we got up to get ready for school, there was a loud knock on the door. I heard mama getting out of the bed to answer the door. Before she could get to the door, the door was kicked in. When I looked up, guns were in my face. Men with guns were everywhere. It was the police, looking for drugs. They scared all of us to death. They searched the house and didn't find anything. They found out they were in the wrong building. They apologized over and over to us. Mama and I would later go to the store. We seen two of the policeman who kicked our door in. They apologized again. I told mama to sue them; they had terrorized her and five children. She refused to sue. This made very me angry.

We had so many bullet holes in our house; we thought that was the way it was supposed to look. When mama would get angry with us, she would start shooting. Not shooting at us, but all over the house. We would take off, running. Even our baby sitter would run. We weren't afraid because we were used to her doing this. (When we moved out of that apartment, my husband's cousin moved in. She asked me where all the bullet holes came from. She said there were bullet holes in every cabinet, and every door in the apartment. All I could do was laugh and shake my head.) Mama had one eye. She was shot in the eye with a BB gun when she was five years old. Her mother also died when she was five. Her aunt, Willie Ann Barber, raised her. (We called her aunt Will.) I remember she came to visit us. We were living in the projects and the elevator was broke. I was worried about her walking up five flights of stairs, because she was ninety years old. She began to walk ahead of me. By the time I made it to the fifth floor, I didn't see her. I called her name and she answered, "Where do I go now, I can't go any further." She had walked all the way to the ninth floor.

Mama's stepmother passed away when I was a little girl. I remember our lights blew out and the phone rang. It was someone was letting us know that she had passed. After she died, she haunted me in my dreams for months. Each time it was the same dream. I would dream that I was running from her and she would point her finger at me. I would begin to run in one spot and never going anywhere. She would be walking up on me and when she caught me she would tickle me, until I could barely breathe. It was not her being friendly, she was being evil. These dreams made me afraid to go to sleep at night. She was very mean to us. When we went to visit her in Tennessee, she would make us sit in the sun. She didn't allow us to get anything to drink. The children who lived there, she treated them different. In my mind, I planned to give her the whipping of a lifetime. She had steel gray eyes and she looked evil. She really didn't care for me at all. She said she didn't like the way I watched her, and that I was evil.

I remember Dada (my grandfather) telling me stories about mama. One of the stories he told was when he would stay out all night and what happened when he would come home. He would throw his coat or hat in the house first. If he heard the wind, he would take off running. The wind was mama swinging with the blade in her hand. Mama told me he ran so fast that his hat jumped off his head on to her head. He said one day when he got away from her that his coat was cut in half down the back. Mama also told me stories of how she was the babysitter of Rev Clay Evans, and Tina Turner while their parents were in the field. Mama was a child of a pastor, Rev. Robert Reed. He had children by at least three women that I knew, but there were probably more. I only know of three of his children by the three different women. I sat many of days at the table talking with her, while everyone was outside playing. I sat under her more than any other child in the house, learning how to cook and listening to her stories. I was her daring grandchild. She would tell me, "Ronnie stop being so mean." I was also a very silly child. I would get in all types of trouble about laughing at things. Once I started laughing, I couldn't stop. Mama and I were walking down the fire lane, headed home once. All of a sudden, mama took off running. I laughed because I had never seen her run and she looked funny. She ran off the fire lane and fell into the grass. I walked over to her to help her up. I was bent over, laughing so hard that my side was hurting. After she got up, she slapped my face. I asked her why did she hit me. She told me that she had tripped and was praying that I would catch her. She was running to keep from falling on the concrete. She ran over towards the grass to keep from injuring herself and all I could do was laugh. I told her I thought she was just running. I didn't know she had tripped. She looked at me and said, "They don't come any sillier than you." And she shook her head while looking at me in disbelief. Mama taught me how to fight, and how to use a knife. Mama was a diabetic. I was the one that gave her insulin shot twice a day, at the age of 9. I remember how she would give each of us a whipping. She would whip us according to our age, so I was always the first one to get the whipping. I got the worse of the beatings. She would take me to all the funerals. We were terrified of dead people so we would sit at the back of the funerals. Once when we were leaving a funeral, she told me, "When I die, I'm going to come back and scare the hell out of you" and laughed. I cried all the way home on the bus, begging her not to come back and scare me.

Mama stopped drinking in 1977. She and her friend, Ms. Hazel Carter started going to church. They became members of Greater Harvest Baptist Church and they were very active in the church. I never thought I would see a change. She gave her life over to the Lord. Mama may have been a fighter, but she was more than that to her six grandchildren. She was the one that taught us how to live, love and forgive. She taught us many good values that we still carry with us today. She took care of us and made sure we went to school. Mama became sick in 1979. During this time, the fire department was on strike. She was having difficulties breathing and we couldn't get an ambulance. They finally arrive and got her to the hospital. When she came home, she was on dialysis. The last day I saw her, we were playing cards. She wanted to play my hand, but I didn't want her to. She kept at it until I finally gave in. As she was playing the hand, I noticed her breathing was not good. She had told me that she dreamed of Aunt Will the night before. Aunt Will had on all white in the dream.

That night I went home. I had to be to work the next day. I set my alarm to ring at 6 a.m., so that I could wake up on time. (It was on a Tuesday.) My alarm didn't go off for some reason. At around 11:30 a.m., I got a call from my sister. She had something to tell me. There was no way that I could escape what she had to tell me. Mama had died. I dropped the phone and fell to the floor. I cried hysterically. I felt as if my life had ended. I had lost my mother, my teacher, my rock and the woman I loved so much. She passed away on May 27, 1980. That night, I went to stay at my mother's house. I slept in the dining room on the couch. When I opened my eyes, I'd seen mama standing in the doorway. I blinked my eyes, praying she would go away. She began to walk closer to me with a smile on her face. I screamed! My sister came running in the room to see what was wrong. I told her what had just happened. I slept with her that night. The next day, I asked, "What outfit did mama wear to the hospital in?" When they told me what she was wearing, I couldn't believe it. It was the same outfit she had on when I saw her. Mama did exactly what she said she would; she came back and scared the hell out of me. That was the only time she would visit me. She never came back to me again.

Now I must introduce you to my other grandmother, my father's mother, Bessie Oby. (This is whom everybody says I look so much like.) Grandma Oby is what I called her. She was a beautician and well known around Chicago. She was the daughter of a Pastor Rev Scott. Grandma Oby never bothered anyone and she didn't allow anyone to bother her. Grandma Oby was a fascinating dresser. There were not many that could out dress her. She took care of me as well. She made sure I had my school clothes and anything I needed. She stood about 5'10 and she didn't take any mess. I remember riding with her in the car, and a man cut her off. When we got to the light, he began to curse her. She raised her knife at him and told him to pull over. I prayed the man would keep going. Fortunately, he did.

When my uncle died, she took over his cleaners. I would help her. There was a man that came into the cleaners, claiming that Grandma Oby lost his wife belt. He told her, "You need to find that belt, because you don't want my wife to come in here." It was right around the Christmas holiday. She looked at the man and told him, "If you want your wife home for Christmas you better keep her at home."

When Grandma Oby would get angry she would lose her mind, she couldn't see anyone except for the person she was trying to get to. One of my scariest moments is when she was putting my father and his wife out of her house. His wife told her, "I will leave when I get ready." Not to mention, she had my little brother in her arms. Grandma Oby told her, "I don't mind giving you a whipping with him in your arms, if you don't mind talking to me that way." She kept talking. That's when my granny kicked her and she landed on the bed. Granddaddy Oby had to pull her off of my stepmother. She was very angry with him for stopping her. She went in the closet looking for the gun and didn't realize she had tossed it out of the closet. I was so happy she didn't see the gun. I knew she would have shot him while he stood there like a dummy. I was saying in my mind, "Why don't he just run." Later that day, my stepmother's mother came over. She asked Grandma Oby, "Why did you put my daughter out?" She began to walk toward my granny with her hand under her coat. Grandma Oby grabbed the big punch bowl and hit her upside her head. She gave her exactly she was looking for. Later, the police came and arrested

Grandma. She set in the back of the paddy wagon, begging them to put my stepmother's mother in the back with her. I was a young child. Even if I were older, I wouldn't get in her way. She had four sons. Neither of them would get in her way.

Grandma Oby was a very smart woman. She always handled her business and paid her bills on time. She was a woman of wisdom. We laughed many of days together. When we would talk on the phone, we would be on the phone for at least three hours, laughing and talking. I would listen to her advice. I loved my grandmother and she loved me. I was on the phone talking with my granny once. All of a sudden, the phone went dead. It sounded as if someone had hit her in the head. I called the police and they went over to check on her. She called me back and thanked me for calling the police because it could have been something wrong. She laughed and told me the cord came out the wall. We both laughed. She said the police scared her to death when she opened the door.

Grandma Oby was strong and forgiving. I think back to the time Granddaddy Oby decided he was going to leave her. They separated for about a year. He stayed in the house at 6805 S. Parnell, the house they had purchased in 1955. She moved into her building at 5327 S. Michigan. I was so hurt that they had separated. I felt they were too old for this. I believe she was in her 60's and he was in his 70's. He eventually had taken ill. She went, got him, and brought him home with her. She took care of him. He acted as if he had not done anything wrong; I just shook my head at him. They carried on as if nothing happened. I asked her "Mama how do you do that?" She told me, "When you have a man like him, who doesn't have any sense; you have to keep your senses. You don't be silly because he is silly." He was so loving and stubborn. He had some very mean ways, but he was sweet.

I can remember when Grandma Oby became ill. I went to visit her in the hospital. I had taken her a plaque that I had made. The plaque was letting her know how much I loved her. She cried so hard, I didn't know that she would cry like that. The hospital released her, sending her home. There was nothing more that they could do for her. Although, I hated to see her in such a state, I would visit her often. I was sitting in her room, talking to her. She was trying to get on the pot and I was frozen, not thinking to help her. I was thinking that I never thought I would see her this way. She looked over at me and said, "What you are just standing there for? Get up and help me." I just couldn't believe I would ever see my grandmother needing help. She had always been such a strong woman.

March 5, 1998, I remember that day oh so well. I was at work. I got off work, and headed home. I pulled up to my house and was opening my car door, to get out of the car. Before I can get out of the car, my daughters met me, delivering the dreadful news: my Grandma Oby had passed away. Upon learning the news, I fell apart. Once I pulled myself together, I went to her house. When I went to the door, my uncle opened the door. He jumped and said I scared him. I scared him because I looked so much like my grandmother. I went into the room where she once laid. I had laid across the bed and cried. My thoughts were how I would miss talking to her, for long periods of time. How I would miss her Ham and Potato Salad. She could make the best potato salad and ham. I had once again lost my other mother.

I had a step grandmother named Mary Matthews. We called her Grandma Matthews. She was saved, sanctified, and filled with the Holy Spirit, as she would say. Going to church with her was punishment. It was never a beautiful place to be. She was something else she made me not ever want to go to church. Grandma Matthews raised my middle sister and did she suffer at her hands. I believe this is the only way she knew how to show love. She would tell us that she had been saved since she was 32 years old. Her husband came in the club and cut her face with a bottle. In doing this, he put her eye out. She shot him six times and killed him. Her pastor came and got her out of jail; she was saved ever since then.

Now Grandma Matthews did have some nice ways about herself. She was a very hard worker; she was the head seamstress for Evans furrier. Even after she retired, they paid her to come back and work for them. She was an excellent cook; she could cook the fire off the stove. She made a hamburger taste like a delicacy. She could bake any type of cake, or pie you wanted from scratch. She was just so mean and strict. I never understood how she could be so mean, and shout all around the church. We would have to leave for church at 7 a.m, taking the bus to the west side of Chicago. She lived on the south side at 65th and Marshfield. We would stay at the church until the church ran out of services. We would then head back home at 9 p.m. on the bus from Douglas Blvd. We better not go to sleep in the church or we would be hit up side our head with the bible or a comb. I often wondered how she could be so spiritual and natural messed up.

Grandma Matthews had a nephew that had spent twenty years in jail for murder. Upon his release, she would pick him up from prison. She brought him home to stay with her and assigned him to the room next to my sister's room, which was upstairs. They would sleep upstairs, while she slept down stairs. He began to have sex with my sister when she was thirteen years old. He was in his late 30's. He threatened to kill her if she told. In the back of her mind, she's thinking, "He just got out of jail for murder." Now do you think my sister would tell? I guess you already know he was a faithful member of the Church of God In Christ. On Sundays, he did his devil dance and chanted in tongues to the devil. Meanwhile he was thinking about the next time he could get in the bed with my sister. We do know he was not dancing unto the Lord or speaking in the heavenly language. He was dead when I found out. I cried, not only for what he had done to my sister, but also because I wish I had known. I know I would have killed him. I begin to sit in church and watch the men dance. I wondered how many of them was bothering children. Mama had already passed when my sister told us. I know if she had known, she would have died sooner.

Grandma Matthew was also a licensed babysitter. She would leave my sister at home, so when the parents came to pick up their children, someone would be there. One parent, which was a male, would come to get his son. My sister was about eleven years old at the time. He was also using her body as a toy. He would tell my sister he wanted a mother for his son. He was a sick man! I often wondered, if Mrs. Matthew was so connected to God, where was her wisdom? There was no God involved. She was so busy punishing us, abusing us, and keeping us in church but yet she had lost touch with the true and living God.

Once, my youngest sister and I decided that we weren't going to church. She told us if we didn't go, we would not eat dinner in her house and she meant it. I looked to my stepfather for help but he was not about to go against his mother. I think he was afraid of her himself. My two sisters had the same father and she would make a difference between them. She would take my younger sister shopping with her to buy my middle sister clothes, and wouldn't buy my younger sister anything. I remember my sister and I broke open a bank to get the money out, so that we could get on the bus to go home. Charles came just so happened to come in. He took us home.

Everyone who goes to church, stands on the pulpit, dance in church, speak in tongues or carry a bible is not of God. I was blessed to learn this at a very early age. Satan can do everything but tell the truth and save your soul. He presents himself to be whatever you desire. He operates in many areas in the church from pastors to just plain members, looking for someone to devour. He even stands over the children in the church.

I mentioned that mama (my mother's mother) had one eye. Grandma Matthews also had one eye. Mama was shot in her eye with a BB gun, at the age of five. Mrs. Matthew's husband cut her in the eye with a Pepsi cola. Mama taught us a song that went like this. "Grand mama pee peed, she wasted her water knee deep, she climbed the mountain high, and didn't have but one eye." We would sing that song with her all the time and have a good time. We went to Grandma Matthews house and we thought it was ok to sing the song.

We got the beating of a lifetime. We didn't understand why we were being disciplined for singing the song. After all, it was mama who taught us that song. She too had one eye. Grandma Matthews drove a Cadillac and she loved to drive. She wanted to continue to drive, even after she gotten too old. She would drive so close to the doors of the parked cars, and it took her forever to hit her brakes. We would be in the passenger side putting on brake for her. She had a couple of accidents. I was so happy she finally stopped driving.

Grandma Matthew had taken ill. I went to visit her at the nursing home. When I walked into her room, I was blown away by what I heard. The lady was cursing up a storm. I had never heard a cursing word ever come out of her mouth. Not to long after she had gotten sick, she passed away. On the day of her funeral, many people spoke nice of her. She sang with many well-known gospel groups in her day. All of the gospel singers from the groups she once sang with were all saying nice things about her. Meanwhile, the family, we just sat there as if we didn't know whom they were talking about. My cousin got up and did she put the icing on the cake. All I could do was smile as I looked at the faces of the holy rollers. She told them, "Yes I loved my Aunt and the rest of the family loved her also. But we never got to know the part of her you all are speaking about." Their faces were broke in one thousand pieces and I loved it. They weren't looking for a speech like that. The speech my cousin gave was fit for an academy award. Grandma Matthews may have had some evil ways, but in everyone you can find some good. I learned how to cook. I learned what it was like to run my own business because she was a woman of business. I learned how too much religion was as harmful, as not enough religion. I learned that you can be so focused and yet out of focus on reality. I learned that too much of anything is not good. I learned that people treated you according to what they thought was right, or according to how they were treated. People found love in which they are surrounded with. She was only doing things in the way she knew how, or the way she was treated.

My grandfathers, I loved them dearly. However, they were rank sinner whores. My mother's father, Robert Waddell (Dada) was the life of the family. He would come over and assist mama in taken care of us. Dada would give us a dime when we would see him. The next week, we would see him again and asked for money. He would ask, "What happen to the dime I gave you last week?" Mama and Dada had been separated for almost thirty years. Their separation didn't stop them from loving one another. If mama got sick, Dada would come over and take care of her. If Dada got sick, they would reverse the roles, leaving mama to take care of him. He never missed a week of coming over to see her. If there was anything she needed, he would give it to her. Dada went to church every Sunday just to see the women. He had plenty of women too. He would sit and tell us stories and kept the family laughing. All of our friends loved him. He told us a story once about how he beat a young girl to a seat on the train. He said that he'd elbowed her, sat down, and opened the window. The girl's stop came up and she got off the train. As the train was pulling off, she reached in the window and slapped his face. He told us, "She slapped the hell out of me. If I had a gun, I would have shot her." He told us that everyone on the train was laughing. He decided that he wanted to get off on the next stop. There was one problem: the train went express. So, he was stuck on the train with everyone laughing him. Dada would ride the bus every morning to work. He said everyone on the bus knew which stop he got off on. They wouldn't move when it was time for him to get off. He decided the next day he would fix them. They next day when he got to the door to get off the bus, he turned around and fell off the bus backwards. When he fell backwards, nine or ten people went out the door with him. He said he didn't have a problem getting off the bus anymore. Dada would put his arms up so that no one would get on the bus before him. My neighbor tried to go under his arms she said that he almost broke her neck. He told us a story once about a man and woman trying to rob him. The man was holding him and telling the woman to go in his pockets.

He said every time the woman reached for his pockets, he snatched some of her clothes off. He said when he got finish with her all she had on was her bra and panties.

Dada kept the laughter going, as he told his stories. He was a lot of fun. If you wanted to laugh, all you had to do is come over to our house. His stories weren't the only thing that kept the laughter flowing. Dada was comical, overall. He would be in his 70's when he attempted to sale marijuana. He would sit by the door and wait on his customers. His bags were short but no one dared to bring the bag back or complain about it. He had a butcher knife and an ax sitting right next to him. (These are the same weapons he slept with under his pillow. He said they kept the witch from riding him.) I remember when he was in the basement using the bathroom once. My cousin knocked on the window really hard. Dada came running out the bathroom with his pants down. We laughed so hard. Once, I came in the house and noticed that he had strings tied around the bottom of his pants. I asked him what he was doing. He told me that he had seen a mouse. He was making sure it didn't run up his pants leg. I pulled up to the house once, in my car. When I got to the door, I noticed that it was open. I thought to myself, "I'm not going in that house with the door open." So I called Dada's name and he didn't answer. I went across the streets and called the police. When they arrived they went in with their guns out. Dada came out of the basement. He screamed when he'd seen the police with the guns out. He told them he was the one that opened the door when he saw me pull up. He told them he was looking out the window when I pulled up. I didn't see him looking out the window. Oh, Dada was so angry with me; he told me he would never open the door for me again in his life.

There was a lady who lived down the street. She told everyone that a naked man tried to climb through her window. A girl who lived across the streets told us that a naked man tried to get in her car with her. We wondered who in the world was this naked man. One night, my sister, Dada and I were sitting in the kitchen. Someone had knocked on the back door.

We kept asking her who was at the door and they wouldn't say anything. My sister went to answer the door. When she came into the kitchen, behind her was a naked man. My sister, Dada and I fell on the floor laughing. It was my mother's boyfriend sleep walking. He walked into the bedroom and got in the bed as if he had clothes on. Dada never stopped teasing him, calling him the neighborhood rapist.

When he got sick, I had borrowed some money from him. I went to give him his money and there was something different about his eyes. His eyes looked as if he was staring into space, he didn't look the same. He had been getting Motrin's from me, and he was getting too many. I asked him why he needed so many. He told me that his leg was hurting. We tried to get him to go to the hospital. He was declined, saying that he was fine. The next day, he was in his room turning the bed upside down. The whole room was torn apart. He told us he was looking for his money. We knew something was wrong. We finally got him to go to the hospital. They found out he was bleeding out of the brain. Dada passed away Dec. 19, 1989. He is surely missed by the family.

It was very strange because he and my stepfather Charles were sick around the same time. Once, I was lying in the bed reading my bible. There was a door to the bedroom that led to the bathroom. I looked at the bathroom door and my stepfather and grandfather were standing there. I thought that was God's way to let me know they were both leaving. The next day, I got a call from Grandma Matthews telling me that my stepfather passed away that morning. Charles passed in November and Dada passed in December. I never understood how I was able to see both of them in the door way, they were standing together looking directly at me. What was strange was it was daylight. If it had not been I would have thought it was my imagination.

Granddaddy Oby was a very kind man. He was very appreciative for anything you did for him. He never complained about anything I did for him. He would eat his food and never complain. I remember when he got sick once. The ambulance came to take him to the hospital. As they were taking him down the stairs, we noticed a group of children across the streets. One of the girls asked me was he my father. I told her that he was my grandfather. She told me, "Don't worry. He will be fine." She then waved at Granddaddy Oby. He waived back at her. It was something about this girl that stood out. She was different from the other girls. Two days later, I saw the same group of girls. I asked them, "Where was the girl that I was talking to?'" They didn't know whom I was talking about. I asked them, "Don't you all remember me talking to a girl that was with you all?" They still didn't remember me talking to anyone. I described what the girl had on, and no one knew whom I was talking about. I couldn't believe that they didn't remember. I pulled one of the girls to the side. I asked her about me talking to the other girl. She told me no one was talking; they were just watching. I asked my grandfather did he remember waving at a girl. He told me yes. I asked him, "Do you know that no one remember who she was?" He replied, "I knew it was something different about that girl. She just looked so different from the other kids."

I was working, going to school, taking care of him, my daughter and my granddaughter. It was as if God had me in a zone, I was only focused on what I had to do. I remember I sent my daughter next door to ask the neighbor would she braid her hair. (This was in March) Mr. Jay told Taineeka that she had passed away in November. I was about to have the elderly woman's grass cut. When I returned, her brother was cutting it. I told him that I was about to have her grass cut. He told me that she had passed away in January. I asked God, "How could I not know that my neighbors on both sides of me had passed?" How did I miss that? I told my grandfather the death angel had skipped over our house the time he was sick. I was really confused with that. How could I be so busy that I didn't notice both of my neighbors had passed away?

When Granddaddy Oby became ill, I received a three-day suspension from my employer. I told them I was not going to come in and take care of others grandparents and I couldn't be with my own grandfather. They told me that if I took off, they would suspend me. I took off anyway. Granddaddy Oby was in critical condition. His intestines had tied up into a knot. He was taken to one hospital. They wanted to do the surgery, but they found out that he had two bubbles, one on each side of his heart. This hospital didn't have a cardiology team. In spite of the hospital not have a cardiology team, the doctor still wanted to proceed with the surgery to untie his intestines. I refused to give my consent for this. The doctor responded, "If his heart goes, out he's old anyway." I replied, "I will not allow this to go on without giving him a chance. I want him transferred to another hospital." My grandfather was transferred to another hospital that had a cardiology team. They called to let me know that he had a 50/50 chance of surviving the surgery. Granddaddy Oby came through like a champ. What was really interesting is he refused pain medication. The doctors couldn't believe that this ninety-four year old man would not take any pain medication. He was a very strong man, they had cut on his intestines and put a hole in his stomach, to give him a colostomy bag and he refused pain medication.

I remember before he had gotten sick he had locked himself in the bedroom. He refused to open the door. I left for work. When I returned home from work, he still refused to open the door. I told him that I was going to have the fire department to open the door if he didn't open it. He finally opened the door. We walked to his room, and I made a wild discovery: He had mess all over the bed, on the mattress, the rails, in the carpet and all over everything in the room. I took my uniform off and put on my scrubs that I would clean up in. I took his clothes off and put him in the shower. I took all the clothes and linen, rinsed them off, and put them in the washer. I scrubbed the room and cleaned as much as I could. It took me about five hours. When I finished he looked at me and said, "Darling, I'm so sorry. I really feel bad that you have to do this for me." I told him, "You better be happy that I love you." We both laughed.

I had a privilege of caring for him for three years before he passed. He passed away at the age of 95. He actually passed away on his birthday in Las Vegas. He had moved to Vegas with his baby son in August 2006. I talked to him that Tuesday. He told me, "Baby the Lord is calling me home." I told him, "Daddy, you can't leave now. Your birthday is Saturday." He asked, "This Saturday?" I replied, "Yes." He then asked, "What is today?" I told him, "Today is Tuesday. I want to be able to say that my grandfather lived until he was ninety-five." He replied, "Ok darling. I will wait just for you." December 16, 2006, he passed away. He waited until his birthday. I am able to say that my grandfather lived until he was 95 years old

My mother's name was Barbara Jean Ford. People knew her as "Piggy". As a young child, I had difficulties pronouncing the letter "P". As a result, many knew my mother as "T.T" My mother and I were more like sisters, than mother and daughter. We were only sixteen years apart. We did everything together, from partying to going on trips. My mother loved to party and she could out dance all three of her daughters. She was a sharp dresser. She always dressed nice even when she was going to work. She would dress me in very expensive clothes, when I was in grade school. My pants, tops and shoes all matched.

Although T.T would give me money, and dress me in nice clothes, at times I felt that she treated me unfair. I had $5,000 saved in the bank. I was planning to take a trip to Hawaii in 8th grade. She asked me, "If you go to Hawaii, where will you sleep when you return?" I had to cancel my trip. She went and bought my sister and I bedroom sets. I asked her about my money. She gave no explanation. She would never show me the account book. I found out later that she had taken my money and bought her a car. She promised me she would give it back to me tax time. I never saw the money. There were times that her and my sister would double-team me. She asked me to co-sign for my sister a car once. She agreed that she would be responsible for the payment. When my sister got behind in the note, I went to my mother for assistance with the note. After all, the car was in my name. She cursed me out and said she wasn't paying anything. Once, I was hospitalized for nine days. I was near death. I looked for my mother and sister to visit me they never showed up. I thought maybe they were too busy, but I over looked it. It seemed she would mistreat me purposely. When microwaves first came out, I bought her one for Christmas. The microwave cost me $300. After Christmas, one of her neighbors asked T.T how was her Christmas and what did she get. She told the lady right in my face that she didn't receive anything. I asked her, "What about my gift?" She responded, "You didn't buy me anything." I was so hurt. I looked at her and told her, "You will remember the next gift I buy you." From that day on, I didn't buy another gift. After a while, I would give her money. I was tired of being mistreated. I felt that she didn't want me to get ahead in life. She wouldn't attend anything I participated in. She went out of her way for my sister. I asked her why she doesn't let me stay with my father's mother, like she gave my other sister to her father's mother. She cursed me out. I didn't understand her. She would get my hair done and buy me some of the finest clothes. I felt as if I was being dolled up to be humiliated.

We were playing cards one afternoon. During the card game, she talked about me to my friends. I couldn't take it any more; I decided to leave. When I tried to leave she blocked the door, not allowing me to leave. I was so angry that I tore a chair apart with my bare hands to keep from hitting her. I was an outcast in my own family. I knew she loved me but she would do things to provoke me and laughed. I was told because I looked so much like my father, and he didn't marry her is the reason she treated me the way she did. I grew up not really being able to trust my mother. I never knew when she would turn on me.

T.T and I had a share of good times, and got along well sometimes. She saved my life once. I was a sophomore in high school. I had a friend named Rhonda who sat next to me in class. There was a Valentine's dance at another school. She wanted me to go with her to the party. I begged T.T to let me go. She refused to let me go. I cried and I was so angry with her. That Monday, I went to school. I was waiting to talk to Rhonda about the party. She never came into the classroom. The teacher came into the classroom and announced that Rhonda was killed at the party. There were some boys they had confrontation with. One of the boys pulled a gun, firing a shot. Rhonda was hit in the back; she died instantly. I had to leave school early that day. I didn't want to be in the classroom anymore. I couldn't stand to see the empty seat next to me. I thought my mother never stopped me from going to parties she would let me go even on school days. My cousin and I could party every day of the week and still get A's. We were allowed to party because we knew how to keep our grades up. I thought my mother must have felt something that day. I'm so happy she did. When I asked her the reason she didn't allow me to go to the party, she told me she felt something was wrong that day. I know my life was spared, I know in my heart if I had gone. I would have caught the bullet.

I spent the last 48 hours of T.T's life with her. I knew she was sick, but I didn't know she was as sick as she was. We would talk a lot about a lot of things. She kept speaking of going to the cemetery to visit her mother. While we were out, T.T. talked about what she wanted me to do if she died. She told me where to have her services and to make sure we cremated her. She said she didn't want anyone standing over her body lying. She felt many would just come to see what she had on or looked like. She even told me the music to play for her service. She wanted to hear the Clark Sisters, "Jesus is a love song" and Frankie Beverly and Maze "I want to thank you" She called me at three in the morning with my niece was on the phone. We laughed and talked for about two hours. We were having a conversation about a pastor that had checked into the hotel my niece was working at. She was talking about all the women that were visiting his room. When I was about to hang the phone up, T.T. said, "Goodbye." It was like I had never heard it. She said it so sweet, it so different that it caught my attention and stayed on my mind. I thought about a question I wanted to ask her. I was so tired I thought, "I would ask her tomorrow." The next day never came for me to ask the question.

The next day, at 3 p.m. I received a call from my middle sister. She had informed me that T.T was sick and that the ambulance was taking her to the hospital. I called my husband to bring the car. I needed to go and check on her. He told me that he was on his way. I waiting an hour and a half, he never showed up. A friend picked me up and took me to the hospital. T.T was having seizures back to back. The doctors wanted to put her on a machine to breathe for her. They told me that this was the only way to stop the seizures. T.T told me to never allow a tube to be put in her and a machine to breathe for her. I stood there in the room, watching over her. I called her name and she rose up with tears in her eyes. I told her the machine was only to stop the seizures, not to breathe for her. She was fighting as if she didn't want it. I stood there crying for about 10 min, not knowing what to do, I asked God to help me make the right decision. I didn't want to go against my mother's wishes. I reluctantly went along with the doctors. I figured that it would cease the seizures and she would be fine. The doctors told me to go home for a while, get some rest, and come back.

I went home until they got her in a room. I then called Mr. Jay again for the car. I waited four hours. I had started calling him at 3 p.m. and he arrived at 10 p.m. When he arrived the first thing he told me was, "If it were my mother, I wouldn't have continued to call and wait. I would have walked to the hospital." I couldn't believe that he would say something like this to me at a time like this. My mother was fighting for her life. He was out with his girlfriend and cared less about me or my mother. I often wondered what kind of woman my husband could have been with. If it was me, I would have made him leave. He was a quiet storm. People would find every excuse for him and why it was my fault that he treated me the way he did. I guess people don't care until it becomes them.

I took the car and went to the hospital. I stayed there three days, sleeping on the floor. There were times when I was the only one there. I prayed constantly for her recovery. I cried for three days in the waiting room. I would go into the room and talk to her. The last time I talked to her tears came down her face. The nurses kept telling me to go home and get some rest. I didn't want to leave. I knew if I left that she would die. I would finally leave that evening. I went home, and fell into a deep sleep. I was sleeping so peaceful, until the next day when the phone rang. It had to be about 11:20 A.M. It was my husband. He wanted to know who was at home with me. I asked, "Why? Why, what's going on?" He wouldn't say anything. I screamed, "She isn't dead, is she?" My husband must have drove 100 mph. He was there within seconds. Meanwhile, I had lost it. She waited on me to leave so that she could die. I knew she would leave once I left the hospital. My mother and grandmother died on the same day and time, May 27 11:15 a.m., nineteen years a part. She died at the age of 56.

I don't speak of the bad times that I had with my mother to show bitterness. I speak on them to show what people go through in life. I wouldn't say my mother didn't love me. I would say these were just her ways. I don't know what she experienced in life. We never know what a person has been through.

I truly loved my mother and I know she loved me. She was a great teacher for me. She taught me to be strong and not to let people turn me away from the things I wanted to do. There were things she wanted to me to do after I was grown that I refused to do. I told her when I was a teenager, "When I am grown, anything that I want to do I am going to do. No one would ever control me but God." I would only allow God to control my life and not others, this is the life he gave me I'll live it the way he want me to and not man.

My mother had three sisters, Mary Louise, (who was from my grandfather's first marriage), Yvonne, and Patricia. Aunt Mary Louise was always kind. She never ended her conversation without saying, "I love you." She had such a sweet personality. She would come around to all the parties or the family outings.

She loved to drink, party, and have a good time. Aunt Yvonne, (we called her Butch) kind of stayed to herself. She loved to party, drink, and gamble just as all the family did. She was a hard worker and was always on the go. God changed her life. She would become a woman to serve him and I would like to thank God for that. Aunt Patricia (we called her Pat) loved to have a good time, drink and loved to party. (She still loves to party.) She love to be around people and would always invite people to her house. She feels that no one in the family love her, yet we love her so much. She is a great skater and a very good dancer. She love to entertain, and she's very smart. Aunt Pat was once a nurse and a Sheriff.

My stepfather Charles, as I said before was a very nice person to me. I would have so much fun with him. He would let me sit in his lap and pretend that I was driving. He also loved to scare us as children. Once, he put on a wig and had a fishing pole. He stood in the dark in our bedroom. We screamed, for he had scared us to death. He turned on the light, laughing so hard. Nothing in this world scared Charles. He was a man who had no fear.

I have some of the craziest memories of Charles. One of the fond memories is when I was in kindergarten; we had a Doberman named Blackie. Charles had called me from my room. He wanted me to help him do something, concerning Blackie. He asked me to hold Blackie for him and I did. Charles had taken a hatchet and cut Blackie's tail off. Blackie screamed in agonizing pain. Me, I just set there with my mouth open. Blood was everywhere. I was flabbergasted. I could not believe that he would do that, and ask me to help him. Blackie tried to get away. I almost let him go too. That was until Charles said, "Oh no, don't let him go now. I'm not finished with him yet." In my mind, I'm thinking, "What do he mean he's not finished with him? The dog is in pain. What more do he want to do to him? Maybe he's going to clean him up." At least I was hoping that's what he meant. Well, I thought wrong. Charles had grabbed a pair of scissors and clipped Blackie's ears. I was outdone. Charles had a seizure in the living room once. I stood there and watched him tear the room up. He even pulled up the floor. I watched him and laughed. Mama asked me, what all the noise in the living room was. I went to her and demonstrated what he was doing. That's when they realized he was having a seizure.

When I was third grade, the children at the school would pick on me. There were two brothers that would fight me every day. One particular day, I decided I would run home. The school was right across the streets from where I lived. I ran home and they were behind me. I put the key into the door and Charles snatched the door open. He pulled both boys in the hall and took off his belt and gave them a good whipping. He told them, "Bring your father and your mother back with you." I never had a problem out of them again. Charles would take us on picnics every holiday. He would take us to Starve Rock, where he and mama would fish. Once he caught a catfish and threw it at me. The fins caught my leg and stuck there. I was afraid of fish ever since. Charles teased my cousin and I with some candy. We chased each other for the Razzle candy. She ran into the wall. I was right behind her, hitting the edge of the wall. We were both lying in the bed with big knots on our head. The only difference was that I had a cut from the corner of the wall.

Charles was living with a cousin who weighed about 600 lbs. He would try feeling on me and I would tell him off. Once I walked by him and he grabbed me, putting me on his lap. I fought him, hitting him in the head with a cup. The cup had broken. That's I tried to stab him with the cup. I didn't want to be there anymore. I would tell Charles to take me home. I didn't feel comfortable being around his perverted cousin.

Once when I was 4 years old, Charles left a knife on the bed. He was going to the bathroom and told me not to touch it. As soon as he got out of my sight, I picked the knife up. When I heard him coming, I tried to put the knife back in the case. I missed the case and split my hand almost in half. He was so angry with himself for leaving the knife and trusting me not to bother it. Charles was diagnosed with cancer and passed away in November 1989, a month before Dada.

My father had three brothers, Claude, Leonard, and Clarence. Uncle Claude was something else. He had no shame in his game. He would embarrass everyone couldn't care less. He would answer the door in his underwear (Fruit of the Looms). Not to mention, he was 400lbs. He would answer the door and walk away as if he had clothes on. If you thought this was something, he would sit in the living room in his underwear and hold a conversation with your company. My grandparent's would become so angry.

In 1977, I went to Grandma Oby's beauty shop to get my hair done. When I arrived, I would learn that she was not there. There was another beautician present. She had told me to have a seat. That's when I would learn that Uncle Claude had just died of a heart attack. I walked out of the beauty salon an emotional wreck. I cried as I walked to the bus stop, (which was five blocks way) and during the entire bus ride. In attempt to make us feel better, Uncle Butch took Uncle Claude's two children and myself horseback riding. When I got on the horse's back, he decided that he wanted to fight another horse. He stood up on his hind legs, and took off running, through the woods. I only had one foot in the stirrup, as I held on for dear life. As my horse ran by, there were two men standing by, laughing at me.

Uncle Leonard always had me looking forward to an airplane ride. Every time I would see him, I asked him for an airplane ride. Once, I'd asked him for an airplane ride. He looked at me and chuckled. I didn't know my legs were almost as long as his. That's when I realized I hadn't gotten too big for an airplane ride.

My Uncle Clarence (we called him Butch) he spent a lot of time with me when I would visit my grandparent's house. We had so much fun together. He would take me everywhere he went. He would cook some of the most tasteful dishes that I couldn't find anywhere other at than his house. I loved to be around his friends; they were so full of fun. They kept me laughing each time I was in their presence. Uncle Butch would take me shopping to buy my clothes. He was a very good dresser and coordinated his clothes so well. I loved to see my uncle dance. No one could dance like my uncle Butch. As a child, he was just a joy for me to be around. I loved him so much. We would do real silly things. A friend of his cooked some Salmon Croquettes. He over cooked them and they were so hard. Uncle Butch grabbed a Croquette and threw it at his friend. When it was all over, we were having a Croquette fight in the kitchen. We really had fun that day. While I was writing this book, my Uncle Clarence passed away. I will truly miss him. He was a blessing to me. He taught me so many things about life and how to deal with the pressures of life. I wish he could have lived to read my book. He would have been so proud of my accomplishments. Nevertheless, I thank God for sending my uncle in my life. He created many fond memories for me at my grandparent's house.

Revelation: It has been revealed to me that everyone I came into contact with and every situation I encountered was involved in molding me to be the person that I am today. There is a love for your mother regardless of what you go through to receive the love. Children can see through many things that are considered immoral, or wrong to find the love from their mother that makes them comfortable. My mother had her ways but I knew there was love in her heart. When speaking with my mother on several occasions, she told me that people would say to mama, "I will babysit the other two, but not that black bad child." I know this had to make her feel bad as a child. It caused her to be the person she was. She was only reflecting on me what she had been through. I didn't understand it as a child but now that I'm spiritually mature. We can't be so quick to jump to conclusion and make accusations until we have investigated the problem. I feel she would have done much better if someone had reached out to help her. She growing up.

There is always a root to every problem we are encountered with. We can't get rid of the weed unless we pull it up by the root. During my journey with these people, I was taught how to love and have compassion for others. I was taught how to care for others. I was taught how to enjoy myself and how to deal with different issues that have come my way over my lifetime. Most important, I was taught how not to be by being around others that was not good role models.

I was introduced to God through all three grandmothers. I can't go through life living in yesterday. If I did that, I would never enjoy tomorrow. I had to learn to take the weights off my ankle and become who God ordained me to be. Many things that hurt me in my lifetime have made me to be a strong person today. One of the things that use to hurt me is when a person had wronged me, and they'd walk around me as if they have not done anything. They even feel they can come back and sit in the same position in your life, as if you are suppose to trust them again.

Many times they don't apologize for what they have done to you. I have learned to deal with them at a distance; forgive them and keep moving. I'm still afraid of fish, mice, and birds. These are the things that Charles used to scare us with as children. When I look back at my childhood I never remember being hungry, or without a place to stay. I thank God for that. I had plenty of clothes, and I was never without love. When one person didn't show love, God always gave me someone else to show me love. He constantly bought people into my life that loved me. I was never without a person to talk to; I always had someone to listen to my problems. I always had someone that was there to give me advice. This was truly a blessing.

Chapter 11

Touch Not My Anointed

Mama had a first cousin that would visit periodically. He was about ten years older than me. My cousin Selene and I were sleeping in the dining room on a bed. Selene was about seven years older than me. I was about 5 years old, probably no more than six. I was asleep and I felt someone taking my clothes off. It was pitched dark in the room. I was terrified, afraid to scream. I knew who it was. It was mama's cousin. I begin to push him away. He began to choke me, in attempt to keep me quiet. He was on top of me, licking and feeling on me. Selene woke up and was shocked by what she'd seen. She pushed him off of me, threatening to tell. I told mama what had occurred that night. Shortly after I told her, she kicked him out. He promised me not to do it again. I didn't believe. After all, why should I believe him after he tried to violate me in such a way? I would always carry a weapon, waiting for him to appear.

I was 9 years old. Mama told me that we were going to her uncle's house. I became fretful and began to cry. I didn't want to go because I knew that I would see her cousin. That's where he lived. She demanded that I go. I went in mama's room and grabbed her ice pick. I put the ice pick in my pocket, taking it with me. I was determined that he wasn't going to bother me. When we arrived at the house, he was sitting on the porch. When he saw me, he began to smile. We spoke to one another, and I walked by. I went into the kitchen to get some water. Out of nowhere, he appeared. He said to me while smiling, "When everyone goes to sleep tonight, I'm going to get you." I smile back at him and replied, "Not tonight. I'm going to get you." I said that and I meant every bit of it. I was waiting on him to put his hands on me, or anyone in my family. My plans were to kill him that night. I waited and waited for him to carry out his threat. It never happened. When I threatened him, I don't know what expression I gave him but it worked. As a matter of fact, he never bothered me again. I've seen him several times at funerals since I've been an adult. He would hug everyone except me; he only speaks to me. I watched how all of the girls in his family begin to have babies at very young ages. I know in my heart that if I had a talk with them, I would learn that he has molested them also. I'm quite sure he has molested the boys also.

When I was young, I was taught that the people in church were nice people. I was taught that you could trust the people in church, but oh did I get a rude awakening. Yes, there are some very nice people that are in the church. However keep your eyes open at all times. Satan lurks everywhere, including in the church. The way I was treated by Grandma Matthews, and the long periods of time I was made to sit in church, I often wonder why I stayed in church. I know it had to be God that kept me there. Satan was using my grandmother. He thought if he made me dislike church at a young age that I would turn away. But God had a plan. Satan did everything he could to turn me away from God, yet I was drawn closer. Now what if I was turned away because of the bad experiences in church. What would have become of me? Would I be the spiritual mature woman I am today? This is what happens to many people that we can't get to come into the church.

When a child doesn't want to go certain places or want to be around certain people, pay attention to them. They may be afraid to tell you what's going on. It is a reason that they don't feel comfortable in certain environments. Please know that mama taking me around her cousin was also a form of abuse. I should have never been taken near him again. He shouldn't have been allowed around any of her grandchildren. We as guardians must make wise decisions. I was very careful who my children spent nights with. Most of the time, it was T.T or Mr. Jay's mother. I didn't allow them to sit on men's laps. I didn't care if the men were family member or not. Satan does not discriminate in whom he use. As a matter of fact, family members, or someone well known to the family committed most cases of molestation. Ladies: Don't bring so many different men around your children. It's very dangerous. By doing this, you are setting a bad example. In addition to that, the intentions of these men may be something other than just visiting you. They may be looking at your children, male or female. They may have plans to molest your children. Please take heed. It's better to be careful than to be sorry later once your child's life is destroyed.

I recall visiting my uncle and aunt once at the age of 11. There was a lady that asked could I babysit for her. I didn't mind. The baby was new born and I loved children. I went over to her house to babysit. When I walked in the door, I seen that the baby had a sock stuck in his mouth. This angered me. I took the sock out of the baby's mouth and picked the baby up. She told me, "He hollers too much." I pleaded with her not to hurt the baby. The baby was only two weeks old and was the cutest little thing. I cried as I held the baby. I was so afraid for the little boy. I hate to say it but I the thought of getting rid of her crossed my mind. I would do get rid of her so that she wouldn't hurt the baby. He seemed to be so happy I was there. He wouldn't stop laughing and smiling. That would all change. As soon as she walked in the house, he began to cry. I was so afraid to leave him with her. I knew the baby was in danger. I went and told my aunt and uncle. To my dismay, they along with other neighbors already had knowledge of what was going on. I was told to mind my own business and that they would try to talk to her. I told them that they should call the police. My advice fell on deaf ears. So I planned on calling the police when I got home. By this time, it was too late. That evening, I saw the police and ambulance outside of the building. I asked my aunt, "What's going on?" She told me that the woman had thrown the baby against the wall. The baby was found dead, with a sock in his mouth. I cried for an entire year for that baby, I blamed myself because I didn't call the police. I couldn't get the babies face out of my head. I kept seeing him smile at me. I was sick and I went into a depressed state. I would cry for no reason. I couldn't concentrate, I dreamed of the baby every night. I could see her throwing the baby against the wall, although I wasn't there. I was told to stop all the crying because I didn't know the baby. I couldn't understand for the life of me why I was the only one that seemed to care about the baby dying. Why was the mistreating of the baby kept a secret amongst everyone? Although the mother was in jail, I even regretted not getting rid of her.

Revelation: Every person or situation that you encounter and everything that harmed as a child you will become a part of your molding as an adult. We don't realize that everything that we pass through is like shopping in a store. We pick up things; some we use and some we don't. Some things we try for the very first time and some things we know the taste because we've had them before. Many things we like because of the taste and they are not good for us.

It's very nice to have memories of your family members. Memories are pictures that never fade away. They don't require a frame, nor do they require a stand to sit upon. They stay with you until you block them out, or you leave this earth. Don't frown upon the bad events that have happened in your life. Don't glorify yourself of the good things that happen in your life. Give all glory to God for both. These events are used by God to shape and mold you and help you reach your highest potential in life. He's preparing you for the work he has ordained you to do for his kingdom.

CHAPTER 12

Gifts being revealed

I can remember saying things as a child and they would fall right in place. I never paid it any attention. When Mr. Jay was having an affair, there were many times the Holy Spirit would lead me right to where he was. I remember looking all over the west side for him, not having any idea where the woman stayed. God gave me directions right to her house. I thought, "How in the world did I find his car and didn't know where I was going."

I once dreamed of a train wreck and was telling a friend about it. I told her, "I don't know how to stop it but there is going to be an accident today on the train." One hour after I told her that, the news flashed and showed the train downtown hanging off the tracks. She looked at me her eyes were big as bow dollars. I couldn't explain it; I just knew it was coming.

God showed me the gift of healing in my hands with Taineeka. I remember doing nursing home ministry and there was a man that would sit in his wheel chair, watching every move I made. I once stopped and asked him, "Why do you watch me like that?" He just smiled; he couldn't talk because of a stroke. He was about in his 40's. Once when I went to the nursing home, the Holy Spirit instructed me to put oil on his legs. I did. He was slumped over in his wheel chair. He was having a hard time sitting up. A month later, when I returned to the facility, he was sitting up in the chair without assistance. He also looked different. HE called my name. I turned around and asked, "Did you call me?" "Yes", he answered. I went to see what he wanted he told me he was now walking. He thanked me for praying for him. I was so happy. I begin to praise the Lord.

There was a time Pauline lived in Virginia, my cousin Robin lived in St Louis, and I was in Tennessee. We would do a three-way conference call every nigh. We spent three to four hours on the phone, laughing and talking. I remember Robin and I would fight over a dress that she had given me. She would steal the dress back and I would take it back from her. We did this for two years and I finally got the dress. Robin was one of the sweetest people you ever wanted to me. The only problem is she would steal anything that was not nailed down. She couldn't help herself. She would even steal things she couldn't use. She would return what she had stolen. She would apologize and cry; you couldn't help to forgive her. Everyone in the family loved her. We all overlooked her problem. She had a beautiful spirit that we loved. Once when one of my cousins died, we had people coming in from out of town. I asked Robin not to steal because we were trying to put him away peacefully. She promised she wouldn't steal. After the funeral, she came to me and said, "Ronnie I didn't steal from anybody." I thought that was so beautiful that she could refrain from stealing. I knew it was hope for her.

One morning, Robin called me at 7 A.M. She was on the phone fussing, about the Veterans hospital. She was so angry that they wouldn't pull her sons tooth. She would also exclaim, "I'm bleeding so heavy, I don't know what's wrong with me." I told her she needed to go to the hospital herself. She told me she would call me back later. I waited on her call. I laid down because all of a sudden I got real sleepy.

Once I got into the bed, I went into the most peaceful sleep I had ever had. I could do nothing but get up to go to the bathroom and get back into the bed. I was so sleepy; it was as if the bed was sucking me in. I woke up at about 8 p.m.; I had been in the bed all day long. When I woke up, I felt refreshed for the first time. I looked at my caller ID and noticed my cousin had not called me back. I called her house; her son answered the phone. He told me his mother was sleep. I told him when she wakes up to have her call me back. The phone rang thirty minutes later; I answered it. It was her son. "Hello Ronnie, my mother is dead", he said. "Who is this", I asked. "Man", he replied. I asked, "Man who?" "Robin's son Man." A feeling of anguish hovered over me like a cloud would before a storm. I couldn't believe this. She was just 49 years old. I knew then the reason I couldn't get out of the bed. It was her sleeping away and I was being affected by it. This was a gift I had. I knew she was dead when I first called. That is why I was able to get out of the bed. She was supposed to have been at my house. She was coming to visit and she changed her mind. Her dream was to go to Jamaica, that's all she ever talked about. I cried until I got sick. We would get into disagreements and argue all the time. But she had a way of making up with you and you couldn't help but forgive her. She had a beautiful smile, and had no problem telling you she loved you. Her favorite saying was "Lord." She may not have gotten to Jamaica, but I really believe she's in heaven. March 2003 was very sad for me

February1996, Robin came to Chicago for her mother's funeral. She ended up staying in Chicago. She stayed between my aunt, my sister and my house. I remember the day of my aunt's funeral. I waited for the others to line up. No one ever came. I went back to see what was going on. To my surprise, everyone was fighting. The whole family was fighting with the funeral directors. One of the funeral directors had grabbed one of Robin's sons out of the car by his collar. He told them it was too many people in the funeral car. After he grabbed Robin's son, the brawl began. The funeral director was lying across the car. His glasses were on the ground, bent up. The other funeral directors were running back into the funeral home. They told us we couldn't have any more funerals if our last name was Waddell. This was nothing new to the Waddell clan; we were barred out of many places. We were barred out of a hall we rented for the repast of my mother. The fight broke out when one of my cousins hit another cousin upside the head with a forty-ounce beer bottle. What can I say? This was the Waddell's for you. Robin and her mother both died in their sleep. God has his way of doing things.

This gift was revealed to me twice since the death of Robin. Once, I was lying in the bed and I had gone into the deep sleep again. This sleep is one that I can't describe. Again, it was so peaceful. It's as if you are floating away and you are so relaxed that nothing can touch you. It's like you are being welcomed by the bed, to rest in the most comfortable place in the world. I could hear myself speaking in my sleep saying to myself this is the best sleep I've ever had. The phone rang and I ignored it. I didn't want to come out of my sleep. The phone rang again. Once again, I didn't answer. All of a sudden, Taineeka screamed from downstairs, "Mom, Auntie Dina is dead." I knew something was going on because the sleep was so peaceful.

I then had another incidence that revealed me my gift. I had a friend who was at my house. He was about to leave to go meet another friend. As he was about to leave, a strange feeling came over me. I was pinned to the bed, and I had the same feeling I had when the peaceful sleep came upon me. I looked at him and told him something was not right. I felt the same way when Robin died. He sat on the side of the bed as if he didn't want to leave. He then headed towards the door. He came back as if something was drawing him back towards. I can tell that he could feel something wasn't right as well. He was hesitant. When he left out the door, I followed him to the porch. I watched him run down the streets to the bus.

I will never forget the strange feeling that overcame me. I felt as if I would never see him again. I was supposed to pick him up at 9 p.m. I was headed to get him and the phone rang. It was my friend. He told me "Don't worry about picking me up. I'm in jail". He ended up doing three years, being in the wrong place at the wrong time. When we had a chance to talk, he told me that he had never seen anything like the day I was laying in the bed talking to him. He said, it was like a higher power had taken over me, and I was myself. He said it was hard to explain, because it was me and then it wasn't me speaking to him. I found this interesting because no one was ever around when this feeling came upon me. This was the first time that anyone had witnessed this. He asked me why didn't I stop him. He was given free will and I had no control over it.

I never knew what to do when this feeling came upon me, until I was later taught what to do. I had many things that have happened to me, that I can't explain. A friend of mine took me to her relative's house. When I went up the stairs, I stopped and told her, "I've been here before." I told her how many bedrooms were in the house, and where each room was located. She looked at me with her mouth wide open, and she asked me how did I know that. I told her, "I don't know but I've been here before." I don't remember visiting the house, but I knew I had been there. I don't know when. I had a dream that a car had almost hit a person. In my dream, the person ended up on the side of the tire. A couple of weeks later, a friend and me were running across the streets. A car was approaching. I hollered for her to stop. She slid out of in front of the car. The car turned his wheels and she ended up on the side of the wheel. I stood there thinking, "I dreamed of this."

Years later, I was pulling in front of my mother's house. I had Taineeka in the car with me; she was about 6 months. My oldest daughter was across the street with my niece. My niece told her, "Tyra, there's your mom." She ran across the streets. I was trying to stop her because I saw the cab pulling off. I seen my daughter running and the cab hit his brakes. I just knew my daughter was hit. I jumped out the car, never putting it in park. My car was going down the streets with Taineeka in it. A young man ran and caught my car. I was afraid to look on the other side of the cab. When I did look my daughter was in the same position that my friend was in 16 years before then. She was also in the same position as the person was in the dream, leaning up against the wheel. I stood there and all I could do was remember the dream.

There was another moment something happened and I can't explain it. I had not seen my cousin for about 5 years. As a matter of fact, the last time we talked her mother was very ill. God put it on my heart to call her. I begin to search for her number. When I got in touch with her, I asked about her sister. She told me that her sister had passed away three years ago. She also told me that the day I called would have been her sister's birthday. I then asked about her mother. She told me that her mother was in a nursing facility and she wasn't doing well. I continued on with the conversation. By mistake, I asked, "So, your mother passed away huh?" I didn't mean to say that. It just came out of nowhere. I apologized to her. I felt so bad for saying that. Later on, she called to inform me that her mother passed away. I then felt so bad; I didn't know what to say. I couldn't stop apologizing. I thought, "Was that why God had me to call her, to give her a sign that her mother was going to pass away?" There are many things that happen in our lives that we can't explain, and no one will be able to reveal why but God.

Revelation: God gives each of us gifts to use for his glory. 1 Corinthians 12: 7-11[7] to each is given the manifestation of the Spirit for the common good. [8] For to one is given through the Spirit the utterance of wisdom, and to another the utterance of knowledge according to the same Spirit, [9] to another faith by the same Spirit, to another gifts of healing by the one Spirit, [10] to another the working of miracles, to another prophecy, to another the ability to distinguish between spirits, to another various kinds of tongues, to another the interpretation of tongues. [11] All of these are empowered by one and the same Spirit, who apportions to each one individually as he will. We receive gifts and we don't recognize our gifts until we have fully accepted him. I had fully accepted him and did not know what to do with the gift it was all something strange to me.

I enrolled in an intercessory prayer class with Prophetess Dean. Till this day, she doesn't know what she has done for me. She opened my eyes to my gift. I learned that what was coming upon me was the Holy Spirit. I was to begin praying when it happened. I learned that even when I had the dreams that I was supposed to pray. I learned that I had a gift of seeing things, healing, wisdom, faith, discernment, prophecy, I am a dreamer, visionary and I have the gift of speaking things into existence. I have to be very careful of what I say. My words come to pass quicker than most people could fathom. One thing I learned is that God will not reveal your gift to you until you are ready. I was very afraid when these things first begin to happen to me. There were times I was afraid to go to sleep. I was afraid that I would go into a deep sleep and something would happen. When God is ready for you to use the gifts he has given you, he will send the person he wants to reveal them to you. We must stay in the face of God and continue to worship and pray. God is a God of revelation. When your time comes, nothing can stop it. I thank God for all the gifts and blessing he has given me. The word of God says that your gifts will make room for you and bring you before great men.

CHAPTER 13

Blessed Coming In

As I look back at my early childhood, I realize that I was blessed from the beginning. God had his hands on my life before I was even born. There were many things that could have easily killed me. I remember as a child I loved to eat the plaster off of the walls. I would wait until it was dark in the house and I would go get a spoon and then dig into the wall and eat the plaster. Whenever I was caught I would hide the spoon behind me, and say I didn't eat anything. The evidence would be all around my mouth and I would deny it. My cousin Sweet Man (nickname) and I were playing in the bathroom sink. He told me to put my foot in the sink and I did. He then turned on the hot water and I received third degree burns on my right foot. When I was taken to the hospital, they tested me for lead poisoning and the test was negative. I could have easily tested positive, but God saw different. He took it out of my system.

When I was in the seventh grade, my right breast swelled up, it was hurting me to touch it. I told mama about it and she took me to the hospital. I was told I had a tumor in my breast and they had to do surgery. I went into the hospital around Halloween. The nurses decorated my room so pretty. My seventh grade teacher came to see me and brought a card that the entire class had signed. I couldn't understand why she stood over my bed crying. Everyone was so concerned about me. Grandma and Granddaddy Oby, Mama, and Dada came to see me. They all cried. My mother and aunts all cried when they came to see me. I asked the nurse, "Why is everyone crying?" She told me, "They are just concerned about you, that's all". I told T.T "You act like I'm going to die, all he's going to do is remove the tumor." She started to cry. I thought they were crazy, I didn't understand their reason for crying! The removal of a tumor wasn't that serious. At least, that's what I thought.

The next day I had the surgery. When I woke up the doctor told me everything went beautifully. When I was taken into the room, it looked as if I was having a party. My room was full of people. They had big smiles on their faces. The only person that was crying was Ms. Dorothy (my aunt) and that wasn't anything new. She cried all the time. T.T came over to my bed and she told me if the tumor had been cancerous she had given them permission to cut my breast off. Heat came all over my body. I was very angry that the doctors had to give me medication to put me to sleep. I asked T.T "Who gave you permission to tell these people what to do with my body, and not tell me what they were going to do?" I felt I had a right to know what was going on with my body. She told me she didn't want me to worry. I replied, "Worry! Suppose I woke up without a breast? Then what were you going to do?" I told everyone in the room, "You should be happy that they didn't have to cut my breast off. If they had cut my breast off, I never would have spoken to any of you again for life". I was angry about that for a long time. Mama waited until I got home and had a long talk with me.

Mama told me that, "Sometimes it is best not to know everything. When you know something, it makes a thing worse than it really is. If God wanted you to know, you would have known".

Grandma Oby told me, "What you need to be doing is thanking God that everything went ok. This is not the time to be complaining about the blessing God has given you. We loved you enough not to tell you, because we didn't want to hurt you". It took me about three months to really calm down,

I was angry with my teacher and my doctor. I didn't speak to my teacher for two months. One of my friends in the building became sick and died. They found out he had meningitis. He was only 9 or 10 years old. That's when I realized what my grandmothers were telling me about being blessed.

When I was about 10 years old, I was reading the newspaper and ran across an ad that wanted young children to participate in a McDonald's commercial. I called and set up an appointment for all the children in the house to go. I told the woman on the phone that my grandmother would bring us to the appointment. No one wanted to take us, so I walked downtown on my own and spoke to the woman. She told me that we needed $50.00 per child and they would allow us to be in the commercials. The woman was very impressed with me. She told me that she thought I was older than I was when she spoke to me on the phone. She told me you are very intelligent for your age, she wanted to put me in the commercial without the rest of my family. I told her she had to take all of us. I wouldn't participate without my family. I went home and told my grandmother about it. She asked our mothers to pay the fee and no one would come up with a dime. The woman continued to call. I talked to her several times, but no one would give us the money. I explained to them that we would be the first Black children, on a McDonald commercial and no one cared. Each time the commercial came on television with the Black children in it I got angry. I didn't understand why our mothers wouldn't invest in us. It probably was a good thing because we may have had to sue them about our money later. I thought at least we had a chance to move on to other things once we were in the commercials. Well that was one opportunity that blew away in the wind.

When I was in the 1st grade, I attended Blackstone Elementary School. I had a teacher that loved me. I was her favorite. When there was an assembly, she would always choose me as her spokesperson. I was always chosen to lead her class.

When the Christmas break came around she took three of her students' home with her. She bought us all kinds of toys. We had a lot of fun at her house. When the summer break came, she took me home with her for one month and bought me clothes and all types of toys. I loved her. She was very nice to me. She loved to have me read stories to her. It was as if she was a child listening to me read stories to her. Before she took me home, I think I had read every book in her house. I loved to read. I think she enjoyed me because she didn't have any children of her own. I was her child and I enjoyed every bit of it. She continued taking me home with her even on the weekends, until I was in the third grade. This was during the time we moved from 6252 S. Stony Island to residing right next door to Hyde Park High School. We had to move because an extension to the high school was being built. I really didn't want to leave because I had lived there since I was in preschool.

When my teacher heard we were moving she came to our house and asked T.T if she could have me. She promised to allow me to stay with my mother when school was out. T.T told declined the offer. When Grandma Oby heard about it, she had a fit! She told T.T, "I wanted my baby for a long time and you won't give her to me. You better not give her to anyone other than me." T.T replied, "I'm not giving her to anyone." We moved and I lost contact with my teacher. I was so hurt. We moved to the Harold L. Ickes projects, 2320 S. State Apt 507.

I had to fight to live in that building. We were new in the neighborhood, which meant we had to prove ourselves. I would always fight because I was not afraid of anyone. My cousin Sweet Man and I were the oldest, so we had to fight for everyone. Sweet Man and I were just fourteen days apart. Soon I was adjusted to living there and it became fun. I would take the other children places on the bus. I knew my way around when I was just 9 years old. I took them to Riverview, Fun Town at 95th and Stony, the movies on 63rd St. and the Met Theater. My friend Patricia Evans thought I was older than them and I was actually the same age they were. As a matter of fact, many of them were older than me.

People looked down at the projects, but we were more like family than anywhere I ever lived. Everyone looked out for each other's children. We could go to our friends' houses and eat. When one family didn't have something, you better believe someone was willing to share with that family. We may have fought, but if someone came from the outside to fight anyone that lived there, they had to fight everyone in the building. No one from the outside would dare come there to bother anyone living there. Yes, we had our crime and tragedy, but we also knew how to love.

When there was an only child in any family, they always had brothers and sisters in the building. They were never lonely. We always had activities to keep us busy. Once, I was walking down the "lane" with some friends. I felt pain in my leg. When I looked down my leg was bleeding. Immediately, I realized that someone had shot me twice in the leg. We found out that I was shot with a high-powered stapler gun. I pulled the staples out of my leg. One of my friends saw the young man that had shot me in the leg. I went home to tell mama and she refused to call the police. She loved peace when she was sober. I thought, "Suppose he had shot me in my eye." Nothing was ever done to him.

I saw the man twenty years later and asked him if he remembered me. I asked did he still ride his motorcycle he told me yes. I told him to come by my mother's house because I wanted him to teach me how to ride the motorcycle. When he pulled up, I told him to show me the gas and the brakes. I got on the bike and took off. I picked up my friend and we hit the expressway. I drove by everyone's house I could think of, we were gone for about 5 hrs. When I got back, T.T and the guy were on the porch. She shook her head at me. He was so glad to see his bike in one piece, he wasn't angry. He looked me and said, "I thought you didn't know how to ride a bike?" I told him, "I didn't know how to ride a bike. I never rode a bike in my life." He looked at me in disbelief. Before he left T.T, he told her that he was so worried. She asked, "How in the world are you going to pick someone up to ride and you don't know how?" I told her anything I thought I could do, I could do it. I didn't feel sorry for him he shot me in my leg 20 years ago. I told her, "It's in my blood. You and my father rode bikes, I didn't need any lessons." My mother looked at me and shook her head.

Mama was a Cubs fan, although we didn't live far from the White Sox Park. My Aunt, Ms. Dorothy lived in Stateway Gardens, which was located down the street from White Sox Park. Since Ms. Dorothy lived by the stadium, we were able to go there quite often. Mama watched the Cubs every chance she got. I would also become a great fan of the Chicago Cubs.

In the projects, tutoring took place on Tuesdays and Wednesdays. We had to sign up for it. Tuesday night, the tutors came from Inland Steel, and on Wednesday night they came from Quaker Oats. Everyone wanted to go on Wednesdays because they were known for giving out the best Christmas gifts. They would also throw big Christmas parties for us at the company. I applied for both nights because we were allowed to attend both nights. I was so angry that I didn't get a tutor on Wednesday nights, I went home crying to mama. She told me take the tutor on Tuesdays because they all serve the same purpose. I told her if I couldn't have a Wednesday tutor I wouldn't go on the other night. She looked at me and said, "Don't be stupid, you may miss out on your blessing being stupid." I went there on Tuesday night. I was so angry. The lady who was in charge of the program told me to cheer up and put a smile on my face. I told her, "For what I didn't get what I wanted." She looked at me and said, "You don't know who you are going to get now smile young lady." She told me she wanted to blindfold me so that it would be a surprise. I let her put the blindfold over my eyes and she sat me at the table. I heard someone sit at the table with me. She told me to take the blindfold off. When I took it off, I screamed to the top of my voice I jumped up and started running, holding my head. She had to calm me down. It was Ernie Banks number 14, first baseman for the Chicago Cubs. I didn't learn anything that day. I was too busy taking pictures with him and running the other children away from my table. They were asking if he could be their tutor, the lady told them he would only be my tutor.

I was blessed because there were usually two children to each tutor and she only allowed me to be with Ernie Banks. I couldn't wait to get home to tell mama. She thought something had happened to me because I was screaming so loud. Ernie Banks took me home with him to play with his children and I had the best time. I told him my father had just died that year. He replied, "Well I guess I arrived right on time huh?" We were only allowed to stay with our tutor for 9 months, but it was like years for me. I received all kind of gifts with the Cubs on it. I was very depressed at that time because of the loss of my father and God fixed that! He knew just what to do for me. Mr. Banks treated me like a little queen. I once again felt special. He would always tell me that I was a special little girl.

He came into my life, when I really needed him. He helped me make it through the loss of my father. He was very good with talking to me. He was more like a counselor, and he was the therapy that I needed. The length of time that he was there was perfect. It allowed me time to heal. Mama looked at me and she laughed every time I came in from tutoring. She even had me getting autographs to bring to her. She thought she was being tutored. She had a chance to come down and meet him personally. She sat and talked to me. She asked, "Do you see how God blesses you when you are patient and wait on God?" I couldn't answer her because she was right once again.

I hated when the tutoring was over. I knew I would lose contact with him. He kept in contact with me and for about a year he would call to see how I was doing. He would bring me gifts for my birthday and made sure I had my school supplies and received Christmas gifts. He even came and picked me up one summer holiday, and bought me once again to his house. We eventually lost contact and I have not seen him since. I would love to see him again and ask him if he remembers me.

I was a kid that never wanted for anything. My mother worked and she would take care of us. Grandma Oby was a beautician and she made sure I had everything I needed and more. Granddaddy Oby worked at International Harvester, and my mother's father he worked. My Uncle Claude owned cleaners and he would give me money. I had uncles that would always look out for me if I needed anything. My Uncle Claude would allow me to work at his cleaners on Saturdays to make extra money. I worked at the cleaners so long; I could run that place, blindfolded. I had been working there ever since I was 10 years old. I would work the counter, by taking the orders in and retrieving clothes for the customers that came in with their tickets. My uncle even taught me how to use the presser, so I was able to press clothes also. I would even go to Grandma Oby's beauty shop and sweep the floors to make money. I would run errands for the customers.

There was a man in the projects that allowed us to sale Jet Magazines to make money. We would get a bundle of ten and get on the train and sell them. My friends were trying to find out how I sold so many more than they did because I would sell two to three bundles a day. I did two things different than what they were doing to sell my Jets. One, they would walk through the train hollering, "Jet, Jet, Jet." I would not only holler Jet, but I would holler what the top stories were in the Jet. Since I knew everyone was selling theirs on the train, I got smart and would get off of the train downtown and stand on the street and sell mine. I would get customers they would never get a chance to see.

Mama was actually a wealthy woman. She was so afraid that Public Aid would find out what she had that she allowed her wealth to slip through her hands trying to hold on to Public Aid. Mama owned over a thousand acres of land in Brownsville, Tennessee. Her brother knew she was trying to hide her property from Public Aid and he took advantage of the opportunity. He offered to help her, by having her to sign her property in his name so that no one would know she had it. He also had taken land from her, because she would trust him to take the trips to Tennessee to make sales for her. She didn't know how much money he was making. She sold timber, beans, chickens, cows and hogs. He would return and give her a couple of hundred dollars and she was content with that. His oldest daughter once told her he was cheating her, and she didn't believe her niece. Her nephews and many other family members were involved in the stealing. She trusted him with her life because she loved him. He took most of her land from her, and passed it on to his children and other family members.

When she passed away her three children only received thirty thousand dollars each for the land. The family members were like wolves trying to buy it from them. They were just greedy because many of them had money and they didn't need her money. If mama would have listened, her children and grandchildren would not have struggled so hard. This was a lesson for me to trust only in God. You can't listen to others and think everyone has your best interest at heart. Everyone who tells you they have your back don't. Many are trying to get in front of you.

When people mistreat you, don't get angry. Those people are no more than a ladder. They are actually giving you a boost to your destiny, to be the great person you are predestined by God. Without him, you would have not made it. I want to thank all the great warriors in our lives. Thank you! You all have done an excellent job. I couldn't have made it without you. Keep up the good work.

I mentioned earlier that I held many jobs. One of the places that I tried to work when I was younger was McDonald's. For some reason, they would never hire me. When I was 18 years old I went to work as a ticket agent for CTA as a seasonal employee for almost a year. It was an experience for me. I enjoyed the job but every day it was something different happening. I can remember a little girl walking up to my booth telling me she didn't have enough money to ride. She asked if I could allow her to get on the train free. I told her I would pay her way and to go ahead. She hollered, "Hey everybody she said go ahead she'll pay our way." Before I knew it, there were about twenty children running through my turnstile. I couldn't believe it. I just stood there and shook my head in disbelief. I was working one station on the midnight shift once. A man came up and tried to open the door to the booth where I was working. I pushed the button for the police. The CTA security came three hours later. He told me there were only three CTA police and they had to cover the entire rail.

Once, a teenager became angry with me because I wouldn't allow him to ride free. He spit in my face. I was working on State and Lake at the time. I was so angry I forgot I was at work. I ran after him and caught him at the top of the stairs. I gave him the fight of his life. He received a good whipping with the transfer puncher. When I let him go he just sat there, he couldn't move. The passengers were all laughing at him. I left CTA and went to attend Dawson Skills Center to study to become a Licensed Practical Nurse. I enjoyed nursing and I was also being paid $400.00 a month to attend. It kept money in my pockets. It was over when I was assigned a patient that was suffering from "blue balls". His scrotum had swollen so large. I had never seen anything like it. When I walked into the room, he was smiling, looking at me, and telling me, "Come on baby and take care of daddy." He was licking his lips. I left to ask my instructor what I was supposed to do for him. I was getting instructions because I knew what I wanted to do to him and it had nothing to do with nursing. She told me to put an ice bag on his genital area. I went back into the room with an ice pack and handed it to him. He told me, "I want you to do it baby." When I refused, he spit in my face, grabbed my arm and twisted my skin. That was the end of my nursing career. I took my stethoscope and used the metal part of it to beat the heck out of him! I was about to wrap it around his neck until my instructor walked into the room. She heard him screaming because I hit him all over his swollen scrotum. Before the instructor could say anything, I told that her she could take this job and shove it! I walked out of there and never returned. Two weeks later I received a call to work for the Social Security Administration.

I worked for the Social Security Administration for one year and transferred to the Post office. I walked in the door knowing this was not a place that I would retire from. I was hired as a LSM operator and I later transferred to a FSM operator at the Post Office. I left there and went out to carry mail. Now this was also an experience for me. I was putting mail in a box and I heard a man hollering. When I looked up three men were dragging a man in the building with guns in their hand. I pleaded with them no to shoot the man. I was trying to get the key out the box and it was stuck. I tore the pocket off my pants and left the key hanging in the box. I was so scared. Another time I couldn't get the key out of the box, bees were attacking me. I was even attacked by birds. I never knew that they were that smart until after my attack. I, at one time loved Robins until this particular day. I was putting mail in the box. When I turned around, the Robins were right in my face, trying to peck my eyes. I dropped everything in my hand; the owner of the house came out and told me that they had to go through the back door because the bird was attacking them. She told me that the bird had a nest over the porch and I could drop her mail next door. I thought that was better so that the bird would not bother me. Well the bird fooled me. I was coming down the street the next day on the opposite side of the house. I saw the bird sitting on top of the house. This bird flew across the street to attack me. I asked myself, "How did the bird knew who I was and I wasn't even on his side of the street?" That Robin was dangerous. He was swooping down at my head like a mad bird. I also found out how prejudice and mean people could be. They would let me drop their mail and as soon as I walked off of the porch, they would let their dogs out.

My most traumatic experience is when I was delivering the mail and there was a man shoveling the snow. He asked me my name and I told him. He then begins to walk with me, holding a shovel in his hand. He told me that he wanted to marry me. I told him I was already married. He told me he was a millionaire, as a result of being struck by an ambulance. He told me about the scar that was left on his body and asked me did I want to see it. I told him no it was too cold. I went up the stairs to deliver the mail. When I turned around, he had taken all his clothes off and it was below zero outside. I told him to put on his clothes before he freeze to death. He had a scar that went from his neck to his ankle. I knew I was in trouble. I didn't see a soul on the street, so I told him go home and prepare dinner. I would be there after I finished. I was trying to get him away from me so that I could get in my truck. He left, so I thought. When I went to get in the truck, he pushed me from behind; both of us ended up in the truck. People were looking out the window. I was praying they would call for help, but they didn't. I was not driving away with him in my truck. Whatever he was going to do, he had to do it in the truck. He kept asking for a kiss and I kept refusing, telling him to get out the truck. I was trying to move him, so that I could get out the door. He kept grabbing my face trying to kiss me. As I was trying to get out of the truck, I kept watching the shovel that he had in his hand. I was afraid he was going to hit me with it. We had already been in the truck for about thirty minutes. I thought, "Well it's about to be me or him. I'm going to have to fight this man." I made a break for the door and got it open. He grabbed for me and we both fell out the truck to the ground. Now I had to wrestle for the shovel, because I knew what was next. We were in the snow and sliding on ice, wrestling. A lady came out of her house and called his name, "Gary." She told him to let me go before she called his parents. He told her, "They are in Florida spending my millions. Stay out of me and my wife's business." Her husband came out and picked him up with one hand, throwing him to the ground. I was shaken up. I left and went to the station. My supervisor didn't want me to make a police report nor did she want to write it up. I went to the police station and was explaining what had happened. The officer asked me, " Is his name Gary"? I was out done. He told me that Gary was harmless and was in fact a millionaire. I told him I want to press charges and I didn't care what he was. He wrote the report up.

The next day, when I went to work my supervisor told me, "I wish a millionaire would grab me. I bet I wouldn't report him." I told her, "Then you go out there and deliver the mail on his block." She laughed and told me, "No you're going to do it." I told her that I was not going anywhere near that man's block. She insisted that I go back out to the same block. I had to call the union and the area manager in. The area manager told me to go home for a couple of days because I was being transferred. He told me to report to my new station in a couple of days. This was one of the many incidents that I had to deal with. I hated working at the Post Office because all of the supervisors had their picks.

Once, two women who worked there were for no reason, harassing me. My supervisor wouldn't do anything to stop them. I wanted to kill them. I was about to lose it because I wanted to get them. The only thing that stopped me was the fact that I didn't want to lose my job. I flied every complaint I could against them and nothing was ever done. My supervisor was getting angry with me. I became so depressed; I went to see a psychiatrist. This was one of the biggest mistakes I had ever made. I never knew the trouble I was headed for. I went to see the psychiatrist and I was explaining everything I was going through. She asked me, "Do you want to hurt any of the women?" I told her, "Yes I want to kill both of them". She left the room and came back with three men and a stretcher. She told me because I wanted to hurt them she had to admit me into the hospital. I told her I didn't want to go in the hospital. She told me I had no choice but to go. She and the three men wrestled me down to the stretcher and off to the hospital I went. They took me to the psychiatric ward, as if I was crazy. I couldn't believe it. I never knew I was headed for more hurt and pain. Mr. Jay is the person that talked me into going to talk with a psychiatrist. He told me maybe they could help me. This is the reason I went into the hospital.

Now I here I am sitting in the psychiatric hospital. Whether you believe it or not, I was really enjoying myself in the place. I had no responsibilities. I could rest and get up and watch

TV and I had no one bothering me. I was at peace with no worries. I was told I only had to stay in the hospital for about a week, until they could find out what my problem was. So I felt like I didn't have anything to worry about.

The place was not as bad as I thought it would be. I could at least rest. Well that's how it started off in the beginning. I went into the hospital a couple of days after Thanksgiving. I figured I would be out by the first week of December. I had found people that I could talk to. There was even a lady there who never said anything. They told me her family said she had not talked in three years, since the death of her son. I didn't find this out until later.

They would allow us to play music and dance in the afternoon. I decided I would play a song I liked and I got up to dance. When I turned around the lady who never talked was smiling at me. I asked her, "Why you are always smiling at me?" She shrugged her shoulders. She would just sit and watch Conaan and I, clown around. Conaan was a gay guy. He was great when he and I clowned around. He kept me laughing. He would have me on the floor and the nurses were getting angry. They felt he was showing off in front of me. Once, they pinned him down, with the assistance of security. They gave him a shot in his buttocks. He was screaming to the top of his lungs and at the same time flirting with the security officer. He told the officer, "If you give me the shot I won't holler baby". They took him to another ward. I really missed my friend. He made the time go by. There was never a day without a laugh.

They begin to give me medication and I couldn't sleep. The medication made me feel like I wanted to take off running. I told them I will not be taking any more medication so don't bring it to me. I was lying in the bed and they brought the lady that couldn't talk and put her in my room. They called themselves being funny telling me, "She will keep you company." I laughed and looked at the lady and I told her, "You are company to me, although you can't talk." She sat on the side of the bed and smiled. I told her, "For some strange reason, I think you can talk. You act as if you want to say something to me." She just smiled. I told her, "You don't have to talk if you don't want to. You're probably better off because you don't have to be bothered with people." I continued, "People get on my nerves. I wish I had my own island. There would be no one there except my children and me." I noticed she watched everything I did, with a smile on her face. I told her, "Keep watching sweetheart. You will learn something. I have learned something from you. Silence is beautiful." I told her that I wasn't taking any more of the medication. The medicine was making me feel sick and I don't need it anyway. I told her, "You better talk to me because I will be getting out of here in about two days." I was sleep in the bed one night and someone was shaking me and calling my name. I turned around and it was she, the lady that didn't talk. She told me, "Don't eat the food they are planning on putting something in your food. The doctor talked to your husband, and I don't think you are going home tomorrow." I forgot the lady couldn't talk. I was getting angry I wanted to go home and be with my daughters.

The Christmas holiday was coming up. I got up and went into the TV room, praying that they would say something to me. The nurses never said anything to me about not going home. The doctor came in to see me that morning and he told me that he had talked with my husband. He had told my husband that I would be coming home in a day. My husband told the doctor that he was very concerned about his safety and the children's safety. He asked the doctor if could he keep me a little longer. I jumped up and told the doctor, "There's nothing wrong with me, he's the reason I'm in this place and I want to go home." The doctor replied, "I can't release you without his consent." I looked at the doctor and told him, "His life is in danger now. It wasn't, but it is now, I don't want him visiting me." There was a look in the doctor's eyes that I will never forget. He's the one that was crazy it wasn't me. He looked at me and said, "I can't release you." I asked him, "How long do I have to stay in this place?" He told me until after the New Year. I told him, "You and my husband are crazy; man

153

I'm going home to be with my children for the holiday. If you don't let me go there will be all type of problems in this place, do you understand me? I'm building up a hell fire inside me, and water won't put it out. The biggest problem is I don't care anymore." I asked if I could use the phone. I called a friend of mine. She told me he was keeping me locked up, until him and his woman comes from their vacation in Vegas. This is the woman he is married to today. I hung up the phone and sat down trying to get my thoughts together, thinking of a way I could kill him and get away with it. I was doing ok until one of the mental health workers walked in the door. He said, "I told you that you were not going home." I got up and went to my room. I didn't want to hear anything negative. I just needed God to begin to talk to me. Right now, I needed someone to give me direction.

The mental health worker came into my room because he needed to do an assessment. I told him I didn't feel like it. He told me he had to have it done before his shifted ended. I told him I wasn't concerned with his work, I did not feel like it. He became angry and began to pick at me. He told me I wouldn't eat, unless I allowed him to do an assessment. I told him I didn't have an appetite anyway so it didn't matter to me if I didn't eat anything. I gave my food to my roommate; the woman who people said couldn't talk. I was astounded to find out that she actually did talk! As a matter of fact, she talked to me a lot. No one knew she could she talk, except for me. I asked her why she didn't talk. She said it hurts her to talk and she didn't have anything to talk about. I couldn't argue that. I understood her because it was hurting me to think.

That evening, they brought a new patient in. I could look at him and tell that he was trouble. I told my roommate, "We have to keep our eyes on him." He was a white guy, standing about 6'2, weighing about 240 lbs. He was a pretty nice size guy and he looked very strange. He would sit on the couch and stare at my roommate and me. He really seemed to have an interest in me, and I had an interest in him also. I knew he couldn't be trusted. I was one step ahead of the game.

Every night when everyone was ordered to go to sleep, he would constantly walk by our room, looking in. By the room being dark, he couldn't tell whether I was awake or asleep. Since we couldn't trust him, we had to watch him. I took the night shift and she took the day shift to watch him. My roommate couldn't stay awake at night, and I couldn't sleep at night. We were a perfect team. By no one knowing she could talk it was even better. The next day, he appeared to be kind of anxious. I figured this is the day he's going to try his attack on me so I had to be ready. We were allowed to do puzzles and they would give us pencils. I had to figure out how to get away with my pencil, because they counted everything. When they took him downstairs to see the doctor, I took two pencils and gave them to my little friend. I told her to put them in his room under the mattress while I kept the nurse occupied. I told her to also take two of the pencils and hide them in our bathroom, under the trashcan. I don't know what they did to that man but when he returned, he was like a wild man. I believe he needed medication and they were taking their time doing his assessment. But in the meantime his meds were wearing off. I asked the nurse if they could lock us in our room at night and she told me, "He's not going to bother you". I knew that was a lie that man was going to bother someone he was even bothering himself. I asked the nurse, "Why don't you give him some meds, he needs his medication." The only thing that was good about this man is that he kept me from thinking about killing Mr. Jay. I didn't have time to think about that, I had to watch him. When it was time to go to bed, the nurses came looking for the pencils. They began to search everyone's bedroom. I went to my room against the orders of the staff. I told them, "You can't stop me from going to my room. I'm getting in the bed you are not searching my room". I wanted them to think I had the pencils in my bed, I knew they were going to strip my bed this is what I wanted them to do. They came and dragged me out of the bed, while I fought them. While they were searching my bed one of the workers hollered we found two of them. They left my room and they all went into the man's room and begin to tear his room up looking for the other two pencils. I knew they were finish looking in my room and they would never go into the bathroom and lift the can up. I heard the nurse ask him where the two other pencils were, he told them he didn't know. The worker said, "He probably took them downstairs with him earlier." They asked him where the pencils were, he told them, "Downstairs." My roommate and I looked at each other with smiles on our faces. I told her, "I will get the pencils when I go to the bathroom." That night, he paced back and forth. Every time he got near our room, he slowed down, looking in the room. I was laying in the dark, waiting on him. I noticed my roommate was still awake. She must've had the same feeling that I had. I went to the bathroom. As soon as the light was turned off, I opened the door to come out. I heard another door close. I stood in the doorway of the bathroom. I knew he couldn't see me. He walked right over to my bed and began feeling for me. When he realized I wasn't in the bed, instead of looking for me, he went right to the roommate's bed. Before he could even feel for her she jumped out of the bed, on the other side. He rushed to the other side and I was right behind him. She started screaming and the nurses came into the room. By that time, he had her by her neck. I had the sharpened pencil, jabbing him everywhere I could. I saw that this wasn't working. I got on the bed and jumped on his back and begin to choke the living daylights of him. My Grandma Oby taught me how to choke a person, and cut their wind off and it was working. He let my roommate go and was trying to get me off his back. The nurses were screaming for me to let him go. For some reason, I was really enjoying what I was doing. I knew if he had gotten a hold to me, he wouldn't have had mercy on me. I finally let go of his neck. He was holding his neck trying to breath. The next day, I was questioned about the pencils, I told them, "He brought them into the room with him." He was sent to another unit. I was happy that I could now sleep again.

Mr. Jay came to visit me. He brought a friend with him to show him that I was in the mental institution. They looked at me, laughing and ridiculing me. I really didn't have anything to say to him. But I had to behave accordingly if I wanted to be released. The doctor was coming into my unit the next day. I was going to see if he was going to release me. If I let Mr. Jay have it, I might as well revoke the thought of asking the doctor about discharging me. So I carried on in a respectable way. I started the conversation off by asking him, "When will you and your woman be returning from your vacation?" His face turned pale in disbelief. He didn't know that I knew about the vacation. He gave me the answer that he'd always give whenever I caught him by surprise, "I don't know what you're talking about." He was lying. He knew exactly what I was talking about. What boggled him is that I knew about the vacation, yet I was separated from the world. The element of surprise is something else. I wanted to knock him from amazing grace to a floating opportunity. This would be the first holiday away from my daughters, and it was his fault. If looks could kill, he would have been crucified. However, I had to be civil. My freedom was at stake. Although I knew he was a lying, I remained calm and carried on the conversation, cordially.

The next day, the doctor had informed me that they needed to do a procedure on me to cease my depression. He said he had already spoken to my husband and he didn't have a problem with the procedure. They were putting drugs in my food; hence I would become drowsy after each meal. I was called informed that the procedure would take place the following day. I asked, "What kind of procedure am I having?" They told me again, "It is a procedure to keep you from being depressed." Thy told me that my husband signed the papers. I told them I didn't want the procedure. They told me because my husband had already signed and I was not capable of making my own decision, I really didn't have a choice. I was heavily medicated I didn't understand what they were doing and half of what they were saying.

The next day, it was time for the procedure. The doctors came and took me out of my room and into another room.

The room had a table with a TV screen, in front of the bed. There were prongs lying on a table next to the bed. They put me on the bed then put the prongs around my head and explained to me what they were doing. They put an IV in my arm, to administer anesthetics. I had to be put to sleep for this procedure. I found out the next day I was given Electroconvulsive Therapy (ECT). This is when the brain is given electrical shock and this is supposed to help a person that is depressed. The shock makes the person have a short seizure. The therapy does not last a long period of time. When I recovered from the procedure, I wasn't in any pain. However, I was very disoriented. I could not remember anything prior to the treatment. I wondered how long this would last. The fact that I could think after this electric shock treatment, I guess was a good thing. I remember trying to remember how my children. I was afraid that I would forget how they looked. I didn't care about forgetting anything else. I struggled to remember my name, but every day it seemed as if my memory would get a little better. I continued to struggle to remember many things like my address, phone number, and my birth date. I thought I would go crazy. I was soon released to go home. I found out that my husband did ask that I stay in the hospital so that him and his woman could take their trip to Vegas. My thoughts were not clear enough to fight with anyone. I was just happy to be home with my daughters. It took me a complete year before I could get most of my memory back, and I still didn't get it all back. I thank God I could still pray. I prayed a lot consistently and I read my bible a whole lot. Reading the bible and praying gave me the peace I needed.

When I went to the clinic, I would see others that received the same treatment that I had. They weren't doing half as well as I was. Seeing these people made me realize that I wasn't in bad shape at all. I would sit and pray for the people as God instructed me to do. There were people that had the treatment six months before I did and they still couldn't remember many things. Many of the people that were with them were surprise to know that I drove myself to the clinic. I found it strange that I was to the point I didn't care what my husband did anymore. I don't know if the treatments made me not care what was going on around me, but that's the way I felt at the time.

I remember delivering mail and I saw the police riding up and down the street. They were looking for someone. I had seen a man running down the street. I said to myself, "That must be the man they are looking for." The police stopped and asked me if I saw a man running down the street. I told them no. The police left, and continued their search. I refused to involve myself in their affairs, when there was no one to protect me. I knew they weren't going to protect me. I went in a building to put the mail in the box. All of a sudden, man came walking down the stairs. He looked at me and said, "Thank you for not telling the police you hadn't seen me." I was outdone. Now suppose I had told the police that I had seen him. That man would had been waiting in the building, plotting to do Lord knows what. I was so happy that I told the police that I had not seen the man. I would have been in danger if I had told them anything different. The man was waiting in the building and there was not one policeman in sight. Thank God I did the right thing.

Revelation: Yes I was a bright child and never did I think I would endure what I have in my life. Many times, God will show us what he has for us. He doesn't tell us what lies ahead or what we must go through to get there. Many times, we think we are suppose to walk and just pick up the blessings that God has promised us. We don't want to go through anything. We feel that because we are Christians and the word of God speaks of blessings in our life, that we are to have an easy walk. If I had not went through the things I did, I know in my heart I wouldn't be the person that I am today. My struggles molded me to be who I am today and who God wanted me to be. I was being molded to do what God wanted me to do for his kingdom. Therefore, it's not about me. It's all about the kingdom of God. When going through, we can't see why we are suffering. We can't think of one reason why we should suffer. This is because suffering is not a part of what we expect in life. When we dream, we never include suffering. We only dream of the things we want to happen in our lives. If we could get a peek of what lies ahead for us we would probably give up, or turn around. We will never reach the place, where God has predestined us to be. It seemed throughout my life that I had to fight every step of the way, and it wasn't easy for me. It seemed as if every time I stepped out of one situation, I found myself in another situation. God placed people in my life to assist me in my walk. The people were placed in my life just when I needed them. God made sure I always had someone to accompany me through my trials and tribulations. God even sent people that I never thought would be in my life.

God gave me wisdom and discernment at an early part of my life. He equipped me with what I needed to make it through my walk. God had even blessed me to be a blessing to others all through life. I was able to make children my age happy by taking them around. I was able to experience many things when I was young and others that are older would probably never experience. Even when I was going through, God allowed me to reach out to others and bless them. There were many that looked up to me, and I never realized that I was a walking example for those that were watching me. When I was in the mental hospital, I thought it was the worst thing that could happen to me. I never knew I would go into the hospital and help those that were there. My husband thought that he was hurting me when he was actually hurting himself. He thought he was on top of the world and he was in control of everything he was doing. He never knew that for every trick of the devil he was pulling, God had a ram in the bush. He was creating the diamond carats in me, and didn't know it. He and all his women have suffered more than I have. He thought that he would live happily ever after with this wife, on easy street. They are working happily ever after. No, there are no laid back days for retirement. They are not enjoying vacations. Everything they took me through, they are going through right now. They have to hit the floor each morning to go to work. Tick tock, watch that clock. This is the life they built for themselves. If there is a crack in the foundation, everything built upon it will fall.

There were many that lost their memory when they received the ECT treatment. I lost my memory for about a year. Some memories, I didn't get back for a couple of years. If I was to look at how the treatment affected others, and how they lost their memories, I realized how God has blessed me. When I look at the others, I realize I could have lost most of my memory and never regained it. I may have lost something because I never thought of leaving my husband, and I can't tell you why.

When I look at the situation now, I think I was just comfortable with the way he was treating me. I was still searching for love in the wrong places. Accepting anything just to feel love. The man was a feeling drainer. He would drain all the feelings out of you and he didn't care how he did it. He didn't care whether he had to hurt you to leave your heart dry. It was all about him and only him. I was no more than a welcome mat, and he didn't even care about wiping his feet on me.

I was at the point in my life where it didn't matter to me and I didn't think about it. God has a road for each of us to travel, and the road is different for each individual. God has a purpose for each of our lives, and your walk is in alignment with the purpose God has for you. We become bitter about the things we go through, and bitter at the people for taking us through it, and we don't realize that God sets everything in place. It's just like a stage play; with things set in place for each scene, with each person in place for the scene they are suppose to be in. We have learned that God does things decent and order.

Things may not look decent, because of the encounters we have throughout our lives. We don't see things being in order because of our hurt and pain we endure while going through. In the end things seem to fall in line with the order of God. God always have a plan for us when we think things are out of control and there's no way out of our situations. I learned that God always give you the right things to say in situations. He would lead you down the right path, if you will allow him to lead you.

CHAPTER 14

Toe-to-Toe battle with Satan

I would have thought I had conquered all the greatest battles in my lifetime, until I was introduced to Mr. Cocaine. Mr. Jay was the dealer who introduced me to the drug. At the time, I couldn't understand why he would introduce me to it, but today I will tell you why. It was his way of controlling me; he was out of control and used me to gain control over his life. He just walked into the house and gave me a package, and he told me to try a little of it. He then sat down and took him a hit of it.

I eventually I developed had a habit doing Premo's, this is when you take the tobacco out of a cigarette and loosely put the tobacco back in the cigarette. Then you stick cocaine into the cigarette, twist it at the end and light the cigarette. This habit was not nice, because more cocaine was needed in the cigarette to get high. This was the only way I knew how to get high. Thank God I never knew how to smoke the pipe, because I was having trouble with this particular high alone. I was working every day at the Post Office; therefore I didn't have to worry about having money to support my habit. Also, when Mr. Jay had it I didn't have to worry about money. This drug changed my entire life around. I lived for this drug, I worked for this drug and I dreamed of this drug. This drug was the pimp of my life. The main thing is that it didn't change me morally. I still had values and there were things I wouldn't do for the drug. I never turned a trick for the drug, because I had a job and it was available to me all the time. I'm not saying this to make myself look as though I am better than others that did turn tricks for the drug, but I never neglected my family or myself. I kept my hair done and kept my appearance up. I kept my children looking nice, but when my priorities were taken care of, the rest of the money went on the drug. I was a real drug addict and enjoyed what I was doing.

The drug was pimping me. I didn't realize it, because I was enjoying it. Mr. Jay thought he was the king on the throne now. He thought that he had me and there was no way for me to escape from his den. I guess he felt that cocaine was not good enough for me, so he then bought Heroine for me to use. He was going to make sure he had me where he wanted me. He would stay in the streets with his women for days. I wouldn't say anything because he would walk in and throw me a stash. This was my "keep quiet token", and it would put me in the "I don't care mode". I truly didn't care as long as he left me some drugs when before he would leave the house. The drugs also kept me from hurting emotionally when he did me wrong.

In the past, if someone would have asked me why I did the drugs, I would have told them that I enjoyed them. I was not one that was in denial about having a problem. I knew I had a problem but I didn't care about it. I would tell people that I had a problem. There was nothing for me to hide, so therefore, I didn't. I wasn't ashamed of being a drug addict, I watched many people try to hide their drug usage, and I never understood why. I would ask people to loan me money so that I could get me a bag. For my get high crew and me, there was no shame in our game. The drugs begin to depress me, and I started to feel miserable.

The more I did the drugs the more depressed I became, and I didn't want to live anymore. I looked at my life and didn't see why it was worth living. I felt like I had let my life go down the drain and I couldn't do anything about it. Satan was trying to take my life, and I could see how he manipulated his way into it. I would go to church every Saturday and help the pastor sale dinners.

I would attend church every Sunday. I decided I was tired of living, and took a bottle of pills and decided to lay down. I woke up with my stomach being pumped, and I was off to the mental ward once again. I couldn't believe five years later some of the same people were in there. I was so hurt when I found out someone had killed my friend Conaan. I was really hurt because he was a nice guy. I had a lot of fun with him. I stayed in the ward for about three days. The interview with the doctor was interesting to me as well. The doctor asked me how much drugs I was doing. I told him as much cocaine as I could get my hands on and maybe $60-$100 a day in Heroine. He then asked me did I hurt if I didn't get the Heroine, and I told him no. He also stated that all Heroin addicts ache when they don't get the drug. I told him I never knew what it is to ache from Heroine. I asked him where was I supposed to hurt. I didn't shoot the Heroine up I would snort the Heroine in my nose. I didn't buy it because I had access to the drug. The doctor looked at me and said, "You are one in a million, I have never saw anyone that did as much as you do and they don't have any aches and pains when they don't have it."

However, I understood what he was saying. I've had many people that told me if they had my body, they would never stop using the drug. They couldn't understand why I never hurt for the drug. I never looked at it as anything substantial, but when I spoke with others they looked as if it was. Many said they had never seen anything like it.

The doctors would listen to me as if I was lying to them. I never could understand why I didn't want to live anymore. The more I didn't want to live the happier Mr. Jay seemed to be. I think that he just wanted me out of his life. In fact, he didn't care if I lived or not, and it wouldn't make difference to him. I believe my biggest problem was that I was trying to get my ex-husband's attention, and he was not paying me any mind. When a person is in search of love, they will often look for it in the wrong places.

I was searching for love and he was taking advantage of it, Satan knew what my weakness was. I never knew that searching for love within my ex-husband would be the wrong place. I have to understand that God didn't choose Mr. Jay, I chose him. This is why things were not going in the favor of God. I allowed my ex-husband to choose me and I never conferred with God. God should do the choosing of our mates and not us. We seem to want things for ourselves. This is what happened to me. I should have known he was not for me. He left me when I first met him at the age of fifteen, because I wouldn't have sex with him. He came around again at the age of eighteen when he felt I was ready. At the time, I didn't know any better and not having anyone in my life to give me spiritual advice was even worse. I wish I could have had a spiritual mother or sister to help me make decisions, or to keep me on the right course.

My mother would tell me not to have sex, but I never was taught how it was a spiritual sin. I had it taught to me but no one ever explained me why. Now here I was, a drug addict with an emotionally, mentally, and spiritually abusive husband, and I didn't know how to get out of the abuse. The more women he had the bigger it made him feel. I believe it made him feel as if he had power when he was actually powerless. The only way he could deal with me was to keep me drugged up; trust me, if I wasn't on drugs I would have been too spiritually strong for him to deal with. Satan knew that I was anointed, and he also knew what I was capable of.

I always had a connection with God, and people that I got high with knew this. I had gotten to the point where I couldn't get high without listening to gospel music. I would turn my gospel music on every time I got high. I would listen to Stephanie Mills, gospel CD of inspirations; the CD had many songs on it that I loved. One of my favorite songs was "everything you touch". For some reason that song really touched my life. The song would speak on how God touched her life as well. I felt like my life was a song and I was waiting on God to touch my life. I knew he was not finish with me. My friends would say do we have to listen to the gospel music, but I didn't care what they would say. It even had gotten to the point where they would no longer would get high with me, but it didn't bother me. It would also be times when I would cry while listening to the music. I eventually came to the conclusion that it was time to stop getting high. I wasn't enjoying it anymore; most of all, my girls were getting old enough to understand what I was doing. I didn't realize that they understood what I was doing, especially on the account that I would make them go to their room when I wanted to get high.

My children were prisoners and I never noticed it until I stopped getting high. When talking to them, they told me it was no secret to them when I was about to get high. They told me they hated it, because I would make them go to their bedroom. I never knew how much getting high affected my children, until I talked to them. I realized they were being held prisoners in their own home.

When we are doing things out of the will of God, we don't care about hurting our love ones, especially our children. We begin to replace them with the drug. We love the drug more than we love our children, and even ourselves. We don't mean to replace them, but the devil is cunning and he's full of deception. He will make you think that everything is ok with you and your children, but in reality he is separating you all. He will not allow you to see that you are so disconnected from one another, and by the time you realize what is going on it will be too late for you to get control of the situation. The situation is too far out of hand for you to easily get things in order. It will take a lot of effort to get things back in order, or back to where they once were. I would go to some of the worse places on the west side of Chicago to purchase my drugs. The drug would make you not afraid of anything, when it came to purchasing it. One would not be afraid of death, when you wanted more drugs.

The drug would talk to you. I can remember when Mr. Jay would hide the drugs from me. When he left it's like the drug called me right to the spot it was hidden in. I remember people calling it a spirit, and I understood why they called it a spirit.

These drugs were very dangerous, and they would eventually lead you right to your death. It was very easy to get caught up in a death trap for the drugs, because you didn't fear anything. I could remember being in uniform standing in line waiting to purchase, not caring if I lost my job or not. I never thought about what if, those things didn't matter to me the only what if I was worried about was what if they were out of the drug. That was my only concern when going to purchase drugs. I was really tired of the drugs before I even thought to give them up. I didn't enjoy getting high anymore the drugs didn't give me the effect they had been giving. I had totally lost interest in the drugs. The drugs began to taste like garbage to me and there was nothing enjoyable about doing them.

I decided I would stop doing drugs; I had set a date on which I would give the drugs up for good. I set the date and I gave the drugs up, I thank God I didn't have to go and enroll into a rehab. I had it in my mind that I tore myself down and I didn't need a rehab. I would build myself up. I set the date for July 5, 1996. I figured I would get high as a kite for the fourth of July, therefore, I did. Once the holiday was over I gave it up and never looked back. I tried to get high about seven years later, and I never felt anything from it. I walked away again from it. I knew I was finished with the drug. You would think that people would be happy that you quit doing the drug.

There were people that were angry with me, because I didn't get high anymore. I couldn't believe there were people that wanted me to get high, and got angry with me for quitting. This showed me that people loved to see you down, and there were many that were happy seeing me down. One of the people was my ex-husband, he felt as if he had lost his control of me. The only control he had was the drug, without the drug he had no control over my life and it was running him crazy. He knew I had stopped doing the drug, so he would bring his friends into the house and get high anyway. He wanted me to continue getting high, so that he could have control over my life. He begin to think of other ways to bring me down, this is why he didn't mind hurting me by sleeping with all the women he had. He had to hurt me some kind of way.

I can remember Mr. Jay requesting a divorce. Furthermore, he had the audacity to ask me to share the money from the process He even told me that he would give me $10,000, then only to remarry. Now I was far from being a fool. However, it didn't hurt me that he would request for the divorce, but it hurt me that he assumed that I was a foolish. So I decided to play his game. I told him that I would only agree to it as long as we consulted with an attorney in regards to getting everything documented. Because of this, he got exceedingly infuriated with me. I just shook my head at him, I don't know where he was getting his advice from, but they certainly had to be misinformed about what I actually would fall for. The devil had really with his brain to make him think that he could fool me, it was sad. I watched him time after time trying to fool me and I would out smart him each time. It's as if God would warn me when he was coming to me with some mess.

I couldn't understand why it was hard for him to see that he couldn't win. He tried every trick to win, but did not win the victory each time he attempted to. He never gave up on the challenge of "pulling wool over my eyes". I often reminisced about how I was the one who launched the "Say No to Drugs" program in high school, and there I was, a drug addict. I was ashamed; how could I allow this to happen to me. I knew that I had got off on the wrong course. I knew I had to get back on course with my life or I would die. I knew Satan was trying to destroy me and take my life. The only way to beat him was to give up doing drugs, or I would lose the fight. I thought that when I gave the drug up, things would fall back in place. I was wrong. It was an uphill battle for me. I knew that the devil had to have an opening to get to me. The drugs were an opening. When I gave the drug up, many thought that I would use again. How I fooled them. I never had an urge for the drugs again. I knew God had delivered me from the drugs and it was over.

When God created the world, man was given dominion over everything. The things around us were supposed to be accessories to us. Man has become an accessory to the things he should have dominion over because we are not taking our position that God has given us. What if God removed everything off of earth that he created, except man. Would we then realize the power we have?

Once I stopped using drugs, I looked around the neighborhood and noticed so many new things that were built. I had never noticed all the new buildings. It's a shame how when you use drugs, you are in a world of your own. When you stop using drugs, there are so many things you have missed. I had to ask people when was certain things built. When people would tell me the amount of time the particular place has been built, I would ask myself, "Why didn't I notice that and I pass by it every day"?" There were so many things that I had missed when on the account of getting high. It was as if I had blinders on and couldn't see but one way and that was how to get the next drug. I had stepped into a new world and the veil was removed from my eyes. I felt as if I had been walking around with a blindfold over my eyes all these years.

I recall sitting in my kitchen once. Some friends had left out to go to the store. As soon as they left, someone knocked on the screen door. I had locked the screen door so that no one could get in. I was sitting in a seat where I couldn't see who was at the door. I asked, "Who is it?" I could barely hear the person answer. I thought, "This is someone who seen my friends leave. They know that I'm here alone and think that I'm going to open the door. This is a set up." The person continued to whisper. I finally decided to peep around the corner to see who was at the door. When I looked, I noticed it was naked women. I thought, "Do she really think that I'm going to open this door? It could all be a plan devised to rob me." I asked her, "Where are your clothes?" She replied, "Miss, please let me in. A man is trying to rape me and I think he's coming." I told her to go in the basement, because I didn't have any keys to open the door for her. She went in the basement and I locked the door with the key. I went upstairs to the bathroom and found her a sheet. I opened the window and threw the sheet down to the basement. I called the police and informed the of the incident. Meanwhile, the lady asked me to call her brothers to let them know that she needed help. I called her brothers; they didn't answer the phone. I left a message on the answering machine for her brothers. I gave them my address and informed them about what happened to their sister. I looked out the window and noticed a police car going by; he looked as if he was lost. I waited for him to come back around, so that I could flag him down. When I noticed that the police was coming back, I ran out the door, trying to flag him down. All of a sudden, something big and white appeared behind me, going over my head. It was the girl with the white sheet that I'd given her. I turned around and took a swing, accidently hitting the her. She fell to the ground. I apologized, redundantly. I didn't know what was flying over my head. I would learn that it was her sheet, waving in the wind. It scared the daylights out of me. I warned her that she should have never ran behind me. When the police stopped and began to tell them the situation. They put her in the backseat of the squad car. She was taken to the home of the man who tried to rape her, so that she can identify him. Then they took her to the police station to file a report. Twenty minutes later, her brothers showed up to my house, looking for her. I had informed them that their sister was in the police car, which was just around the corner. That event has really shaken me up. I began to wonder, "Where my two friends were and what was taking them so long." I would learn that they were standing at the corner, watching. They were afraid to come to the house. It was a wild night. I was so happy to be drug free and I didn't have to worry things like this happening. So many crazy things happen to me in my lifetime, I didn't know what to expect next.

I was scheduled to have what was supposed to be a simple surgery. Before I went to surgery, I said a prayer. I was taken to the operating room. The nurse told me to close my eyes, relax, and count to ten. As she released the medication into my IV, which would sedate me, I began to count. I could feel myself going to sleep. My body was asleep, but my mind was awake. I tried to move to let them know I was awake. I could hear the operating team talking. I heard the doctor say, "Pass the scalpel." I tried to talk, but I couldn't talk. I tried to move, I couldn't move. I begin to pray and ask God to let them know I was awake. I cried out to God to please help me. I didn't want the doctor to cut me while I was still awake. The doctor cut my stomach with the scapula. I completely blacked out, feeling absolutely nothing. I began to travel to what appeared to be another world. I was traveling so fast, I didn't recognize my surroundings. I was going through what appeared to be a tunnel with a bright light at the end. The end of this tunnel was so bright; I could barely look at it. There were two hands reaching out to me as I approached the end of the tunnel. I got to the end and began to back up. I cried out, "Oh Lord please don't take me! I'm not ready to die! If I die who will take care of my girls? Lord, please let me return so that I can take care of my girls. They don't have anyone to take care of them." I begin to go backwards through the tunnel, at a very fast speed. When I stopped moving is when I woke up.

When I opened my eyes, I had seen all the equipment around me. I was inside what appeared to be a tent. There was a tube in my nose and monitors were all around me. The nurse came over to me and began to take the tube out of my nose. I asked her, "Where am I? What's going on?" She told me that my heart stopped twice. I had been sleep for two days. She informed me that I had suffered complications during the surgery. I told her, "I was awake when the doctor cut into my stomach." She replied, "That's impossible. You were sound asleep. You must have been dreaming." "I heard the whole conversation they were having", I replied, "They were having a Christmas party. They didn't want to invite one of the nurses because her husband got drunk at the Thanksgiving dinner. He had gotten so drunk; he'd knocked the table over with the dinner on it. They didn't want the same thing to happen at the Christmas party." When I told her that, her became widen with surprise. She looked at me and said, "You were awake." I told her, "My heart had stopped because the doctor cut my stomach while I was awake. God protected me by putting me to sleep." She couldn't believe what she was hearing. She just shook her head in disbelief. For the remainder of the day, the nurses were coming into my room, asking me to repeat what I heard. My story never changed.

I was over to T.T's house when Tyra had became sick. She had a fever and an earache. It was twelve midnight and I didn't want to go out that late. With Tyra's condition, I had no choice. I had a feeling that something would happen once I left the house. I took a butcher knife and put it on the door of my car just in case something happened. We went to the emergency room. Tyra was diagnosed with an ear infection. I was given a prescription that had to be filled. I had to drive to 95th and Cicero, which was a 24-hour Walgreens. Afterwards, I stopped in across the street to White Castles to get us something to eat. I pulled in the parking lot to purchase the food. I looked over to my left, and there was a white man in a red truck, licking his tongue out at me. I pulled out of the parking lot. To my surprise, he followed. I made it to 95th and Western and he continued to follow me. As we approached the forest preserve at about 91st street (a wooded area), he ran me off the road, forcing my car on the sidewalk. My car cut off after it jumped the curb. That's when I began to pray. I could see the truck behind my car. He turned his lights off. I grabbed the butcher knife, waiting for him to approach me. At the same time, I didn't give up on trying to start my car. I turned the key in the ignition, the car started up. As the man was approaching my car, I sped off, doing 100mph, driving off the sidewalk back into the streets. Immediately, the man jumped in his truck and resumed the chase. I had gained ground because he couldn't make the sharp turns in his truck that I was making in the Firebird. The man followed me all the way to my mother's house. I was blowing my horn as I was driving down T.T's block. I was hoping that maybe her, Dada, or even some of the neighbors heard me. If they hear me, they'll open the door. I could avoid running from this crazy man with Tyra in my arms. Meanwhile, the man had disappeared. I knew he wasn't gone. As a matter of fact, he was far from gone. I jumped out of my car, while watching my back. I looked around me. There was no sign of the man. I looked to the end of the streets, near the train tracks. Low and behold, there sat the man, in his red truck. He was watching me, with a big smile on his face. I ran to the house, leaving Tyra in the car with the door open. I screamed while beating on the door, loud as I could. I was relieved when Dada answered the door. "What's wrong with you?" Dada asked. I was in such a state of panic; the words wouldn't come out right. Dada stood on the porch, watching me as I got Tyra out of the car. The man pulled off down the alley. I never saw him again. Thinking back, the man followed me from 95th and Cicero to 75th and Winchester. He was persistent about catching me. I was terrified. I knew something was going to happen I felt it, which is why I grabbed the knife in the first place. One of my good friends had just been found dead in the area around that time. Her killer hadn't been caught. For all I knew, he could have been the killer. I didn't know what the man's plans. I knew one thing; I wasn't taking any chances finding out his plans either. I will never forget the feeling that I had that night before I left for the emergency room. I prayed to God before I left. He protected my daughter and I.

Recently, I had a talk with a friend of mines. She told me that years ago, she was working in the streets with a church. At that time, a man, driving a pick truck, was killing women. This was happening around the same time I had my encounter with the strange man. It's strange that I would find this out 26 years later. God has his way of allowing you to find things out. He knows just when to release the information to you. When you are trying to get an understanding about a certain situation and it's not coming clear to you, it is not your time to understand. Stop looking for understanding. When it is time for you to receive clarity on any situation, you won't have to chase down the understanding. Understanding will chase you. I often wonder was this man who was killing women the same man who chased me that night. Sometimes life is like a winding road; you don't know what lies up ahead because of the curves you are facing.

Tyra's bed would squeak whenever she moved, while laying in it. I was lying in my bed after Tyra and Taineeka had left for school. I heard Tyra's bed squeak; her bed was squeaking as if she was in it. This was strange. After all, I knew she was gone to school. I got up to go in her room to investigate. The door to her room was closed. I opened the door, entering the room. There was no one there. I turned and walked out of the room. As I was leaving, the door slammed behind me as if someone had closed it. I reopened the door. I placed a phone book at the bottom of the door to hold it open. I returned to my room and laid across the bed. I felt a cold breeze go across my body. I felt the bed sink in as if someone had sat on it. When I turned around, no one was there. This experience was baffling. I thought to myself, "What is with all of these strange encounters?" Shortly after pondering that thought, I received confirmation. One night, one of the drug dealers came over to my house. He looked towards my daughter's room and said, "That was once my friend's room before he was killed." I reflected on how my daughter would always tell me about a little boy who would come in her room to keep her company. I never paid her any attention. But that night, I would learn that many of the things she told me about the little boy matched up with what the drug dealer was telling me. He told me that his friend was thirteen years old. He was shot and killed while gangbanging. A week later, my friend and I were sitting at the kitchen table. All of a sudden, we heard someone running up the basement stairs. We both waited to see who it was. They never opened the door. We both thought this was strange. There were a lot of strange things going on in that house. I would just ignore them.

When I was a teenager, my friends and I would take a short cut across the train tracks, to get home. Once, we jumped down off the tracks, and onto the grass. When we landed on the grass, a bird arose from the grass, with a wingspan as long as my body. I was in total shock. I had never saw a bird that large! What kind of bird that was, I have no idea. I know one thing for certain; we didn't take the shortcut after that. We would take the long way home, just to avoid that bird. It took us maybe 15 minutes longer. We didn't care; we would have walked an hour to avoid seeing that bird. The incident on the train tracks was the first time we would see the bird. But, it would not be the last. During the summer nights, we would be sitting on the porch. The bird would fly over our heads. Not only did it frighten us, it also gave us a breeze from its wings. Eventually, the bird disappeared. To this very day, the species of the bird remains unknown.

That summer was the strangest summer that I had ever experienced. We had an owl in our back yard. There was even a snake in the back yard. I looked out the window once, and saw a bird running like a man. Dada told me that the bird was a Pheasant. I had never seen a bird lean back and run like a man. The next day, I called my cousin, who lived next door. I wanted to see if she had any sour cream for my baked potato. I went to get it from her and there was an animal that resembled a cat on her porch. I took a second look and realized it was a giant raccoon. The raccoon walked down the stairs and went up in a tree. All these animals were present in one summer, which I found to be very strange. Not to mention, I was afraid of animals.

My friends, my cousins, and I went to a basement party. When we arrived to the party, we learned a girl was upstairs, being raped. Upon hearing this, we decided to leave. When we tried to exit, a man put his arm up, blocking the doorway. He told us, "Y'all aren't going nowhere!" I looked at him like he'd lost his mind. When we opened the door to leave, there was a man standing at the door, with a gun in his hand. He came into the basement, intimidating everyone. For some reason, I wasn't scared of man. Everyone in the basement was shaking. The man went back upstairs to finish what he'd started. Before he left, he looked at us and said, "One of you will be next." This didn't scare me one bit. I headed to the door and shoved the man out of the way. I told everyone that was with me, "Let's get out of here." I proceeded to leave, and my party followed me. When we got to the front of the house, the gunman came running behind us. Everyone began to panic, screaming and running. The gunman told everyone to freeze. They did exactly what he said. He told us to get in the car that was parked on the streets. It was a station wagon. I know I wasn't getting in the car. I told everyone that I was about to leave. He told me, "You are not going anywhere." I replied to him, "You are not a man. You have to pull a gun on women. What kind of man does that? I'm not afraid of you and I am getting ready to go." He put the gun to my head. I could feel steam coming out of my ears. I told him, "If you put the gun down, I will give you the worse whooping you ever had in your life." As I walked away, I told him, "Be the big man that you are and shoot me in the back, Hero." I went through the alley. When I looked back, he was standing still, holding the gun. He looked as if he couldn't believe that I had walked away. When I turned the corner, realized what I had done: I left my friends. That's when the fear set in. I took off running. As I was running, I came across a man whom I knew with a CB. The man was from the CB Club, which consisted of men with CB's. These men were good Samaritans. When I told him what happened, he radioed for help from others in his club. They went back to the scene, searching for my party. They didn't see them, or the offenders. When I got home and was headed up the porch, the station wagon turned the corner. To my dismay, my dumb entourage got out. They actually let the men bring them home; I just shook my head in disbelief. I saw the man that had the gun about a week later. We were walking towards each other. Once he noticed who I was, he crossed over to the other side.

There was another incident that took place, which was confirmation that God was on my side. Mr. Jay had bought his cousin to our house. I was asleep when Mr. Jay decided to go to the store, leaving his cousin home with me. In my sleep, I felt someone standing over me. When I opened my eyes, there was his cousin, towering over me. He had a blank look in his eyes as if he was not himself. He snatched the cover off me. He started talking to me, trying to intimidate me. I jumped out the bed and grabbed the lamp. That's when I heard the door open. It was Mr. Jay. His cousin started laughing as if he was playing with me. I knew better. He had a cold look of death in his eyes. If Mr. Jay had not came back as soon as he did, his cousin and I were going to battle. From the look on his face, I knew that I would be fighting for my life.

When they left the house, I noticed that a knife that I'd purchased a week ago was missing. I searched the entire house; the knife was nowhere to be found. Mr. Jay's cousin had taken my knife. I guess his plans were to slaughter me. Twenty minutes later, the phone rang. It was the Chicago Police, asking for him. I told them that he had just left with my husband. I asked them, "What's going on" What did he do?" They informed me that he had cut two women up the night before. These were women that he grew up with. I began to thank God for saving me. I knew that I would be the next victim. He was a sick man. He had stabbed the two women up on the elevator, and cut their throats. If he could do this to women that he'd known since they were children, who was I that he wouldn't attempt to kill me? I was next; I must admit that it was a terrifying experience. I couldn't believe my husband would bring this man to my house and leave him alone with me. All I could do was thank God for saving me. When God has a plan for your life he will not allow anything to get in the way of his plans.

You would think that things were over for me. NO, things weren't over by a long shoot. My life was like a roller coaster. I decided to go to nursing school after I had given up the drugs. I was doing well in the beginning, until one day, things took a dive. I arrived home and decided to wait on my daughters to come home. I sat in the car because I knew this was about the time they would arrive. I wanted to take them to get something to eat. In doing this, I wouldn't have to leave the house later on. I waited and waited for them. Taineeka came home; Tyra didn't. All of a sudden, my cell phone rang. It was a lady, telling me that my daughter had been assaulted and she was in her place of business. I drove to where she was. There was a crowd of about twenty teenagers, standing on the streets. I parked my car in the middle of 95th street. I told the crowd, "Anything I could touch, or in my reach would get cut so it was best for y'all to make room, or I would make the room for y'all." I went into the real-estate office where my daughter was. When I saw her, I became so angry, I could feel the heat pouring off of my body. Fifteen girls jumped on my daughter, and one boy that was with them had stolen her purse. Her eye was swollen, and would later form a blood cot. Tyra had informed me that the mother of one of the girls worked in the corner store, located just a few feet from where she was attacked. I went into the store and informed the mother of what had happened. She tried talking to her daughter. Her daughter talked back to her, and even pushed her. I went back outside and told the crowd, "It's only one of me and about twenty of y'all. Come do me like you did my daughter. They began to walk away. I concluded, "Y'all want war you just signed for it." The police were called, and only a few of the girls were arrested. We were instructed by the police to follow them to the police station. I wanted to press charges, so going to there was paperwork that had to be completed. While in route to the police station, the officers pulled their car over. Since I was following them, I pulled over as well. The officer who was behind the wheel got out of the car and walked over to my car. I let the window down; apparently he had something to tell me. "Where is the knife?" he asked. I was confused at this point. "What are you talking about?" I asked. "The girls told us that your daughter has a knife", he said. I went completely off on that officer. I told him, "First of all, WE called y'all, not them! Second, my daughter was the one jumped, not them! Last, seeing how ignorant and disrespectful they were towards me in your presence, why would you even consider believing anything they say?!!! Furthermore, if we are the victims, why are you questioning us? I am already upset Sir! I am doing my best to remain calm in this situation! Now if we don't get to this police station so that I can file this report, you will see just how upset I really am! Oh and trust me, it's NOT a pretty sight!" The officer walked back to his car, and we resumed our journey to the police station. I stayed there for about four hours to get my paperwork processed. When I arrived home later that evening, I called my nieces and Taineeka called some friends. These girls picked the right one to mess with.

The next day, I went to the high school that a majority of the girls attended. I had them arrested. I had the boy arrested and charged with robbery for taking her purse. That evening, a friend and I went to get something to eat. My cell phone rang. It was my sister, telling me, "Come on, we are at war." I rushed home and noticed that there was a steak knife missing off of the table. I thought to myself, "Tyra took that knife." This frightened me. Tyra was just like me; She didn't bother anybody, unless provoked. She may have been peaceful, but she was far from a punk. As matter of fact, just like myself, Tyra is dangerous once somebody has bothered her. I had to find her. My daughter was only 16 years old and she wasn't going to jail for murder. I headed up to 95th St. When I arrived, people were running everywhere. They were screaming and crying. I found out there was an accident at the tracks. The girls who attacked Tyra were watching the accident. They didn't notice my nieces in three cars behind the accident. When my nieces got out of the cars, the girls ran. My nieces went in the projects, and gave them the whipping of their life. I gathered up my family and took then home. I later reflected on how I grew up. In the Ickes, nobody came to our project to fight us, and made it out in one piece. That was how the real projects were. Those girls ran once opposition was presented to them, on their turf. I should have known that would happen. After all, why would it take fifteen girls to jump one person? That Monday I went to four different schools having them arrested for jumping my daughter. I went to the alderman's office, the 5th and 6th district police department, CHA headquarters, and the board of education. I even called the newspapers. They really didn't know whom they were dealing with. They should have never gotten me started, but it was now too late. I was calling for a meeting and no one could back out because the media was now involved. The newspaper interviewed me. I told them about the female gang that called themselves the "95 Mob Girls." When I did my investigation, I discovered that five other girls that had been jumped by these same girls. One had been cut in the face, another stabbed in the head and yet another was dragged out of her classroom and beat by these little witches. I couldn't believe that no one was doing anything to stop them. The police department offered my daughter protection to and from school. We declined the offer. I figured that they learned their lesson. The board of education suspended and expelled some of the girls. Over all, everyone was cooperative. The only person I had a problem with was, the headman of CHA. He was very rude and even hung the phone up in my face. He told me, "That is what happens in the hood. If you was raised in the hood, this should be no surprise to you." I challenged him on his zero gang tolerance law that he set in place. He had a very nasty attitude. I will never forget him, and the way he spoke to me. I feel that he owes me an apology for the way he talked to me. I have no respect for him as a man, because he didn't respect me as a woman.

I called a meeting at the 6th district police department. The alderman, the commanding officer of the 5th and 6th district, a representative for the Board of education, many of the officers that patrol the streets, and two representatives from Trinity United Church were all present. This was the church that Tyra attended at the time, and they were very concerned about what was happening in the neighborhood. There was no one there to represent CHA. I thought they should have been there because this is where most of the girls lived. There were parents from the neighborhood and one lady from my neighborhood. She was a thorn in my side. Her biggest concern was how bad I was making the neighborhood look. She had been living there for forty years and this has been going on that long. She was saying these incidents were nothing new. They went on when her daughter was young and she's now 40 years old. I couldn't believe the words that were coming out of this woman's mouth. I told her, "Had stopped it when your daughter was younger, maybe we wouldn't be in this meeting. This meeting is so that we can put an end to this issue. Now, if your biggest concern is how the neighborhood looks, you should have stayed at home. I called this meeting. We have heard enough of your beautifying the neighborhood while people are being beat, and stabbed. If you aren't going to cooperate, please excuse yourself." The officers had to separate us twice in the meeting. We finally were able to get things resolved, once we shut her up.

Every time the girls would see my car, they would run. Believe it or not, they were the last thing on my mind. Once, I went to get gas. Some guys approached me. They told me that I was stopping them from selling their drugs, because I had "too much heat" in the area. (The phrase "too much heat" refers to excessive police activity.) If the heat continued, they would have to come at my house. My face turned red. I told them, "Why come to the house? It doesn't fight back. I'm standing right here take care of your business and I'll take care of mine." The boys started talking with the sense that God gave them after that. They told me that they didn't have anything to do with the girls; they just wanted to make their money. They couldn't make money as long as the police were there. I told them, "Well, that's y'all problem, not mine. You want to stop the "heat", stop the girls." They walked off, and never said anything else to me.

Later on that month, one of my friends called me. I told her what had happened with Tyra. She told me, "After today, you won't have a problem." We were in nursing school at the time. Outside of school, I didn't know much about her circle of friends. Whoever she knew they took care of the problem. A man came to my door the next day. He explained to me that we didn't know one another but he had given the word to the gangbangers, that they couldn't touch my family or me. He also informed me that the word came from the top, and his word was his bond. He gave me his number and told me that if I had any problem to contact him and it would be resolved. After that I had no more problems, neither did Tyra. That individual must have had power, because the guys would just look at me when I came around. They wouldn't say anything; they just looked. This was the same young lady who called me when my mother died. One December morning, she called at 9 a.m. We talked for some time. She told me that she would call me back at 9 p.m. When she called back, I was in Mississippi; I had drove there. I got in my car and just kept going and that's where I would end up. I had to quit nursing school. Between the incident with Tyra, and Mr. Jay's infidelity in our marriage, I had too much pressure on me to concentrate on my books.

Tyra had another confrontational incident, when she in the 8th grade. She came home and told me that a girl, who was twice her size, was harassing her. This girl would threaten her every day. Tyra expressed to me, "Ma, I want to get her so bad, but I graduate this year. I can't get suspended. I really can't go into high school with any fights or suspensions on my record." When my daughter told me that, I knew something had to be done. I went to the school and demanded a meeting with the girl's mother. The counselor didn't want to have the meeting because she said the girl's mother was ignorant. I didn't care; I was concerned about my daughter's well being. I knew that this was an issue that had to be resolved. They finally contacted the girl's mother and we set a date to meet. When that day arrived, I was sitting in the office, waiting on the mother to arrive. When she walked in the room, I introduced myself. The woman didn't give an introduction. As a matter of fact, she cursed me out. She told me, "I'm your neighbor. You could have come to my house. Why are you making me miss money for this dumb stuff?" I told her, "Your daughter is making you miss money, not me sweetheart." That woman just kept talking. I remained silent. The woman raced over to where I was sitting, "I will help my daughter whip your daughter", she said. When she said that, my silence was broken. I jumped out of the chair in a flash. All I could think about was the Jerry Springer show, me getting knocked out of the chair and her beating me to a pulp. The woman kept going while she was walking over to me, "You don't know who you are messing with. I'm from the low end." I grabbed her and told her, "You and your daughter will not have the both of us running sweetheart." That's when she took a swing. We tore that office up. I had all the fur from her collar in my hand. They were trying to pry my hand from around her neck, but I had a firm grip on her. She was trying to get away. I said to her, "Naw Miss Low End, don't run! You talked all of that mess, where are you running to?" They called security to separate us. Security escorted me out of the school. I didn't understand why they put me out of the school. I was not the one that started the fight. I stood outside waiting on her to come out. The police pulled up and told me that I had to leave off the property. I agreed to leave. Before I left, I asked the police, "Can you do me a favor?" The officer replied, "What's the favor ma'am?" I replied, "Tell that woman that I am not driving, I'm walking. If she wants a piece of me, I have on a green coat, and I'm walking down 93rd street." The officer pulled off, and I went home. I was then standing in the door of my home. Low and behold, who pulls up? The woman. I noticed that she was one of my neighbors. I didn't know that we lived exactly across the street from one another. It seems as though she was afraid to get out of the car. I stood in the doorway, only to see that she blew her horn for someone to open her front door. I assume that she didn't want to take the chance of me attacking her again. From that day on, I never had another problem out of that woman again; neither did Tyra have any further problems with her daughter.

I also had to fight with the school system about Taineeka. They were telling me that they were going to fail her. I told them that if they failed her that I would sue them. I had asked that she be evaluated and they waited until the school year was over. I sat in a meeting with the counselor, principal, nurse and the social worker. I told them, "You will not fail my child because y'all failed to do your job. If y'all fail her, I guarantee you that I will have y'all in court before the beginning of the next school year." They didn't fail her. They actually did what they were supposed to have done in the beginning; they evaluated her. Whenever I paid the school a visit, it would always take them forever to let me in. I think they were waiting on security. I wasn't a violent person. I just wanted to get my point across.

I had many funny experiences in my life. I can recall arriving home from school one night, and parking in front of my house. It was about 10 pm. Immediately after I parked, police cars pulled up next to mine. There were about 10 cars that pulled up. They got out and went towards my house. I got out of the car and asked them, "What's going on?" They told me they got a call saying that a man was in the house. I was worried because my nieces and Latavia were in the house. The police asked me did I have a key. I let them in. They went in with their guns out. When I knocked on the bedroom door, all three of them came out of the closet to the door. They told the police that the man was at the back door, and had went around to the front door. I told them, "When I pulled up, I saw the man who shovels snow, walking down the streets." I noticed that he had shoveled my porch and the side of the house. What they heard was the breaking of the ice and shoveling. I shook my head at them and laughed.

Revelation: My daughters didn't have any brothers. I was determined to keep the children off of them. As you can see, when it came to my daughters, I fought from the neighborhood to the departments. If you noticed, I was the only one fighting. Mr. Jay never got involved. He never had the time to do these types of things, leaving me no choice but to stand up. I think fighting all my life made me who I am today. I don't have time for confusion. As a matter of fact, I try to avoid confusion as much as possible. If I know a thing or person will upset me, I'll leave the situation.

I'm so happy that I got to know the Lord. I'm learning to allow God to fight my battles for me. I'm still learning to step back I find that somewhat difficult after stepping up for so many years. However, I am learning. God is teaching me and he's taking his time with me. He knows what I've had to encounter throughout my life.

Many people may never understand me. They may never take the time to understand me. They judge me from what they see. They never try to see the good side of me. Everybody have a rough side to them. That side didn't get rough overnight and it will not smooth out in a day. It takes God to deal with that side of us. It's a process that we all must go through to allow ourselves to be changed to the way God wants us to be. When we look at others, we should first look at ourselves.

I know that I'm not perfect. I don't pretend to be anywhere near perfect. When we realize that we all have flaws, we will be able to get along with one another. I knew if I didn't protect my girls, no other person would do it. God sent me to protect my daughters and that's what I did.

My cousin suffered an Aneurysm and a stroke. As a result, he went into a coma. He was put in a rehabilitation center. I had been searching for him because I had heard he was in a coma. I called the penitentiary where he was. They wouldn't give me any information on him. The only thing that they would tell me was that he had been sent to a Rehab. I searched everywhere for him. I knew he was still living because his medical card was still coming to my house. The only thing I could think to do was pray for him and that's what I did. He came to visit me when he was released. He told me that he heard me talking to him while he was in the coma. He thought I worked at the hospital because I talked to him every day. He asked one of the nurses did I work there. They told him that there was no one working there by that name. He argued with the nurses. He just knew that I worked there. He said that I told him he would be alright, and he had to wake up so that I could take him for a ride in my car. He thought, "I have to wake up so I can go for a ride in my cousin's car." He didn't understand how he could hear my voice so clear and I wasn't there with him. I told him it was I, praying for him. My spirit was there, although; I was not there.

It's strange how when you pray, God will allow you to connect with people. God used me to bring comfort to him while he was in a coma. God has his way of doing things that we can't explain. Sometimes things are not meant for us to understand. Yet, we try to understand what's not for us. God is God, not us. We will not understand everything he accept what he does and how he does things.

When I look at the things that I went through, I realize that those things made me who I am. Everything we go through adds on to our molding, whether it's good or bad. Sometimes, we don't realize why we are the way we are. However, if we can take time to think about the molding process we went through, we will then realize that sometimes we have picked up residue from something that we have passed through. You can't go through a perfume factory and not come out smelling like perfume. You can't go through a smoking building and not come out smelling like smoke. You will get residue from many of the places you pass through. Something is going to rub off on you while you're passing through the things you encounter in your life. When we recognize the residue we have picked up is when we can decide what we are going to get rid of. Getting rid of residue is a process, it does not happen overnight. There are many layers of things that must be pulled off. Many people want things to be different in the wink of an eye. It does not happen like that. It didn't happen overnight and it will not disappear overnight. If God allowed things to happen overnight, we may not be able to handle it.

Sometimes things must happen little by little to allow us to get adjusted to the new us. If we changed too fast, we may not be able to adjust to the new, or the new way that we will be forced to live. The answers to many of our problems today are in our past. We must go back and untangle what was tangled up. In other words, we must go back and face what hurt us. We must face what we don't want to. Usually, it's what hurt us the most. Many times, things may have been so traumatic that we don't want to go back to face them. We will pull one layer off, and there appears another layer we must deal with. Each layer is worse than the other. Pulling layers off is like pulling skin off; it hurts. There is nothing you can put on the layer to take some of the pain away.

Prayer is the only healing for this process. We look for God to begin the healing process right away. Many times, God will not soothe the pain right away. He wants us to feel the pain. This will keep us from returning to that area. Remember, God has the last word in everything in our life. We must have an ear to hear what he has to say to us. We can't get directions if we can't hear his voice. God is protecting us when we don't realize we are being protected. Many decisions he makes for us are to protect us. Sometimes, we get angry because we don't like the decisions. We are made to take long routes, instead of short ones for our protection. God knows what lies ahead of us. He protects us and makes decisions for us so that we can avoid what lies ahead.

When we decide to take things into our own hands and do things as we wish, this is when we get ourselves in trouble. We run right into the thing God has been protecting us from. This is why it's important to be able to hear the voice of God and to be obedient to his word. There were times that I didn't appreciate how my mother treated me. I had to learn to embrace the good in her, which was plentiful. The things I didn't care for, I embraced and turned them around. I learned that we could learn from the bad in others as well as the good.

I learned many valuable things from my mother. She taught me independence. As a result, I know how to depend solely on myself and not others. She taught me to think that I am the most important person in this world, when it comes to trying to accomplish something. She was a very hard worker and she took care of us. She provided us food and shelter. She actually was a very beautiful person. I can't dwell on what was. I must concentrate on what is and what I must accomplish in life before I leave this earth. I must concentrate on the good in me that the situation has bought out. There is good in every bad situation. It's up to the individual to find it. Finding it may be difficult at times. Nevertheless, we must realize that it is a part of living.

CHAPTER 15

My David and Jonathan Experience

God has sent many people in my life that I could either consider friends, or associates. There were many I thought were my friend and they had personal motives. I was more of their friend than they were mine. I was a friend as long I met their needs, or made them happy. Many of them turned on me for no apparent reason, after I had bent over backwards for them. I went out of my way for these people, and the only appreciation they could show me, was to lie on me or try to hurt me in one way or another. These people will try to drain you, or control you and when they see they can't hold you back or get anything out of you they become angry. They never looked at you as a friend, you were no more than an asset to them, or a ladder for them to get where they want to go. These people are very unhappy people, and they come in to make your life miserable. They come in to impose on your happiness because they are unhappy.

While you are thinking of ways to help them, they are spending more time thinking of a way to try to bring you down. You would think they would appreciate you helping them, but actually the more you help them, the more they hate you. These people will speak well of you in your face, but behind your back they can't stand you. They are mean jealous heart and evil people, that don't know how to find happiness in their lives because they go about it the wrong way. They are very dangerous people. What makes them dangerous is the time they spend with you knowing they don't care for you. They will pretend for years as if you are the greatest thing that ever happened to them, and they really don't care for you at all. People are dangerous when they can pretend to be in your corner, and no matter how long it takes, they really don't care for you. To achieve this, takes a lot of planning and scheming, you almost have to work overtime to think of ways to hurt an individual.

What's sad is many of these types of people use God to hide behind. They use some type of spirit device to keep your attention off of them. I often wonder why people would take so much time out of their lives, to try and use another person when they can have the same things. These people are no more than burglars; they will sit and watch your house for days, trying to figure when the right time to enter when you are absent. This the same way people do when they want to enter your life, with alternative motives. They are coming to steal something that does not belong to them. This thief can be male or female; it does not matter about their race, color, or creed. Not even religion matters to these people. These people find their target, and drive in on it with no mercy.

If you can hear the voice of God, he will warn you about them coming in the door. We don't want to hear because we feel these are our Godly duties to reach out and help others. We think its Satan telling us to walk away from these people. We must realize that God will have us to walk away from people also, especially when he knows they are not in your life for the right reasons. If we sit back and watch these people, they are always struggling. They can never seem to get ahead. We must pray for these people, although; they will make you very angry. It's our responsibility to pray for people that are messed up. We don't have to be around them, but that does not mean we can't pray for them? Many of these people have residue of things that have happened in their lives, and they don't know how to get rid of it. They have been living this way so long, that they have become comfortable with the way they live. They don't see anything wrong with the way they are living, some of them have been raised in houses by others with the same mentality they have. It's not for us to try and understand, or try and find out what the persons problem is our responsibility is to pray for them. We don't have to allow them to take advantage of us, this is not godly.

These people are very good at trying to make you think they are the most righteous individual on earth. They will also try to make you think that you're the problem. In actuality many of them don't know they are the problem, and many know and don't care. It's about them getting what they want, by whatever means necessary, even if it involves taking advantage of you.

Change of mind can bring great things your way. It allows you to change direction, which allows you to change the people around you. This can lead to a brand new you, new blessings added to your life. Move away from the blessing blockers!

In my life I've come into contact with many types of people, and God had to show me that people fall into different categories; even I fail in a different category than others. Some people are glorified when they see you hurt. These people are in pain, they have at some point in life, been hurt and are carrying the scars of the past. They feel that mistreating you is alright. If you looked into their past, you will discover you are not the only person they have misused. Some of them don't know any better, but some do. They don't want to see you get ahead, or do better than they have. Many times they attack those that are doing better than they are, for no apparent reason.

These people are what I call "blessing snatchers". They can see the God in you and they know you have a blessing, they are working for Satan. Their assignment is to keep you from receiving the blessing that God has for you. These people are very dangerous, they don't care how you feel, or how they hurt you. They will go to any extent to stop you, they are cunning, deceitful, and jealous people. They will pretend to be your friend, while they plan your fall. These people will speak of God, and they will speak against exactly what they are. For example; they can always analyze another person, but can't see their own problems. They are always giving you advice on how to deal with others, and they are the ones to be watched. They don't care about anyone but themselves. You can bless them in many ways, but for some reason they think you owe them, and are quick to tell you that you haven't done anything for them. These people will drain you spiritually, mentally, and physically. They get energy from draining you. They hang around until you either move them, or you have nothing to offer them. You can't ever tell these people about being wrong, because they are never wrong, they are always right. They can't see past themselves and what they are trying to accomplish. They will tell you things like they don't like gossiping people, and by the time you are out of their face, they are on the phone talking about you. They never realize what a blessing you are to them, remember you haven't been a blessing this is something you are supposed to do. In their mind you have done more harm to them than help. They are so focused on you doing them wrong, that they can't see themselves. They have not looked in at the man in the mirror, as Michael Jackson would say, "What these people don't realize is, when you mistreat a person that God has sent to bless you, God will give that person a blessing, and they will receive a lesson".

Then there are others that pretend they want your spiritual help, and all the time they are trying to get what they can out of you. In their heart they know changing is the last thing on their mind. They have a motive behind their friendship with you. They are controlling and manipulative people. These people know they have a problem and they don't want to face their problems, but they will try to make you think they want to change. They use people, and their past, to hide. It's always someone's fault other than theirs. They can never say these things are happening, because of what I'm doing. If only they could see themselves, they could then receive help for themselves. They have friends that will agree with them to keep their friendship, rather than tell them the truth.

We must then talk about what I call the Leech people. They suck the blood out of you by attaching themselves to you with their special needs. You lose focus of what's going on; because you are too busy trying to assist them with their needs. The more you help the more they need. They are very comfortable with asking for things, it's their way of life. You find many of these types of people in church.

They will usually try to attach themselves to a person in the church, or the pastor. If they can't get to the pastor, they will try to get to someone that is close to the pastor. They will go as far to join the church, to gain an inside position to beg. They use the church as an enabler. They have it in their minds that no one can see what they are doing. They are so caught up in their needs, that they walk over others to fulfill the void in them. When these people can't get what they want or they get what they want, they will disappear out of your life or the church. They will then give the church, and its members, a bad name. They begin to look for others, or another church to attach themselves to.

Then there is what I call the manipulative pilot person. They come into your life to take full control. They use all types of tactic to gain control of your life. They will tell you how much they love you, when they don't love themselves. They have done just as Paul was teaching the Romans. Romans 12:2 "and be not conformed to the world, but be ye transformed by the renewing of your mind, that you may prove what is good and acceptable and perfect will of God." They have a worldly mind, the world tells them to take care of themselves. I have run into many pastors with this attitude, false prophets and men and women of God. They teach the word of God and yet they are out of control, or they have their own situation they can't control. They look for someone that will allow them control, or someone that is weak enough to allow them control. You will find that most weak people don't want a strong person around them, if they are seeking control. They must find someone that will allow them to present themselves as the stronger person. These are the worldly minded people. The wise person is looking for a stronger person, or more powerful person than they are. They know they can be lifted up and learn something from that person. They realize that God put these people in their life for a reason.

The person of the world looks at the person as an enemy to them. This person is looked at as a person that is trying to take their place. Surprisingly they are seen as the controlling person. The controlling person spends a lot of time and energy trying to plan your life or your downfall. Then there is the aristocratic needy person. These are people that think they have everything intact, and can't see they need help. They will tell you how good God has been to them. They will show you how God has blessed them. They refuse to take Godly advice, because they don't think they need it. They are comfortable living the way they live; they have become comfortable in their struggle.

People have been sent their way countless times to assist them and they refuse. If only they would accept the help life would be less of a struggle for them. They will tell you I'm comfortable, I'm alright, and they go on through life struggling and barely making it.

Then there are the too good to ask. They will assist everyone, but when they are in need, it's embarrassing to them for people to know they are in need. They will be surrounded by people that can help them, and they refuse to ask. If you ask them why they don't ask for help, they will tell you they don't like asking for help. Matthew 7:7 "ask and it shall be given unto you, seek and you shall find; knock and it shall be opened unto you," this is the word of God. You will never receive if you don't ask how anyone would know you are in need.

We have people that are always in need of something. They don't have to be poor; many have everything they need and more. They are usually compulsive in everything they do. They never have anything to offer you, unless they are going to gain from it. They are very miserable people, and they usually have too much of everything. Their houses are over furnished and cluttered. They will rather let something dry rot than give it to someone. They buy things just so they can say they have it. They are hoarders of many things. They don't see anything wrong with the way they live. They are sad to watch.

Now there are others that God will allow in your life to become your true friends, these people will love you in spite of your flaws. They are not only there for you, but you are there for them. You'll have the friendship of David and Jonathan, a friendship not even your family members can separate. These are what you call true friends. They love you for you, and not for what you have, or what they can have. These people will often forget about themselves, to assist you. They are friends that will tell you when you are wrong, and you don't mind listening because you know they have your best interest. They see no flaws in you, even when you may have many. They will worry themselves to where they can't sleep, if you are in need. They seem to show up when you need them, even if it's just to say I love you, or share words of comfort. God has allowed me to have several of these people in my life. Many times I was not looking for them, they appeared out of nowhere. I realize that we don't get many of these people to come in our lives, so I've learned to cherish the ones that are in my life. I have had encounters with many types of people and I never knew why. There is a reason for everyone we meet in life. We don't meet people by accident, because God does not make mistakes.

Revelation: I recognize that I must move on with my life. I must put things behind me. I often have run into many types of people, since I worked as a Case manager for the mentally ill. I found that many people had problems putting things behind them. People get confused with putting things behind them, and forgetting things. I don't think anyone forgets anything that's done to them when it hurt them.

I think it's okay to remember, as long as you can function normally, and you don't hold any grudges against the person. There should be no vengeance in your heart for that person. Forgiving is a part of healing. When you don't forgive, you are putting yourself in prison, while the other person is running free. Being unforgiving, you hurt yourself, more than the other person. Once you forgive you don't forget, but it allows you to forget the hurt in a way that it does not make you angry. Putting things behind you allows you to move on with your life. Both are important in order for God to move into your life and take control of your situation.

You can't righteously go to God without forgiving first. We can't worry about what a person has done, that person knows they have wronged you. God will deal with that person in a way that you can't. We can't change people from their wicked ways; this was the biggest problem throughout the Old Testament. We can only change from our wicked ways. Many times if we apologize for something it would make our lives more pleasant to live. I've apologized to people when I know I haven't done anything. When you hold anger against someone, the other person has usually moved on with their life, and you are the last thing on their mind. You are the only one that can't sleep, or eat. You can't move forward unless you forgive, you are putting your life on hold. The word of God says, Romans 12:19-20, "Dearly beloved, avenge not yourselves, but rather give place unto wrath: for it is written. Vengeance is mine. I will repay saith the Lord. "Therefore if thine enemy hunger feed him if thirsts give him drink: for in so doing thou shalt heap coals of fire on his head." Paul is saying, the shame and guilt will be on the other man's head, not yours and maybe it will lead to repentance. Matthew 5:44 tells us "But I say unto you, love your enemies bless them that curse you, do good to them that hate you, and pray for them which despite fully use you, and persecute you." Jesus says it doesn't matter how much they hate you we must love them; he says they hated him first.

People think that you must be friends or hang around people to love them, but you can love a person from a distance. You don't have to be around them. The most important thing is to show love in their presence. There will be many readers of this book that will be angry with me, because of its content.

The devil hates to be exposed, he hates when the covers is pulled off of him. Once covers are pulled off, a person is now able to repent or change from their wicked ways. Rather than change from their wicked ways, many become angry. I realize that I wasn't received by everyone when I was in world, and I won't be received once I've made a change in my life. Matthew 10:44 say, "And whosoever shall not receive you, not hear your words, when ye depart out of that house or city, "shake the dust off your feet." That scripture allows you to know you will not be received by everyone. You must shake the dust off your feet and keep moving. Jesus was hated without a cause, and he died for their sins. It was his own people that hung him. Why is it that people think they would be treated any better. I've had people that stop speaking to me for no reason, and these were the same people that I tried to help. Now am I supposed to worry about these people, or move on? I have done what God has required of me, they're the ones that have the problem not me.

Everything happens for a reason. Maybe God wanted you'll to separate for whatever reason it may be. Let it go and move on with your life. Life is too short for you to sit still and worry about people and their problems. Their problems shouldn't become your problems.

When people are pulling on you and wearing you down, you should remove yourself from the situation. You're not being helpful. You are creating for yourself an extra burden, which you don't have to be bothered with. People come into your life for various reasons, some for good and some for bad. You'll see these people years up the road, and they are in the same position, leaning and pulling on someone else. Let these people go, give them direction and let them walk on their own. They don't need you they want what you have what they have and that is misery. If they really want to make it, they would take the advice that you have given them. Yes, it may be a struggle, but it's not easy for anyone. If they are struggling and you're trying to assist them, it makes your journey a lot harder, if they are refusing to move on their own. You are dragging dead weight around. Imagine holding someone's hand that's willing to walk with you, that walk is easy when they are walking with you. They can even be assistance to you if you fall, or vice versa. But, if you are walking with someone that is dragging, they will pull you down. If you fall who will pick you up? More than likely the person that has been dragging will pick themselves up, step over you, move on looking for someone else to pull down. That's why it's important to pray before you make a big decision, to assist someone.

You hear many people saying "God said this", many of them don't know the voice of God any more than they know their dogs bark. There are many people reading into your life, claiming to be prophets. If the prophecies do not come to past, you know God didn't give them the word. All the prophets in the bible prophecies came to past. God will give you confirmation on anything you want to know. Read your word so that no one can tell you anything, and if someone gives you a word, listen to what they have to give you. Many people take advice as criticism. They don't receive the advice, because they have heard it before or they know it's true. Many times someone has already told them the same thing you're telling them. Constructive criticism is to build you, not bring you down. When God sends you a friend cherishes, embrace, and thank God for that friend.

There are many people that have never had a friend they can call their own. Friends are special gifts, and they are not to be misused, or mistreated. Treat your friends as if they may be the last friends in your life, you never know, they may be. God send the people in your life that he wants to be there. We must be careful because Satan will also send people into your life, that he wants to be there. That is why people should know Satan when they see him. If you stay connected with God he will warn you of the people that surround you, and he will remove them.

When people pull up weeds they grow back fast, and begin to spread and destroy the life around them. There are people that are like weeds, they stay around just to squeeze the life out of others and spread their poison. If we could have the endurance of a weed we would be an awesome people. The more you are mowed, the more you grow, the deeper you are rooted in God and the more you spread God's love to others.

CHAPTER 16

God Was Still Preparing Me

I never knew what my gifts were. I never knew why God had me to begin to write the prisoners from my home. I never questioned it; I just did what God told me to do. He told me to name the ministry, "You Are Not Forgotten International Pen Pal Ministry." God gave me the name. I never knew why he gave me the name until I began to have encounters with people of all walks of life. I worked out at the hospital as a Nurse Care Technician. I had never worked in a hospital before. I worked in the Northern Suburb of Chicago, therefore; there were not many blacks there at the hospital. I was placed on the Neurology/med surgery floor dealing with strokes and head injuries. When I was being interviewed for the position, the director of nursing and I had a very good talk. I explained to her that I had never worked in the hospital, so everything was new to me. She told me she would put me on the day shift with two good workers.

So my journey began and what a journey I had. The two ladies she assigned me to work with were demons from hell. They never trained me, they didn't like me. They told me they didn't know why the director of nursing chose them to train a Black girl. Yes they were white. They asked me why you didn't get a job with your own. Why did you come out here? I would look at them and try my best to remain calm. In my mind I was thinking they really don't know who they are bothering, but I'm going to ignore them.

I went to the director of nursing and told her the things they were saying to me, and I also told her I was not being trained. I told her I had been there a month, and everything I learned came from others, or the three ladies on second shift. She told me she would put me on second shift, but I had to wait until the next schedule came out, and it would take about a month. Did I go through plenty abuse in thirty days! They went to the director of nursing, and told her that she should fire me, because I wasn't fit for the job. They didn't know I had already talked to the director of nursing.

One day I was called in a room to assist them in turning a lady that had hip surgery, she had clamps in her hip. I was turning the lady real easy trying to be gentle, they told me move you're too slow. They flipped the lady over so hard, as if nothing was wrong with her. The lady screamed in pain and she began to cry. I was feeling the pain of the lady. They gave me tissue, laughed, and left the room. I stayed in the room with the lady apologizing for what had just happened. I began to pray for the lady. I told her to report them, I told her I was the only black on the floor and no one would pay me any attention. The lady reported it and I was called in as a witness. I told the truth of what happened, the two ladies received a write up, and they were furious with me. The heat was on, so they thought. They didn't know I was ready for them. I was still angry about how they treated the lady.

I came in to work one morning, and discovered everything had been taken out of my locker, and placed on the floor. I shared lockers with the Polish girl, who was the ring leader. She had put all my belongings on the floor. She and the other girl were standing in the locker room watching, and laughing. I begin to pray for myself, because I didn't want to lose my job. I knew once I went there, I wouldn't know how to get home. (My mind would leave) I began to pick my personal items off the floor. The Polish girl waited until I put them in the locker, then she pulled them back out, and put them back on the floor. Before I knew it, I grabbed her in the collar; I had my right hand in position to put her to sleep. I told her as her friend watched in fear, "I'm not who you think I am I'm not the person you want to bother". "You don't know me, but you will get to know me." "I will hurt you or maybe kill you". "I'm fed up with both of you, and this will be the last warning I will give you." The other girl ran to get the supervisor. She told her I was beating the lady. The Polish girl was still being smart. She told me, "You don't know who you are bothering, I put roof on my house." I told her," I would be the one to take the roof off the house." I told her I came to work and not make friends, as long as she didn't put her hands on me, we could get along. The DON (Director of Nursing) came running in the locker room. This time I had my stethoscope in my hand. She asked me, "What are you going to do with that". "Are you going to hit her with it?" I told her if I was to do anything it would be to choke her with it. The DON changed my locker, I begged her not to. I wanted to stay in the locker with the Polish woman. The DON also changed my shift. I screamed "Hallelujah!" I was so happy.

The women on second shift were so nice. They were two women that were from India and one was a Mexican. They would teach me in the thirty minutes we shared, during the change of shift. I was assigned to a lady I had been taking care of all week. She was 36 years old, she had gone to Vegas for her anniversary and she suffered a stroke. I was always assigned to care for the worse patients. She was in bad shape, when I first start taking care of her. She was lifeless and had to have total care around the clock. Her husband and two small sons would come to see her. I asked the husband did he want to pray and he agreed to pray. The first day I started taking care of her, in two days she opened her eyes and began assisting me. I would talk to her; I did this even when she was in a coma. I would pray over her every day. The weekend came around and it was time for me to be off. The two trouble makers were laughing, because they thought she was a hard job. But, I was really enjoying taking care of her. When I returned to work, she had gotten worse. This was my last day on the first shift. I went to her room I was totally out done. I asked the nurse, "What happened she was doing so well the other day?" I prayed for her and did what I had to do for her, I went to lunch. While I was on the elevator, a strange feeling came over me; a voice whispered in my ear say she is gone. Sure enough when I arrived on the floor she was dead. She was the first person I had to die in my care. I was torn apart I cried as if I had lost a family member. We were the same age; I was assigned to cleaning her up and placing her in a body bag. I finished early I asked to leave early; I was not any good for the rest of the day. I asked myself over and over, what went wrong after I left for the weekend. Her death bothered me for weeks.

Each time I passed her room I cried, and would get a strange feeling. My journey on second shift was much easier. I would rotate between first and second shift. The three ladies on second shift had trained me, and I was an expert in thirty days. I was assigned to an elderly lady, she was 90 years old. She had one son and no one wanted to care for the lady, because they said the son was very mean. I knew I was going to get the patient if no one wanted her.

One day I was taking care of her and the son arrived, came in demanding things, I didn't say anything because I knew his mother was dying. I asked him, "Would you like me to pray for your mother?" He looked at me and began to cry. He told me yes please pray for her, and he asked could he join. I prayed for his mother and afterward, he began to share with me that he was the only child. He told me he and his mother had lived together all of his life. He told me he had come to the hospital several times and his mother didn't have enough cover on her, she hadn't been turned, and the people thinks that he's not supposed to say anything. He said, "You're the nicest nurse I've met up here in the last eight days." I thanked him and gave him a hug. After he left the other nurses were laughing saying things like, "I know you are glad he's gone, I know he worried you and you are tired." I told them I enjoyed myself and I had no problem with him. Later the D.O.N came in she told me, that I would be assigned to the lady every day. Her son called and he didn't want anyone other than me assisting his mother. Later the phone rang it was the lady's son, he told me he had talked to the top administrator and if I see anyone taking care of her while I'm there to give him a call. He said he could sleep at night knowing his mother was being taken care of. He gave me his phone number.

The following day his mother passed away. The son arrived with a handmade pillow. I thought what I he going to do with that his mother is dead. He gave me the pillow and told me he would never forget me, I would always stay in his heart. He thanked me for taking good care of his mother. He told me that I had made his mother's transition much easier for him. He said, "God is truly going to bless you, because you are an angel and God sent". These same words were written on the pillow. He cried, and so did I, we both stood in the room crying. What they thought were the worse patients, turned out to be my best patients. I was then given a Russian patient, he couldn't speak any English. When he left the hospital he was praying in English. I had fun teaching him English. I was assigned to a Spanish man that spoke no English, he taught me Spanish, and I taught him English.

My job was getting better every day. The nurses would ask me which room I wanted, I would tell them give me the patient that no one wants. They would look at me like I was crazy and I would smile at them. I looked forward to going to work, just to see who my patient would be that day.

I was assigned a 21 year old man. He had taken some drugs and jumped out of a moving ambulance, they thought he had brain damage. He stayed in a coma for two weeks. I would go to his room and pray for him, and talk to him. I would introduce myself each time I entered the room. I came to work on day and God had answered my prayed he was out of the coma. The nurses were calling for the doctor, because he was fighting everyone that entered the room. One nurse looked at me and said, "Veronica your hands will be full today he's assigned to you, be careful because he's violent." I smiled and told her thanks.

I entered the room and introduced myself as I did every day he was in a coma. He stopped cursing and got very quiet he began to stare at me watching every move I made. He then said, "So you're the nice lady huh?" I turned around and asked him what he meant by that. He told me, "While I was in the coma I had terrible headaches, but when you walked into the room and introduced yourself my headaches would stop". "I heard everything that was said in this room". "I heard the nurses say nasty things about me". "I even heard you praying for me". "I want to thank you, because you could have been like the rest of them". I was standing looking at him in shock, I was speechless. He didn't allow anyone to take care of him except for me. Look at God! He promised me he would find a church to join, once he got out of the hospital. I asked the Lord, "What is going on I was being used to take care of the patients no one wanted to be bothered with why is this Lord?"

I was then assigned to a patient, we will call her Deb. She had a brain tumor, she couldn't walk they were about to remove the tumor. I took care of Deb before she went to surgery she was a 49 year old Italian, I got a chance to meet her husband and children they were very nice. About ten days after her surgery, she looked at me and said, "you silly girl they are sending me to the rehab floor. They are going to teach me to walk. Would you come see me since it's on the same floor?" I told her I would come and see her; I then asked if I could rub her down. As I rubbed her, I was praying for her at the same time. I looked at her and told her," you will walk today". She looked at me and asked, "Do you think I can walk, because I want to walk so badly." I told her get up and let's walk; I told her if you think you can walk so do I. She got out of the bed and we walked to the bathroom, it was slow but she did it. While we were in the bathroom her husband came in, I told him Debbie was in the bathroom. He asked, "How did she get there?" I told him she walked; he sat down and was speechless. She came out the bathroom and told her husband, this silly girl have me walking. I told her God has her walking not me. In a couple of weeks she was going home. She asked for my phone number, she wanted to stay in contact with me. She called me two weeks later and told me the tumor in her head came back, and there was nothing that could be done. She wanted me to come by her house on the weekend; she wanted to prepare me some of her home made chocolate cookies. She had been bragging on her chocolate chip cookies, and how good they were. I agreed to visit her Saturday.

That weekend I couldn't wait to get to her house, I was rushing to leave the hospital. I couldn't make it that Saturday I called her to let her know I would make it Sunday after I got off work, she told me that was good she had the batter of cookies ready to be placed in the oven. When I got off work Sunday I headed to her house, I couldn't wait to see Debbie, she sounded so happy on the phone. I went to the door her husband opened the door, he told me to come in and pointed to the room where Debbie was, and said she's waiting on your arrival. I went to the room and Debbie was lying in the bed, she was in a coma. I begin to speak to her and a tear came down one side of her face. I stood there wondering why her husband answered the door as if everything was OK; I wasn't expecting her to be in a coma. She was breathing heavy, she never opened her eyes. I was there for about five minutes before she passed away. Her husband came into the room, he told me she waited on me, and spoke of me until she went into the coma. She told him "I'm waiting on that crazy girl", that's what she called me. I stood by her bed in disbelief, I was so anxious to see her, but not in this condition. I felt as if I had lost a family member, she wanted to live so badly.

I sat and watched as the family arrived, her husband asked me to stay for the celebration. What a celebration. They came in with food, wine, bread, and pasta. This was something new to me I had never seen anything like it. The food was delicious, and the wine was good too. They ate and went into the room to visit her. I was sitting at the end of the table where I could see directly in the room. I really couldn't enjoy myself looking at a deceased woman in the bed, while trying to eat dinner.

Her husband gave me a bag the bag contained the cookie dough for the double chocolate chip cookies. He told me she wanted me to have the cookies. I carried the dough home and immediately put them in the oven, they were the best cookies I had ever eaten.

I had yet another encounter at the hospital I was assigned to care for a 21 year old male. He had been in a motorcycle accident, an 18 wheeler decided to do a U-turn with him behind it and he went into the side of the truck almost taking his head off. He had brain surgery. It was no surprise to me, as I mentioned before I was always assigned the patients no one wanted.

They thought they were hurting me, but they were blessing me with some of the greatest patients in the world. I really enjoyed them. I would go into his room and talk with him. He regretted riding the bike. He told me he went against his father's will. He wanted me to meet his family they were Romanian. He had twelve sisters and brothers and he was third from the youngest.

I happened to be in the room when the family arrived, they walked in the door praying. My mouth flew open when they begin to speak in tongues. The mother told me they were members of a Pentecostal church. They were a beautiful family. He became one of my special patients. I would spend my lunch in his room, reading the bible to him and praying with him. He was getting better every day, he begin to look for me. He would call the nurse's station, if I was late getting to his room. When it was time for him to go home, he cried. He didn't want to leave me behind. I loved my patients, and they all loved me.

I was assigned to a patient they couldn't determine what was wrong with him. His mother sat in the room crying every day. He was in pain, and he would become confused at times. I read his chart. The doctors had done every type of test on him, and still they couldn't find out what was wrong with him. I wrote his symptoms down on a sheet of paper. I wanted to go home to look on the internet, to see if I could help out.

That evening I got on the internet, and an ad came up on the side, it was talking about a disease that many doctors over look. In order to find the disease there are special test that had to be done. I begin to read the symptoms and they were exactly like my patients. I begin to investigate how to treat the disease, and I wrote everything down. I went to the hospital the next day, and asked the doctor had they checked the patient for the disease, he told me" no". I asked him would he consider checking him for the disease. I showed him the paper I had printed off the internet, he sat down and begin to read the papers. I got a page later that evening, when I arrived there were about six doctors reading the papers.

The neurologist told me they would begin to run the test on the patient the next day. The next day the test was run, and when the results came back, they found out this was the disease the patient had. His mother was so happy, she hugged me and cried. She told me 'God sent you to find the cure for my son". I told her give all the glory to God. I was so happy for her and her son. She tried to give me money, but I refused it. She then asked for my address, she wanted to send me a card. I gave her my address.

A week later I received her card in the mail, when I opened the card there were five one hundred dollar bills inside, and her phone number. I called her and asked her why she sent the money, and I told her I was going to return the money to her. She begged me not to return the money; she told me that God told her to bless me.

Be nice to the less fortunate. You never know who God has put in your path and why. The word of God says, "Don't forget to show hospitality to strangers, for some who have done this have entertained angels without realizing it

I went from working in the hospitals to working with mentally and physically children and adults. Working with the children was an experience, many of them could never express their love but you could feel the love. They had a way of showing their love although they couldn't speak. It was amazing how I would know what they liked and what they didn't like. I really enjoyed working with the children.

I also like working with the adults, they were beautiful. I loved dressing and making them look pretty. I would give them a mirror, and watch their expressions. There were many that were blind, and they would calm down when they hear my voice. I would to them and read stories to them. They were so beautiful; you must have a passion for these types of people to work with them it's not easy work.

I then went on to work with the mentally ill. I found this work interesting, because many of the clients were normal people to me. Many of the people were those that had taken a fall and needed assistance getting back on their feet. I enjoyed speaking with them and assisting them. Many became attached to me, at one place of employment God told me it was time to leave.

I went in with my resignation, and I announced to the clients that I was leaving; not knowing it would cause chaos. The clients begin to, cry they held on to me I had to pry their hands loose. One client got out of her wheelchair with her fist balled up, she looked me in my eyes and said," you can't leave us we don't have anyone that care for us. Who do we have if you leave? Tell me you won't leave me Veronica." In the meantime the others were holding my arms and legs crying. I couldn't do anything but stand there and cry. I felt so bad for them, I couldn't stop crying. I went home and prayed that God would send someone to care for them. I used to hold a bible study at the facility, along with being a Certified Nurse's Assistant. When I held the bible study, many times I would have to bring extra chairs in the room. The bible study would turn into a counseling session; they needed someone to talk to. I heard many stories, and begin to understand what sent them over the edge.

One of the stories that made me sick was told by a young lady in the facility. She was 36 and she cried all the time, many of the workers would get angry at her for crying every day. She asked could she talk with me and I sat with her. I asked why she cries so much, and she began to cry again. She told me ever since she was 9 years old, she had been abused. She told me her eight brothers would fight every night, because they wanted to be first to have sex with her. She said there were many days all eight would have sex with her. They would take turns. She told me there was never a day at least five of them didn't have sex with her. She hated to go home from school. If she didn't come home on time, her oldest brother would punish her by having anal sex with her. She said this went on from the age of nine, until she was fourteen, when she ran away from home. She said her mother was out in the streets, and didn't care about her and her sister. Her sister was three years older than she was, and she left home at 13 leaving her there. She told me the reason she cry so much, is because of the hurt and pain. She felt as if she was dirty and could never be clean. I couldn't help but cry with her, and hug her. I had a chance to minister to her and pray for her. She would come looking for me every day for a hug. My heart went out to her I cried a many of nights for her.

My encounter too many people that were diagnosed as mentally ill, gave me different thoughts for each one. There were many that just needed love and a helping hand. There were others that were being given the psychotropic medication and the treatment was doing more harm for them than good. The clients had been brain washed to believe they needed the medicine, they were afraid to not take them. The medicine were making them worse that what they really were. They had begun to depend on the medicine to survive.

We must understand the pharmaceutical industry is a million dollar industry, and they pay the doctors kickbacks at the end of the year, to pass their medication out. There are some clients that need the medications to survive, but there are many that don't need the medicine. There are some very good doctors out here, that only give the clients enough to stabilize them, and there are some in it for the money. We must use our better judgment when our love ones are being treated for anything. We must make sure they are getting the best treatment offered. I had a chance to work with the substance abuse population; it was heartbreaking to see how they were being mistreated.

Every place I worked, the residents, were at the mercy of others, they were mistreated by the workers. I often got in trouble trying to defend the clients. I was even fired from a job. I will not work anywhere, and watch people be mistreated. Sorry I have to say something. I have seen the elderly be mistreated, me and the worker were about to fight because I wouldn't allow her to mistreat the elderly woman. What was so hurting many of them were being mistreated by people that called themselves Christians? They would listen to gospel music every day, and would break their necks to go to church. I worked at a place for women with addictions, and one of the workers was so mean and evil. She would refuse the clients food, snacks, then curse them out. She would then go to the office and turn on gospel music, and sing every song on the radio. This woman had been in the church 40 years, I wondered why she was there. This bothered me I couldn't take it I had to do some serious praying. I went to her after she had run one of the women out of the center; I pulled her to the side and told her about herself. I told her that, "she didn't have a relationship with God and it was a shame she was spending so much time in church to go to hell. The singing in the choir, and the singing gospel wasn't going to get her in. She had no love in her heart, therefore, there was no Jesus in her and she was a hypocrite. She went and told the coordinator on me, who was a Muslim.

The coordinator looked at me as a threat coming in the door, and she didn't like me. They looked for every reason in the world to get rid of me and they did. Well they thought they were getting rid of me, but God had already told me that my assignment was up. I never looked at my places of employment as jobs; I looked at them as assignments given by God. One week after being removed God gave me a check for the rest of my life, my ex-husband retired from his job. Trust in the word of God and he will never leave you alone. God always take care of those who are doing his work.

Revelation: We never know why we go through things, or why we encounter things in our lives. We don't know why God take us through things that others will never go through. We watch people walk down the streets talking themselves, looking in the garbage cans, sleeping on the streets. We never think this may be this person's comfort zone. Many such as the young lady I mentioned find their peace in the streets. I imagine the 9 year old that was being raped by her brothers every day, wish she could sleep in the streets. I'm quite sure she would have felt she was in a more peaceful place than being home. When we assume everyone is the cause of their own fall, and we have no sympathy for them. We turn our heads away from them and walk past as if they are not there. We don't know what these people are going through, or have been through. We shake our head at the people who seem to be angry at the world, and never ask why you are angry. We look down at the woman that is sleeping with many men and never have time to listen to her story. We look down at the person that is doing drugs, never asking or wondering what made them turn to the drug. We watch the kid that is giving everyone a problem in the neighborhood and in school, do we ever wonder what goes on at home. There are many sick people walking the streets, mentally and physically.

When I took time out with the seniors, the mentally ill, the physically ill, or even those that were in the hospital I couldn't do anything but thank God because it could have been me. Yes, Lord there I go if you had not saved me from that hurt and pain. When I took care of the patients in the hospital I treated them as if they were one of my relatives, and I practiced this everywhere I worked with those that were in need. There are workers that have jobs and treat the people as if they have done something to them, or they don't like the person. They must realize this could have been them and if they don't want the job, they should find another place of employment.

I can remember walking into the emergency room barely being able to breathe. As I approached the emergency room nurse, I coughed. She began to scream at me. She told me to find somewhere else to go with the coughing. I couldn't understand her, because I covered my mouth. I looked at her and asked her for some napkins, she threw them at me. This is when I lost it. I asked why was she still working, why haven't she retired and let someone that is happy to work have the job. I told her if all you are worried about is a cough, what is that you so when people come in bleeding. I told her I came here to be seen by a doctor not to hear her mouth, I was feeling bad enough. If she had a problem treating me like a human being to find someone that could and to shut her mouth right now because I was not feeling well.

There was another nurse that came to wait on me, because I didn't want the nurse to touch me. After I was seen by the doctor, I found out I had bronchitis and double pneumonia. Now do you think I needed anything other than what I already had bothering me? People working with the public must realize that their job is to give service, not beat the person down. When people are not feeling well, their thinking is off; the entire body chemistry is out of balance. When we give a service to others we are expected to give them the best service we can provide. We don't know what we can do that may trigger the other person to react in a way that is not normal for them. Our hands represent service, and if we used them more than we use our mouths we could get more done.

We as children of God regardless of your religion should show love to those that are in need, hurting, or are lacking in any area that keeps them from moving on with their lives. It's us that can make a difference in the lives of those that are in need, it does not matter what their needs are. For many people bad behaviors such as: drugs, alcohol, and any other addiction are no more than self-medicating. They do things to cover up their hurt and pain, or things they can't deal with. This is when we are mandated by God to step in to give service to those that want it. We are supposed to reach out them and lift them up, give them direction, pray and love on these people.

There are many that don't want help; you can't make them get help when they don't want it. I don't care how you argue, or punish them if they are not ready they are not going to accept the help. Maybe you are not the one that God want to assist this person; God has just who he wants to bring a person out of bondage. I will give you a good example, have you ever tried to tell a person something and they refuse to listen to you? Then another person comes along and tell them the same thing, they listen and follow their direction. The other person is who God designated to reach out to that person.

There are many that call themselves recovery, but they operate like boarding homes. They allow the men and women to pay their rent and are no assistance to them when it comes to the problem. They allow the men and women to stay in the recovery homes for years without a care plan for the person. They are collecting money each month for them to receive a service they are not receiving. It's all about the money not the care of the individual. If you are operating a boarding home renting rooms, then say you are a boarding home. It's not fair to the person to think they are going to receive a service and the service is not offered to them.

God sent me to the hospital and other places to work, because he had a plan and it was already worked out. He protected me every step of the way, because he had something for me to do. God will not let anyone stop you when he has even taken care of you after your assignment is up. I'll job is to do what is expected of us by God and he will reward you. Each assignment I was given God would let me know in advance when it was over, so I knew I was going to face adversary when the time was near. The word of God says," Touch not mine anointed, and do my prophets no harm." This scripture let me know I had nothing to worry they about, I don't care what people try to do to you they can't touch you and eventually they will pay. I really enjoyed the places I worked and was able to pray and bless people that were not able to help themselves. I enjoyed the smiles on their faces and watching God heal the people. I enjoyed helping people, whether it was ministering or praying for them.

Many people working in places to give service to others should consider other places of employment if it's not what they want to do. People have a right to have good service when they come to be served and not be treated as if they are not important. If the people didn't come to your place of employment you wouldn't have a job.

Many places are under staffed and they are putting pressure on their employees such as: Nursing homes, hospitals and etc. Nursing homes will give a CNA 20 clients to care for, there is no way one person can give a client what is expected to give. This causes the employee to become frustrated and they direct their anger towards the client. For this reason alone I refuse to work at a nursing home, I don't won't to work where I can't give the clients my best. It bothers me to see people suffer when I can't assist them and it bothers me to see people suffer at the hands of others. It even bothers me to be around people that don't mind watching others suffer. When people can't help themselves, it's up to us to assist them and make them as comfortable as possible.

Many of these people have assisted people throughout their life and they don't deserve to be treated so badly I continue to pray for people that depend on others to assist them. People don't know what a blessing it is to have a kind person to assist them. I thank God for his direction in my life, all he's done for me and all he's going to do for me.

Many think they are getting away with something, because no one sees them, so they think. When you least expect God will show you who's in charge of things. You will pay for what you have done to others. God does not like to see his children hurt by anyone. Your pay will be worse than they punishment you put on others. You need to ask God for forgiveness of your sins. I often wonder does it make people feel big to take advantage of others who can't help themselves. I would feel very small, if this is all the control that I can have. This does not make you a great person, but a very weak person. I don't consider you a man or a woman. You put on a front before others, pretending to be someone that you're not. My question will be to you. Are you the same person when no one's watching?

CHAPTER 17

God Provides Shelter

The things we go through in sometimes hit us so hard, that we feel we are alone. Many times I felt I was all alone in my different circumstances, and I had to remember the words of God to make it through. There were people in my life that made my circumstances worse than what they were. God always had someone to come and lead me out of my storm. After I got out of the storm I developed a passion for those that were going through the things I had been through. I begin to place myself in places to assist those that were in need.

Many times I would get myself in trouble trying to assist those that were being mistreated by their oppressors. As we know, much of our depressions come from those that are sent to help us, or those who claim to be of assistance in bringing us out of our dilapidated circumstances. I have witnessed many agencies that made the depressed state of others a living hell for their benefit. It was not only done by the staff, but by the administrators.

Many times the people that were in charge knew what was going on, and turned their head. Some of the places were places I worked, and others were places I just happened to come into these places. I will share some of my experiences with you.

There was one place that I worked for place that I worked for, that we dealt with the mentally ill and seniors. The staff was so mean and evil towards the clients. If the client didn't do what they were told, the staff would hold back the client's lunch. The lunches were used as a way to control and manipulate the clients.

One day while at work, I walked out of the restroom, just in time to see one of the staff strike one of the clients. I asked her why she hit the client, she told me because she was moving too slow and why are worried about a white woman anyway. I told her I pray I never saw her hitting on another client. I also told her that God was going to deal with her for hitting the client. She laughed at me. It wasn't six months later she died.

I watched how they talked about the clients out loud embarrassing them. There was no need in going to tell management, he was just as bad as the staff was.

The worse thing I had seen happen was one of the clients had an asthma attack. It was about 100 degrees outside. They made the man wait an hour for a bus to pick him up, instead of calling an ambulance. I went to the manager, and asked why they hadn't called an ambulance. I was told it was cheaper to wait on his bus, and if anyone of the staff called they would lose their job. I stepped to the side and called his nursing facility and told them what was happening by this time the bus had pulled up.

That following Monday the man didn't show up, I was told by the other clients he had died. I was really upset. I raced into the manager's office, and told them they allowed the man to die. The assistant manager told me, "I don't know what you are worried about he had a large tumor in his stomach, he was going to die anyway." I told her he was black and she didn't care. I then recanted my statement and I told her you'll are all about the money, you'll don't care about anyone. She sat there with a smile on her face. I could have strangled her. The next week I was called into the office to receive a write up for taking off when my grandfather was in the hospital. I knew this was her way of getting back at me, for challenging her. She asked me to sign the write up; I took the papers, tore them up, threw them on the floor, then looked at her and smiled. I wanted her to come at me, but I think she knew better she didn't move. I left out the office and slammed the door as hard as I could. I didn't care anymore what they did, I was angry about the man dying. I eventually resigned, and went to the state representative and reported them.

The following Monday inspectors were all over the place. They were even investigating the staff that had set up a candy store, and would open on the day the clients would receive five dollars for coming to the program. The clients would leave without a dime, because the five the company gave them they would get it back. When I resigned I was told don't file for unemployment, because I wouldn't get it. God told me to go and file and I followed his instructions.

Watch how God works, on the day the unemployment office was calling them for my conference is the day the inspectors were all over the office. There was no answer, therefore; I received my benefits. When they realized I was receiving the benefits, I was getting my last check. God is an awesome God! This was the second time I was told I wouldn't receive the benefits, and God said yes.

I worked in a nursing facility in Tennessee part-time, I had been working for about two weeks, when I noticed an Afro American client had not been given a bath since had been there. I asked why the man never got a shower and was told he doesn't get visitors and he's too heavy. I asked the director of Nursing could the man be assigned to me the next day and she did just that. I made him my last client, because I knew I was going to have to work. I entered his room and got a Hoya lift to get him out of bed, because he was very heavy and couldn't walk. I took him to the shower it took me three hours to get him clean each time I thought I was finished there was more dirt. I was so angry I had tears coming down my face. I shaved the man, oiled him down, and prayed for him. I begin to look at the photos on the wall. I then realized this man was the first Black police officer in that town, and wow this is how he had been repaid. I looked over at him; he smiled, and gave me a thumb up. I went into the director's office and told her how filthy he was, and that she should be ashamed of herself.

She told me" if you are that concerned you take care of him". I was so tired but I felt good, I decided to take care of him every day I worked. I wanted to make sure he was kept clean when I was there, felt like he deserved it.

I went to work for an agency as a case manager I loved the job because it entailed assisting the mentally ill. I saw some of the clients being mistreated once again. Money was missing out of their accounts, talked down, to by some of the staff. The company had financial problems, and they stop paying. The employees found out we meant nothing to them. They wanted to add more work for us to do, after they didn't pay us. People were being fired for not coming to work, it was crazy. We were being told not to come, and ask about our money. I thought these people were crazy. They had nothing to say to us as employees. I decided it was time for me to resign. I couldn't take the pressure. I was six checks behind in pay. I went and resigned. Then I went to the vice president's office. I went in and he asked me what he could do for me, I told him "you know exactly why I'm here." He then told me "I can't give you all your checks", I stopped him. I told him, "I didn't come here to bargain, negotiate, or make a deal I want my money today." He left out of the office and returned with all my money. I didn't have the trouble everyone claimed they had. I couldn't understand why they didn't lay us off. I felt we should have been given an option. We were treated as if we should be happy to work for them, even when we weren't getting paid. They were very arrogant about not paying us. I didn't have time for the mess, and yes, I received my unemployment benefits, God always provided.

Well I have one more subject to cover and it concerns the recovery homes, shelters, and the homes for the mentally ill being run by ill people. I will start with a men shelter I came into contact with. The men that were running the shelter were placed there by the board members of a church. Yes, I said a church!

The men that were running the shelter were very shady. They were vultures, using drugs, taking the money, clothes, and personal belongings of the men. The food and clothes that were being donated to the shelter, the men would never see the items, unless the people served the food. The food would be bought in and as soon as the ministry would leave, the facilitators would take the food to their car or to a car waiting. They would then serve the men hot dogs. This is the same thing that happened when clothes was bought in.

The facilitators thought they owned the shelter, and they treated it as such. Some of the facilitators were the payees of some of the men receiving Social Security benefits, and they would take what they wanted, and give the men what they wanted to give them. They would tell the men if they reported them, they would be put out of the shelter. The facilitators didn't mind you telling the board, because the head was their pastor. They were deacons in the church, how sad they were. I often wondered what they prayed for when they attended service. I wondered did they even have a conscious, and how could they sleep at night. I prayed for the men to receive help, and God sent help. The facilitators were replaced with new ones. Thank God he answered my prayer.

Now if you think that was bad, check out what goes on in many of the recovery homes that are run by individuals for profit and non-profit. The men and women are charged anywhere from $300-$400 a month. Most of the clients are receiving SSI benefits, and the owner of the recovery home is the payee.

The owner is supposed to take the rent out, and give the rest to the client. Instead they may give the client $100.00; some have kept the entire check, leaving the client without anything and many times hungry. If the client calls the police, the owner would refuse to let them in. This would leave the client locked out, unable to obtain their personal items until the next check. If they cancel the payee, the client would be made to pay to receive their personal items. If a person is caught doing drugs, he has to pay double. Now do you actually think the person that's running the house cares if they use drugs? The more dominating clients were taking advantage of the weak clients. They have their money, food, and personal belongings taken from them.

Many are living in fear in these places. Now let's talk about many of the female houses that are being run by men. The owner deducts money off their rent for sexual favors, he have his choice of the women, if they allow him. Now I want it to be known that the owners I knew went to church every Sunday. The church had a recovery ministry, and this is where they would get their clients from. They would sit in church as if they are faithful members, to get the clients into their homes. It's really a sad thing to watch. The thing that baffled me most was to find out, that neither the state nor the city regulates these facilities, because they are considered for profit. Those that are not for profit no on watches them; there is really no one to report them to. Many are politically connected, and they give political donations so they could get help when they are in need of it. This why the owners are not worried about it, if you tell them they are going to be reported.

I pray that some type of regulation is set in place, so that these places can be monitored. Many of the owners are just pocketing the money, and are living like kings. They are taking advantage of the client, not caring if the person gets better or not. They are driving nice cars, and living in plush homes at the expense of those they are supposed to help. I hate to put it this way, but many are better off on the streets than being in the recovery homes.

How would I ever think the state would care, when they are making the prisoners pay to see a doctor, or dentist. They must pay the money out of the $10.00 they receive each month. Then they must wait up to six months to see the doctor, many have died waiting to see the doctor. I'm not saying the prisoners deserve special treatment, but the tax payers are paying for this. We are billed for the doctors and dentist, and they are allowing the men to die.

I have a friend that worked for a company for 13 years, he was second in seniority. He had mental problems, but he could hold a job. He begins to have problems with a couple of the men on his job, one of them was touching his genitals, and the others would laugh. When the company was ready to get rid of him, they offered him a layoff. He accepted it to get away from the harassment. They then offered to give him the 401k he had earned while working. He didn't know any better and accepted it. He's now without a job, they allowed him to receive unemployment. He thought he was being laid off, and they took advantage of him. His nephew was also beating him up every week and taking most of his pay check, until I moved him near me and put an order of protection against his nephew. He was taking all but maybe $50.00 to $100 dollars from him and sometimes more. He was taking his money as if he had worked for it, until I got involved.

Everyone that knew about it thought it was funny. I didn't find it funny at all and I took action. I wanted to file a complaint with EEO before he left his place employment, and he begged me not to. He was afraid he would be fired, or there would be retaliation. I really felt sorry for him, how could your relative be so low down to do this to him. He should have been protecting his uncle.

I wrote a play about the company where the patient was struck, before I left. The play ended with the company closing down. I was amazed that almost everything I wrote in the play happened just like I wrote it. The company closed down a few years later, and there was nothing they could do about it. The only thing that has not come to pass, is one of the employees have not come to me asking for employment. The name of the play was "Behind the mask". God is awesome! He will reveal things to you without you having any knowledge, of what's going on. I never knew the play was prophetic. I remember telling my supervisor, that when I and another employee leave the place will close down. I told him he should be happy we are working there, because we are the reason the place is staying open. He laughed at me. The other employee left not long after I did, and it wasn't long before they closed down. The power of words God is awesome!

Revelation: There many mistreated in many facilities, that are being paid to give them service. I pray that the government will put stricter rules and regulations over these places. There is a need for a board set in place to watch the recovery homes, whether they are not for profit or for profit. People should also keep an eye on their love ones, when they are placed in the different facilities.

If you have a love one in the nursing home, there should be someone visiting them to ensure they are get what they are paying for. People should make the necessary calls to complain, when they find out their love one is being abused in any type of way. Yes many of them may have wronged you in one way or another, but look in the mirror and show yourself that you are perfect. Many times you are the only voice they have, and if you don't speak out, there is no voice to hear.

The ones that are doing the abusing, or the mistreating, you should recognize that you are sowing a seed. You may think you are getting away with something, but you are not. When you sow a seed your harvest is always larger, than the seed you have sown. You reap what you sow. Job 4:8 "As I have observed, those who plow evil and those who sow trouble reap it." This scripture tells you whatever you put out, you will get back. Many think the trouble will come to them, but God will come against what you love the most. May it be your parents, spouse, or your children; you never know how the harvest will come back. We are to have our brothers or sisters' best interest at heart; they are God's children just as you are.

When you are operating under God's law, you are supposed to help your brother, Many people are being paid, and they still don't help. If you run someone away from the shelter God has sent them to, or if you are the cause of them leaving, the blood is on your hands. If anything happens to that person that you have run away, you are held responsible for that person by God. When you do harm to others you are no more than the Cain that God spoke to in Genesis 4:9. People are offering others shelter from whatever their circumstances are, and operating in another way. This is deception, and they will pay for it, one way or another.

God will use you to reveal things, according to His will. He will use you even when you don't know he's using you. Have will have you speak just what he wants you to say and he will allow it to come to pass. When you are doing God's will, and helping his people, you don't have to worry about anything. God will take care of you, because you are doing what he wants you to do.

People don't be afraid to fight for others that can't fight for themselves, because God will fight for you. For those that are mistreating others, God has a plan for you also, if you don't turn from your wicked ways, and repent for your sins. You can't hide from God he sees and know everything and you will pay one way or another.

For the companies that are taking advantage of their employees and those that do service for the people, I want to say, you are up today, and down at the wink of an eye. You may think you have built the companies, and that you are in control, but you must realize God is in control of everything. There is nothing you have that God didn't provide for you, everything you have comes from God. There's nothing invented or created by man, that God has not created even you were created. You must realize you have been blessed, and it can turn around and be the worst thing ever in your life. People take blessings and turn them into lessons. You will get a chance to see your blessing turn into a disaster.

Don't abuse the blessing God has given you, cherish it and treat it as a blessing. You may never get the chance to do it again, so begin to thank God for the blessing. Treat the people God send your way as a gift.

CHAPTER 18

Divine Intervention

January 25, 2008 I had a case of vertigo. I stayed 5 days, each time I turned my head to the right, the room would spin. I drove myself to the hospital and was asked how I got there. I was asked that because my blood pressure was 196/140. I was later diagnosed with high blood pressure. January 25, 2009 I was back in the hospital my blood pressure was 200/140. I stayed 5 days. Each time I went in the hospital I continued to say I didn't have high blood pressure, because this is what God had told me. I stopped taking the medicine, and my blood pressure would rise, I would then have to take the medicine. As the time went on I needed the medicine less. My doctor changed the medicine three different times, because my blood pressure would be too low.

I went to visit Mississippi to write this book, I was there for 30 days. During my visit, I had only taken two blood pressure pills. When I checked my blood pressure, it was 80/70; this is when I decided to stop taking the medicine. I didn't take the medicine for 30 days. I couldn't understand it. I thought it was maybe because I was at peace in the country. When I arrived back in Chicago my blood pressure began to rise again, and I started to take the medicine again. I would only take the medicine two to three times a week. I couldn't take the medicine every day. As the time went by I needed less medicine.

I was admitted into the hospital again January 18, 2012. I stayed there seven days. I was admitted because of difficulty breathing so I thought. My first roommate was 78 years old, the second was 88 years old, and the third was 96 years old. I was trying to pull together the message in this. I was visited by three Chaplains', each left my room crying. They came to minister to me, and we ministered to each other. They seemed to be glued to my room. They kept telling me they could see the glory of God upon me. My blood pressure was extremely low 93/53, therefore; I refused the medication. I was very congested and had a terrible cough, it was suggested I receive breathing treatments.

One morning I was lying in the bed at about 4am, I felt as if my breath was being taken away from me. I opened my eyes and I saw an arm extended toward my chest, the hand was in my chest. The arm was a steel blue color. I reached and grabbed the hand out of my chest, rebuked the demon in the name of Jesus, pleaded the blood of Jesus and grabbed my breath out of the hand and placed it back in my chest. I then swung and hit it in the face. I know it sounds crazy, but it was crazy for me also. I know I wasn't asleep, because when I looked to the right, there was a lady standing there on the side of the bed. The lady asked me was I alright I asked her did she see what happened. She explained she was there to give me a breathing treatment. I was happy to hear that because I was gasping for air. She then asked me who I was fighting with. I told her I was fighting with a demon, who was trying to kill me. I found it ironic that she was standing there to give me a breathing treatment, after I had lost my breath. I didn't want to talk about it to everyone, because I knew they wouldn't understand me. I know for sure that Satan is after my life, because of the calling on my life. I know that God has something great coming my way and Satan is trying to stop it.

The next day the heart doctor came by to visit me, he explained to me that he wanted me to take a pulmonary test. I went the next day to take the test the lady that was giving the test greeted me at the door. She told me how excited she was to meet me. I asked her why she was so excited. She said, if you could see the report the doctor wrote about you anyone would be excited. I asked her what she was talking about. She told me she had never saw a medical report written the way the doctor had wrote mine. She pulled the report up on the computer and showed it to me. The report was more like a resume it spoke of my life accomplishments. The things that were on the report, I had never told the doctor because he was only in my room a couple of minutes. The lady and I talked and laughed about it. I was confused about the whole situation. I asked over and over how the doctor knew all the things he knew and I never told him. I had just met him the day before for only five minutes.

The doctors were confused because I came in with 11 pints of blood, and in five days I had 8 pints in my body. The doctors were trying to figure out where my blood was going. They did every type of test they could think of on me to see if I was bleeding internally somewhere. They found nothing to give them the answer to where the blood was going. On the sixth day the doctors told me if my blood count didn't rise, I would have to get a blood transfusion. The next day my blood count went up, but they never found out why my blood had dropped. I guess I was just the woman with the issue of blood. God was telling me that I was healed, because I haven't taken any blood pressure medicine in two months. I claimed I didn't have high blood pressure and God healed me of it, because I had faith that he would. Faith is the key to everything in lie even healing. Although, people were angry at me for believing that I was healed from the beginning. Many looked at me as if I was crazy to think I was healed, but I stayed focused on what God had told me and I believed what he told me. I stood on the word of God.

On my way home from a trip to Dallas, I received a text while sitting in the airport telling me that my flight would leave at late. I was originally told it would leave Houston, Texas at 8:40pm after I arrived at 8pm, the text told 9:10pm. When I arrived in Houston I noticed on the board it was scheduled to leave for Chicago at 8:50 pm. I went to the counter and asked, what was the correct time? The lady said 8:50 I decided to go outside because it was cold in the airport. I headed in at 8:30 since the airport wasn't crowded. I was in line and I heard a page, "Veronica Waddell flight 1179 headed to Chicago will be leaving in 5 min." I stopped thinking I know they are not paging me. The page came again, "Veronica Waddell flight 1179 will be leaving soon." I thought I've never had this happen to me. I begin to run in front of the few people in front of me saying, "Excuse me, I'm being paged. They are paging me I must get in front. I heard a lady tell a man she must be a celebrity. I took off through the security screening running through the airport. I felt like OJ running through the airport, I looked at my watch it was 8:38, I was given the wrong time. I got to the desk and approached the lady that had given me the time the flight leaves. I asked her have my flight left, she said, "I think so I heard the door close." I took off running down the ramp, I could hear the lady screaming you can't go down there. In my mind I was thinking, "I'm not getting left here the airport closes at 10:00pm and where would I go with $4.77 in my pocket?" I ran down the ramp I could see the plane moving away from the ramp. I screamed to the man catch that plane, hey stop that plane. I ran up to the man he said, "You must be Veronica Waddell." I replied, "Yes, I am." He pushed a button and the plane came back to the ramp, it seemed to be rolling sideways. The door open and the stewards were standing in the door with big smiles on their faces. The laughed and one said out loud give Veronica a hand she made it. When I got on the plane, everyone began to clap. I didn't know whether I should be happy or embarrassed. That thought changed after I started thinking about how I missed my seat by the window. I looked to the left and there was a whole row empty, I got my seat by the window. The lady across from me said, "If I was running for the plane it would have left me." I told her "God has favor over my life." I sat replaying everything and thanking God. I thought how God was looking out for me.

Revelation: Things are happening in our lives every day and we continue as if nothing has happened. We forget to pay attention to many things that go on in our life. Everything that happens in our life has a message in it. We forget to pay attention and ask God for clarity of the message.

I've learned even when we are going through we are being taught. The teaching of the Lord is with us from the beginning to the end. There's a lesson to learn when you think you are at your lowest. You can't elevate to your highest until you have mastered your lowest sometimes it may just be learning not to go back to what caused you to be in your current situation.

I often stand at the bottom of my mountains and size them up, I put it in my mind that this mountain is not larger than my dreams, it wasn't created to stop me. It was created to exercise my faith and keep me spiritually in shape. I know I'm victorious when I have no fear of the mountain and can stand on top of it looking down at how far I've climbed. I've conquered the wind, rain, solitude, cold, and many storms during my climb. Stand on your mountains whether it be drugs, alcohol, abuse, loneliness, hurt, rape, molestation, pain, fear, or lack of love. Size the mountain up and stand on it. You are greater than any mountain in your life. You may not be what you want to be, but you're not what you could be, and you are on your way to being what you desire to be. You are more than a conqueror.

Chapter 19

Kenosis

I have given all that I can to this book God will not allow me to leave without emptying myself. He has given me so much to touch other with, whether it is words of wisdom, or love to spread among others. My journey consisted of many types of terrain I have gained wisdom to know every day can't be smooth sailing, there may be days you must pull the sail boat to the water, in order to enjoy smooth sailing. You may be required to pull across many different types of terrain and have difficulty in doing so, in order to get your sail boat to the water. Life is full of many unexpected things you can overcome them all through Jesus. When darkness comes into your life, pull out your flashlight by calling on the name of Jesus.

There is no script to life, therefore; everything will not go as planned. There will be times when it seems impossible to fulfill your dreams. What's impossible to man is possible through God. All things are possible for those that believe. Don't stop you can make it. It's not supposed to be easy so when you make it, then it will be much appreciated.

When we learn to trust God many trials and tribulations we will encounter are erased. Many times we receive obstacles in our path to test our faith. When we are faced with difficult situations and we can say but God, in spite of our situations. I use to be lost but now I'm found but God. The devil had a plan for me but God. I couldn't make it but God. I was down for the count but God. People came against me but God. People don't understand me but God. God is the host of my temple, the doorman of my house, the overseer of my life. But God! Life without crooked roads, obstacles in our way, trials and tribulation, haters in our lives, and God taking us through it all would be meaningless. We should give God the Glory when we take the wrong road and God lead us out. We should give praise when we are going through, we should give praise when people talk about us, and we should give praise when God bring us through. We should give God praise at all times! Faith will take you just where God wants you to be.

Many of us are waiting on a blessing and we have already been blessed and don't realize. We must learn to recognize our blessing, when we receive them. Many times the blessing is right before us, all we must do is reach out and grab it. I know I've been blessed, when I look back at the obstacles I've crossed. If we didn't have problems, we wouldn't know when we've received a blessing. If life was all sweet how would you know when it should be sweeter? How would you know how to bounce back and overcome bitter situations? We must learn to accept the bitter with the sweet.

There were times I've watched the different types of nature, and how God has created it so beautiful. If we watch nature we can be taught a lot and we can learn how to live from nature. No matter how many times the grass is cut down it keeps growing, don't let others stop you by cutting you down. When we have beautified our lawns and we notice weeds there, we pull them up.

People coming against you are no more than weeds remove them before they destroy your beauty. Leaves fall off the trees every year, and yet every year there are new leaves on the tree. No matter what your losses are, believe there are new things coming your way. We must realize everyone can't go where God has prepared for us to go. Some must fall to create room for new ones. Trees that are planted too close together, after they become so large they will wrap their roots around each other. This stunts their growth; they get in the way of each other because they have become too large. They must be moved away from each other and replanted so that there will be enough room for them to continue their growth. Don't always look at separation as a bad thing; maybe you had to be separated to continue growing. Some say the glass is half full some say its half empty. How you perceive the glass is the level in which you are. You see things according to the level of your mind.

Tornadoes occur when cold air meets warm air. If you know you have a warm heart why deal with someone with a cold heart, this is sure to cause a storm. The river never flow against itself the river always flow in one direction and it empties into one body of water. We must learn to flow together for the body of Christ, this is why I live and serve. I love the Lord and I feel we as his children should love one another, not attack one another.

When many animals are injured or down the others will try and lift or assist the other animal. Whose human them or us? Let's learn to lift one another up, and watch how God blesses you. We must also recognize that everyone we assist is not our friend. Humility starts in the heart. As rivers flow they are replenished with rich minerals, don't let anyone stop your flow. If you allow someone to stop your flow, you are no more than a pond, waiting to be refilled, waiting to be cleaned and waiting to be replenished. Continue to flow no matter whom or what comes against you God Bless You!

I can't worry about the how people see me, and the different names I've been called such as bi-polar, crazy, special and more. When you know you're special, you don't mind being called special. It only bothers you when you don't know how special you are. There is no one exactly like you... It's awesome that a mastermind can meticulously create billions of people with the same body parts to function the same, but yet the people are all different in appearance. You better believe you are special. I thank God for being special I can't imagine everyone being like me. Yes I'm special and loving it.

Once you can love and understand yourself, understanding others becomes an option. You can't find yourself trying to understand others, it starts with you.

We go through many trials and tribulations we must learn to continue give him praise when we are going through. Many times God allow obstacle to get in our way to teach us and to strengthen us. Without making mistakes is we will lack many lessons and miss out on experience. Once we have been up the wrong road, we should never take that route again. Only a fool travels up the wrong road twice. Obstacles are no more than things put in our path to guide us. Don't be afraid of them. They make us think. They are good for us they bring out the creativity in us. They make us appreciate the blessings. They draw us to God. They increased our prayer life. I thank God for the obstacles they allowed me a closer relationship with God. I received training to hear God's voice as I awaited my answers.

Obstacles are no more than instruments used to measure your Distance (how far you will stay away from God, or how close you will draw to him. Speed (how fast you will move towards the blessing) Cognitive thinking (You visualize see yourself getting pass the obstacle) Faith (although you haven't gotten pass it, you believe you will get pass it) your dark places are not created to keep you down. It is created to activate the kingdom in you, strengthen you and make you appreciate the light. It is created to prepare you for the blessing coming. If you never went into a dark place, how would you know you've come out?

When you think you are at your lowest moment, is when you are at your highest moment to be used by God. It's in your lowest moment God can use you to become creative he can use you to build empires. He will even lift you up to model before people so that they can see his work.

Decisions yesterday determined where you will be today. Decisions today will determine where you will be tomorrow. People we have around us have the exact same effect. Look around and ask yourself who needs to be removed. You can't take everyone with you. Don't let the company you keep make your decisions for today, that's in the past it's call tomorrow.

God uses imperfect people to create a perfect situation. God does not need to rescue those that are well. He's looking for those that dealing with issues. We say we are tired of fighting, tired of struggling, tired of going through. We are tired because we are trying to fight a spiritual fight in the flesh. Jesus is your flashlight in darkness, he's your ladder out of the pit, he's your crutch when you are crippled, he's your pillow to cry on, he your strength when you are weak, he's makes a way out of no way. He says he will supply all your needs. His grace is sufficient. Why are you worried about tomorrow? You have everything. Spiritual warfare's must be fought in the spirit. "For we wrestle not against flesh and blood, but against principalities, against powers, against the rulers of darkness of this world, against spiritual wickedness in high places." Ephesian 6:12

IT'S A SPIRITUAL WARFARE

It's not important whether your friends stay or leave, it's all about the encounter. Not many people have encounters with people they can call a friend. Thank God for the encounter. I thank God for the encounter with each and every one of you! Your destiny is determined by your association. Your association is determined by your walk. Your walk is determined by your endurance. Your endurance is determined by your faith. Your faith is determined by who you serve. Who you serve is determined by wisdom. Your wisdom is determined by you. You were chosen before being known by mankind. Serve God he can give you all these things and more.

When you are mistreated by people they make you angry, those people are no more than a ladder. They are actually giving you a boost to your destiny, to be the great person you are predestined by God to be. Without them you would have not made it. I want to thank all the great warriors in our lives. Thank you! You'll have done an excellent job I couldn't have made it without you. Keep up the good work. Whatever you need in your life God will put just the people there to help direct you. When you need balance he will set people in your life for balance. God will bless you through people spiritually and with love. He always gives you just what you need when you think you are at the end. When you are ready to give up, you are at the break of your blessing.

Don't be afraid to fall, falling is a part of the learning process. You need to recognize Jesus is your flashlight in darkness, he's your ladder out of the pit, he's your crutch when you are crippled, he's your pillow to cry on, he your strength when you are weak, he's makes a way out of no way. He says he will supply all your needs. His grace is sufficient. Why are you worried about tomorrow, you having everything? You need to recognize what made you fall and you will know to move around it the next time around. When you fall get up dust yourself off, ask God for forgiveness and move on. You can't worry about what has already been done. When people realize that failure is the best teacher they would have in life. In failure are the maps and direction to another path. A brick wall does not mean stop or turn around. A brick wall represents the place of preparation. Sit down at the brick wall & determine how u are going to get pass it. As a child we may fall and lay waiting for someone to help us up. Stop worrying about yesterday it's gone today is the present to step into tomorrow for your blessing.

Many children that fall down, they will get up and forget they have fallen and continue running. As adults we let me fall on my back, and lay waiting for others to pick us up. We should think like as child get up and run as if you were a child. Whether run over it, around it, or even taking it down brick by brick. Get pass it and continue your journey. Wisdom isn't determined by the amount of obstacles you encounter. Wisdom is determined by the technique used to encounter the obstacle. Only God can give you wisdom.

Many people don't know how to get up this is why it's important to pray for a person you may be the only one they have to pray for them. The time a person spend putting a person down, they can be picking them self-up. Most of the time you are beneath the person you are putting down. Lifting a person can sometimes be difficult, because many times it's dead weight. Through God all things are possible, that's why prayer is very important.

Many are upset because they are in chaotic situations and they are running not going anywhere. When people learn to embrace chaos, it won't be so frustrating. Chaos is good because it brings resolution. Chaos is a part of God's creation it was created to solve problems. Each time Jesus went to pray, heal, or minister he was encountered by chaos. If you ever pay attention there is always some type of uprising, before peace is ever thought about. You can't fix something unless it's broke.

I have not always made the best decisions in life, and many times I had to deal with situations the best I could when they came my way. Going through life is like going grocery shopping, there are many items on the shelves to choose from. You can have your choice of shelves it's according to what your appetite is. I have not always been dealt the best hands in life, with the presence of God I've played them with such great wisdom.

Although, I was not always a winner, by the time the next hand was dealt everyone knew not to underestimate how I played my hand. My presence was known even when I was not aware of what I was doing. God will allow people to know who you are, before you recognize who you are. You can have your choice of what's on the shelves it's according to what your appetite is. If life has not dealt you the best hands remember there's another deck of cards. There's another hand to be dealt. If it does not work check your dealer and check your game. Don't give up there's always a way out. You must remember that everything in life happens for a reason. Some times for redirection, or maybe for a lesson. We must learn that each occurrence that comes into our life is like a movie for us to watch. We may have to rewind that movie over and over... to get a full understanding of its purpose.

We walk through life and not knowing our why we experience so much hurt. Many of us will ask God to take things away from us, but we refuse to let them go. We don't realize that the hurt and pain is no more than grooming and preparing us to continue our walk. Sometimes we may have to walk alone without a man or woman to walk with us no one but the almighty God. I've had to cross water without a boat. I've weathered the storm without a coat, I've climbed mountains without shoes I've even had heart surgery without an anesthesiologist on hand. The surgery was not to repair, it was done to destroy. God was present in every phase of my trials and tribulations. God send people in our lives for many different reasons.

Sometimes we get confused why people are in our lives and it causes chaos and sometimes hurt and pain. I myself have had more earthly losses and pain than I ever thought I would have encountered. I have been through the ringer by being hurt by others. I have had people that I considered to be friends to walk out on me and never speak to me again, and I don't know the reason why. I have also ran good people out of my life, and never really cared. All I ever wanted was someone to try and understand me, and I have not found many. I grew up being called crazy I felt a piece of me was taken away each time I heard the word being used to describe myself. I took that word and began to use it in a positive way, although it still jolts me when used negatively. Especially by someone I consider myself close to. It seems each time I try to trust I'm let down over and over again. I have made myself adjust to being without others to shield myself. I'm often misunderstood by others and punished because of the misunderstanding.

People really don't have time to find out about you and really don't care. God have sent a few very special people in my life and some have passed away, the others are into doing what they think is right for them. I appreciate them and love them for being a friend to me. I often wonder could someone other than me withstand what I've endured over the years. I've learned to put my trust in Jesus and allow him to walk with me. I know he understands me when no other person has time. I'm content with having him as my best friend. One day he spoke to me, he said "Veronica I want you to put your life down on paper it will help others with their journey." I put it off for years and now and the time to do what was asked of me. God has given me the OK to pour out myself, while he pours into me.

I thank God for the story he has allowed me to share. I feel like Joshua going to conquer an unknown land, with God by my side I can't lose. I have been given specific instructions and I must follow them. I am on my way it's me and God against the world. I was created for such a time as this. The word of God states, "The race is not given to the swift or strong, but to the one that can endure and I made it. Thank You Lord for walking with me! God Bless everyone I will return stronger, wiser, and with the peace of God upon me. I will have a word like never before when I return." Whether you have been abused, lied on misused or going through. Many of us go through because we allow people to choose us as friends. You should choose your friend, not be chosen. God has already chosen you. "But you are a chosen people, a royal priesthood, a holy nation, a people belonging to God, that you may declare the praises of him who called you out of darkness in to his wonderful light." 1 Peter 2:9 I realize to make it in life you must have a vision. A vision is like a map, it gives direction to where you are trying to go. You may run into people that are like storm like ice very cold, some like hail hurt when they hit, some like the wind trying to hold you back, some like rain very uncomfortable, some like the summer very warm, but whichever you encounter just keep going.

You are more than a conqueror through Christ Jesus! If you're trying to change my vision you're on the wrong voyage. I just saw your vision past by yesterday. You missed yours because you were in mine. If you stay out of mine you wouldn't have so much catching up to do for yours. We must let go of our past it will handcuff to the present. Jesus is the key to the handcuffs. Unlock your handcuffs so that you can move on. God has so many great things waiting on you. Now go get it!

When I look back over my life, I realize a greater power than man has taken over, and has become the captain of my ship. I'm enjoying the cruise, never worried about falling overboard or sinking. I'm trusting that things missing in my life will be fulfilled. The hurt and pain will be erased. When I run into storms, I take my mind and move the clouds, and find that beautiful ray of sun.

Sometimes things get hard and I want to give up but I can't. I must fight to keep a level head so that I will know the difference between the inner me and the enemy. Keep speaking Lord! "Then shalt thou delight thyself in the Lord; and I will cause thee to ride upon the high places of the earth, and feed thee with the heritage of Jacob they father: for the mouth of the Lord hath spoken it, Isaiah 58:14

If you want success stay with the Lord, if you want failure pull away from the Lord. This is guaranteed. The word of God says, "I'll never leave you nor forsake you, neither will my seed beg for bread." When I see people begging, I know who their god is. When you give to them, they will say God Bless you. I ask them, "Is your God so small that this is the best blessing he can give you? You're serving the wrong God. God is only as awesome as you allow him to be in your life. He won't knock walls down to get to you. He says if you draw near to him he will draw near to you. Who can match the deity and attributes of God but God? Let him carry you when you can't make it, let him speak when you are speechless let him bless you when you're not expecting it. You've got a blessing in front of you! God is only as far as you allow him to be. He can be a reach out and touch God, or he can be a long distance God. You decided how close you want him in your life. The closer you think you are to God the farther you are from God. Many think they are so close to God that you can't tell them anything. God is not a person that you will fully understand. We may have knowledge of his attributes, but we will never fully understand why he does things. We will never fully understand God. I'm so happy God has favor over my life. You see favor is when you have been kicked to the ground, and something comes from nowhere, allow you to rise above those who have kicked you down. It's when your credit is jacked up and the creditors see good credit it's when people have planned your failure and every time they hammered you down you began to rise a little higher. Favor isn't fair but it's fabulous!

Who will you rely on to move the stone from your sepulcher so that you can be resurrected to reconnect with God? There's praise in my spirit that tells me I can overcome sickness, pain, hurt, and anything that is not of God. I feel victory in my spirit! Hey, it is done in the name of he majestic name of Jesus! Stay connected I'm moooooooving! Anyone want to go with me? God bless you! Amen!

I thank God he does not hold anything against me. He erases my faults and shows me nothing but love. God is a forgiving God he is very graceful. He loves everyone the same. He's no respecter of a person. He is a God of mercy and grace. He's a God that never changes. He will be with you from the beginning to the end.

Although, God does not have to prove himself to anyone, he always proves himself to us. God wants us to turn from our wicked ways and turn towards to him to supply all our needs. He wants us to put him first in everything we do. God is so powerful that no one will be before him and no one will come after. He's the only living God that holds all power.

I thank God for salvation and grace. I thank him for meeting me right where I am without judgment. I thank him for his word, "we all fall short of the glory of God." He knew we would make bad decisions and mistakes. I am thankful that he is the only one that can judge. If it was up to man to judge we would have been dead a long time ago. I thank him for keeping me focused on only him and his word.

No matter what you do in the dark it's in the light when it comes to God he's omniscient. He knows all! You can't hide anything from God he knows what you will do before you do it. Preparation begins with a walk. Your walk is the first step towards preparation for anything you want in life.

Life is full of surprises don't wait on a surprise, you be the surprise. Surprise yourself do something you've had doubts about doing, change something you haven't been able to change, live the way you've always wanted to live, love yourself like never before and praise God like you've never done before and surprise yourself because a change is coming.

When you go before God he's not going to be interested in how your brothers and sisters treated you. He's going to want to know how you treated your brothers and sisters! Everyone will be accountable for themselves.

Jeremiah the Prophet cried out to God, "why the wicked prosper and the faithless live at ease. You are always on their lips but far from their hearts." God responds by asking Jeremiah, "If you have raced with men on foot and they have worn you out, how can you compete with horses." God is saying KEEP GOING THEY WILL NOT LAST It's ONLY TEMPORARY!" Jeremiah 12:1

We must understand that our walk and our talk must same be going in the same direction. Your talk must match your walk they can't be on 2 different sides of the street. Our walk and talk define who we are. People pay attention to everything about you, when you say you are a Christian.

We go through life carrying our past on our shoulders, or holding hands with our past. Don't worry about what your past was like, what you have been through, what people have to say about you. Look the devils in the face and tell them the best is yet to come, you aren't seen nothing yet. Keep your eyes on God and keep moving. We must understand that many people can bring your past up to you, but to get to your past do they ever by past what they once were. They can't get to your past without by passing their own.

When I did drugs you talked about me, Homeless you talked, in an abusive marriage you talked, I even sat and partied with you and you'll talked behind my back. I'm no longer in bondage u still talking you went a step further u lying on me. So what if I go to school, go to church, and don't work. The joy of the Lord is my strength not you. If u must lie on me to make me look bad, I must be a hell of a woman. If you told the truth about me it probably would make you look bad. "You don't have to lie about anybody because the truth about everybody is bad enough" (Louis Farrakhan) I'll pray for the old crew. You'll continue talking and keeping me lifted up before the Lord, and I" pray and keep you'll lifted. Don't lose direction watching me I'm focused and at peace.

I myself have asked why I had to go through so much. God had to speak to me about my life. If peace as supposed to be in my life it would have been there. There were times I tried to buy peace. You can't buy peace when a price has already been paid for it, and you are the owner. I've learned to have peace in the midst of a storm. I learned that I control my environment around me, with the words I speak.

It's time for us to become the architects of our lives. You don't need any special skills to do it. Every morning speak the way you want your day to go, and speak how you want your life to be. Stop letting the devil plan your life, he don't have keys to his own house. Your father has the keys to heaven & hell. Satan has to get permission from your father to operate in your life. When do you go to your father for yourself? Release your hurt and pain into the atmosphere, it has more room for it than you do. Let it go and watch it disappear. God will handle it. God Bless You!

There is more work involved when you dig deep, than it is to scrape the surface. It's more beneficial to dig for that you don't see, than to grab what you see. There is work required, muscles used, brain cells are stimulated when digging deep. Scraping the surface is the result of someone others hard work. Many riches are hidden in the mind of those who work for it. You must dig deep! God Bless You!

Now that you have gotten to know me, do you understand why I'm the person that I am? Can you walk in the shoes I wear? Can you travel the path I've traveled? Would you have survived what I've been through? I may not have been able to handle what you went through in life, because it was created for you. What I went through was for me to become the person I am today. I say this because many have judged me and don't know me. We never know what a person have been through to become the person they are today. Pray for me while I pray for you and your journey God Bless You.

CHAPTER 20

We Are Blessed

A Tribute to my Family and Friends

I thank God for my two daughters Tyranesia and Taineeka, and my granddaughter Latavia. I wouldn't trade them for anything in the world. I truly love them with all my heart. It may seem that we have had a hard time; we are still go through, but God has been watching us from the beginning. He has not taken his eyes off us in our life. We have cried so many tears, but we keep travailing. We will not leave this earth without people seeing the blessing God has for us. I have been knocked down and mistreated on the behalf of each of you. I will go before the same people again if had to because I know that God is on my side. There were many days I have cried. I knew that my tears weren't in vain. There may be many things that we don't agree on but our love will push us to continue walking together. No one can separate us in any form or fashion. Things are going to get better for us.

Tyranesia Veronica Johnson, you have been through so much at a young age, God saw you through every episode in your life. He has predestined you to become a mighty woman of God and a great leader. He showed that when he chose you to become the youngest board member on the Emmett Till Road Scholars Foundation. I watched you fight for justice, watched your passion, and how focused you were. I watch you drive and never give up on the things you want in life. I love when you speak up for yourself with no fear.

What many said you couldn't do you proved them to be wrong and never looked back. You are a fearless young lady, you have no fear but of God. Everything of your past has been erased by God and forgotten. You are a born leader and no one can take that away from you. You are an example to many teenage mothers. You have shown them that through God all things are possible. You have shown them that a child does not have to stop you. I had a chance to witness you walk across the stage and receive your Associates Degree with honors. I watch as you continue your education in your college studies and I'm awaiting your next walk across the stage, which will be very so. I've forgiven you for everything you have done wrong and I want to tell you that I love you and will never stop. I've learned a lot from you. Everything you want out of life and more are already given to you in the name of Jesus. You are priceless!

I pray that God continue to lead you, and he be the direction in your life. I pray he continues to give you the fire to continue to keep going on the path he has predestined you to follow. I pray he keep you in his hands, and hold on to you while you fulfill your dreams. I pray that your hands and testimony be used to bless many of God's people and lead those that don't know him into the kingdom. I pray that you never need or want for anything. I thank God for bringing you into my life. I thank him for everything has done in your life and what's to come.

Taineeka Renee Johnson, although; you have been through so much, God has you in his hands and no one can pluck you out. Don't worry about the latest diagnosis that Satan is trying to place on you. He can't touch you, he can only strengthen you. God has allowed your faith to be built. I watch you as you travail through every circumstance put before you as if it was nothing but smooth sailing.

Whether you know it or not you have showed me many things. You have showed me that there is peace in the midst of a storm. You have showed me how to stay focused in spite of man pains. You have showed me that God is truly a healer and there's nothing to worry about. Many things I've read in the bible, I've seen them work through you. Things such as: miracles, faith, endurance, trust, hope, faithfulness, patience, love, peace, kindness and much more.

I watched the predictions of the doctors put to sleep through your everyday walk. God showed up and showed off in your life. When they said you wouldn't live in 2002, he said you will live and he kept you here. When every organ in your body shut down, God blew life into each organ. They said you will have brain damage and never be able to learn, God sent you off to college. The latest diagnosis I see that as already healed in the name of Jesus. I see you coming across the stage next year getting your bachelor's degree. I see God making every desire in your life a thing of the past. God has allowed you to be an example to many people today, singing in the choir, directing the children's choir, picking the children up and being a role model to the children. God has so much more for you to do and he will continue to bless you over and over again.

There will be a day you will not want for anything, not even a husband. Everything you have ever wished for is at your fingertips. God will send just who he wants into your life, someone who understands and will love you for who you are. Keep shining in the lives of others and the glow will stay on you. I wouldn't trade you for anything in this world. I love you more than you can ever imagine. Keep making the devil out to be a liar. You are priceless! I pray that anything that comes against you will not prosper. I pray that God continues restoring your body day by day.

I pray that God continue to give you the strength to do his work. I pray that God use you in the lives of others. I pray that your mind stays focused on God and only him. I pray that your knowledge and wisdom of his word increases. I thank God for healing you, I thank him for the joy you bring in my life, and I thank him for sending you my way. I thank him for all the things he has done in your life and the things to come. I thank the Lord in the name of Jesus!

Latavia Veronica Johnson, you are the heart beat to my heart. You are a child that was born in one of the roughest time of my life. I was angry because I didn't think I could deal with a child being born at that time. I even had thoughts of making your mother have an abortion. I was so hurt and confused; I didn't know which way to turn. The minute you were born I saw love appear in the world. I knew you would be special because of all the controversy you started before and after you were born. I loved you at birth and I love you even more. You are such a beautiful and brilliant little girl. You are an awesome prayer warrior and I love to hear you pray. You are a child of wisdom, and will be an example to many children and adults. The angelic voice you have will be used to minister to many people. You will sing before many and will be requested by many. You are going to be used by God in a mighty way. God has great plans for you and they will be fulfilled. You will change many lives during your walk for Christ. I want you to know you are a blessing in my life. I wouldn't trade you for anything in the world. You are priceless!

Everything that has ever bought you pain God was right there and he will continue to be in your life. I pray that God continue to lead you and guide your footsteps. I pray that he keep his hands on you. I pray that you continue to have your focus on him. I thank the Lord for sending you into my life. I thank him for the many talks we have. I thank him for the words of wisdom that you have given me. I thank him for allowing you to teaching me and others about love. Grandma heard your prayer and it's already done, your tears for me are not in vain. I love you!

I was on Facebook August 14, 2010 and there was a young man named Chet Pensive Johnson who had been my friend since April 2010. He complimented on something and I told him thank you and he wanted to know why I thanked him. I told him I always thank people for nice things they do. He kept saying he didn't do anything. He became my best friend he helped me through so many things. He's been a listening ear and a shoulder to cry on. I know there were times I really got on his nerves, but he ignores that part of me. He ignores the many things that others can't deal with about me. He is such a kind, quiet and gentle person. He's like cool water on my fire. He came into my life at a time things seemed to be falling apart. God always send someone when you need them. I must say he sent a true friend in my life and I don't have many friends. He is a very exceptional person and anyone that has him as a friend is blessed. Mr. Johnson I thank you for being a friend. I thank you for being a family member. I thank you for being in my life and my family's life. I thank God for having a ram in the bush when I needed it the most. You continue being the person that you are and allow God to bless you. You are truly the millionaire, entrepreneur, real estate investor, media mogul, Philanthropist, Prophet, man of God and more! Keep your head up and move on towards your dream it's just an arm length away. God Bless You! I love you

Thanks to Mr. Jay for the great accomplishments, you opened the door in my life. If it had not been for you I wouldn't be who I am today. You were the ladder to the many blessings I have received. You opened my mind to the many doors that were awaiting my entrance. You allowed me to recognize the greener grass on the other side of the fence. You have truly played your part very well, you were being used by God whether you like it or not. He used you and others to set up the stage for my entrance, and the many scenes in my life, and to set up the leadership role for me to play in my life. If it was not for you and others I wouldn't be who I am today. I thank God for you and the many others that were bought in my life. I can't be angry, why should I be? I may not be who I want to be, I'm definitely not who I could've been and I'm on my way to being what has God ordained me to be. Keep your head up you've done a great job. I must say thank you again! God Bless You!

I thank God for the journey that was laid out for me to travel. Although, there were many ups and downs, but I enjoyed my journey. I have been allowed to encounter many different situations. I learned to trust in God to bring me through each situation. God was building my faith. God allowed me to go through these many things, so that I would have the knowledge to assist others out of their situations. I know God has something special for me to do. I look forward to doing the work that God has for me to do.

I thank God for bringing me to where I am today. He has bought me a long way. There were times I didn't think I would make it and God bought me through. God has bought me from a hurting child, from a poor kid in the projects, from a misused and abused wife, from a drug addict to who I am today. Today I have accomplished many things with God's help. I know it's by the grace of God that I have accomplished theses many things.

I spent 7 years in bondage on drugs, the number 7 means complete. I know of many people that have spent more time on drugs than I have and many are still out there. I know it is a blessing from God that I'm free. I thank God for being free!

In my life, I have endured so much hurt and pain. Each time I was hurting, God had me to look at those that were before me. When I suffered I focused on Job, when I couldn't get help I focused on Joseph, when I went to help other I focused on Esther, and when I felt like giving up I focused on Jesus on the cross.

I give praise to God for where he bought me from. I have reached many incredible milestones in my life. God allowed me to go back to school and obtain a B.A. in Christian Ministry, M.A. in Urban Ministry, and a M.A. in Christian Studies. I have obtained my certification to be a Chaplain. I am an ordained Minister. I am a Certified Nurse's Assistant/ Phlebotomist. I worked as a CPR instructor. I've recorded a C.D of poetry and looking forward to the next C.D. I've been to several cities to speak and recite poetry.

While on my journey I've met so many beautiful people and I've met so many new friends. The beginning of my journey may not have been pleasant to the eye, but it was pleasing to many. They had a chance to watch the miraculous work of God. They watched him remove the layers off me. He took a drug addict that no one ever thought would accomplish these things, and many prayed I wouldn't accomplish them and bought out the best in me. He polished the jewelry in me, until the authentic diamond appeared. I was just a diamond in the rough, or gold being created. Gold is made from repeatedly passing through fire, to remove the impurities. Diamond are created from pressure, the more pressure the more carats. Great leaders are created through their trial and tribulations.

What's so beautiful at one time I felt worthless, now I know I'm priceless worth more than money and I'm on display for the world to see. If I made it so can you. It's not over it's just a part of your story being created for you to share with others. It's your testimony. It tells how you have past the many tests in your life. I pray my story is encouragement to others to show them there's a way out, as sure as it was a way in. If there's a way in there's a way out. I pray that many will see what God has given me for correction in their lives and ministries.

I've played many parts in my life, and I played them very well. When I look back over my life I must thank God because, there's NOTHING BROKEN AND NOTHING MISSING. God Bless You! I'm still whole in spite of what I've been through. It was just a part in my life I had to play. God chose me to play the leading role, with many people contributing to the many scenes in my life. We all have a story to tell about the part we play in our lives. Everyone has a leading role in the part they play, God is the producer, Jesus is the director, and the angels are your coordinator. God is in total control of your life even when it looks like your life is out of control. Let God be the pilot of your life and you will have a smooth landing. God Bless You!

ACKNOWLEGEMENTS
THANKS

Deacon & Mother Brown
Faith Walk Church International
Trinity International University
Pastor Cynthia Bramlett
Minister Loretta Ransberg
Pastor Dwayne Brown
Pastor Sharon Morton
Pastor Lida Ratcliff (Philadelphia, Penn)
Pastor Ronnie & Terrie Simmons (Smyrna, TN)
Pastor Kevin & Regina Wiles (Lula, MS)
Pastor Capatoria Wilson
Pastor Michael & Dorine Stevens
Pastor Deon & Cassandra Hughes
Pastor Doris Nazario
Evangelist Katina Clemons (Carthage, MS)
Pastor Vanessa Hightower (Rivera Beach Florida)
Pastor Howard Hughes
Pastor Keshall (Ghana, W. Africa)
Bishop Luca Wafula (Nairobi, Africa)
Prophetess Spinks (Benton Harbor Michigan)
Prophetess Denise Terrell
ProphetessDoris Fox Davis (Kosciusko, MS)
Rev Dr. Eric Pearman (Colorado)
Pastor Dr. Reynolds
Dr. Alexis Westbrook
Minister Cassandra Bradshaw
Minister Tara Bell
Minister Essie Oby
Minister Eddie Woods
Minister Clara Castle
Minister Lynn Richardson
Minister Joe Blackmon
Evangelist Sharee Blackmon
Minister Phyllis Wade (Smyrna, TN)
Raya Ford (Nashville, TN)
Renita Ford

Stephany Hughes
Mama Marilyn Hughes
Maria Short
Kenneth Washington
Regina Oby (Texas)
Arcurtis Parker
Latanya Bishop
Benetta McPherson
Margaret Brown
George Massey
Sharon Williams
Denise Caldwell
Oby Family (Dallas, Texas)
Oby Family (Oklahoma)
Oby Family (Louisiana)
Bluitt Family (Dallas, Texas)
Janice Kinnebrew
Theresa Fairly (Minnesota)
Pearl Kinnebrew
James Kinnebrew
Wilkes Family
Peteete Family
Braxton & Shadonna Bass (N. Carolina)
Howell Family
Ellington Family
Singleton Family
Parker Family
Healing Hearts Ministry
United Holiness Outreach Ministry
Larry Wilder
Akilah Mines (St. Louis)
Renee Waddell (St. Louis)
Amill Family
Mark Corece Smith
Zsaneika Bass

Eloise Murphy
Mama Nana
Aunt Yvonne Palm
Aunt Patricia Waddell
Patricia Evans (Minnesota)
Mother J. Carrethers
Gregory Showtime O'Neal
Daisy Knox
Linda Brown
Stella Hill (Smyrna,TN)

Zantrece Washington
Zakharria Ford
Robert (Red) (Man)
Ford Family (Nashville TN)
Marcus Oby (Florida)
Tonya Oby (California)
Clarence Oby (Las Vegas)
Kenyatta Oby (Atlanta)
Michelle (Atlanta)
Victoria Wilborn (Antioch,TN)

Thanks to my great editing team: Tyranesia V. Johnson, Taineeka R. Johnson, Monique A. Sargent, and others that contributed.

Contact Information:
veronicajw@att.net
Facebook: Veronica Oby Waddell
Facebook: Nothing Broken Nothing Missing

CPSIA information can be obtained at www.ICGtesting.com
Printed in the USA
LVOW130927271212

313166LV00001BB/1/P